THE RITUALS AND MYTHS OF THE FEAST OF THE GOODLY GODS OF KTU/CAT 1.23

Society of Biblical Literature

Resources for Biblical Study

Susan Ackerman,
Hebrew Bible/Old Testament Editor

J. Ross Wagner,
New Testament Editor

Number 51

THE RITUALS AND MYTHS OF THE FEAST
OF THE GOODLY GODS OF KTU/CAT 1.23
Royal Constructions of Opposition, Intersection,
Integration, and Domination

THE RITUALS AND MYTHS OF THE FEAST OF THE GOODLY GODS OF KTU/CAT 1.23

Royal Constructions of Opposition, Intersection, Integration, and Domination

Mark S. Smith

Society of Biblical Literature
Atlanta

THE RITUALS AND MYTHS OF THE FEAST
OF THE GOODLY GODS OF KTU/CAT 1.23

Library of Congress Cataloging-in-Publication Data

Smith, Mark S., 1955-
   The rituals and myths of the feast of the goodly gods of KTU/CAT 1.23 :
royal constructions of opposition, intersection, integration, and domination
/ by Mark S. Smith.
      p. cm. — (Society of Biblical Literature resources for biblical
study ; no. 51)
   Includes bibliographical references.
   ISBN-13: 978-1-58983-203-9 (paper binding : alk. paper)
   ISBN-10: 1-58983-203-5 (paper binding : alk. paper)
  1. Ugarit (Extinct city)—Religion. 2. Gods, Ugaritic. 3. Mythology,
Ugaritic. 4. Autumn festivals—Syria—Ugarit (Extinct city) 5.
Death—Religious aspects. I. Title. II. Series: Resources for biblical
study ; no. 51.

BL1640.S65 2006
299'.26—dc22

2006004773

For Frank Moore Cross
and Marvin Hoyle Pope,
with greatest gratitude

Contents

Abbreviations

The abbreviations listed in *The SBL Handbook of Style: For Ancient Near Eastern, Biblical, and Early Christian Studies* (ed. P. H. Alexander et al.; Peabody, Mass.: Hendrickson, 1999) and *The Assyrian Dictionary, Volume 15 S* (ed. E. Reiner et al.; Chicago: Oriental Institute, 1984), vii–xxii are used with the following additions, changes, and sigla:

AO	Antiquités Orientales, Louvre
BH	Biblical Hebrew
CAD	*Chicago Assyrian Dictionary*
CAT	M. Dietrich, O. Loretz, and J. Sanmartín, eds. *The Cuneiform Alphabetic Texts from Ugarit, Ras Ibn Hani and Other Places* (*KTU*: 2nd ed.). ALASPM 8. Münster: Ugarit-Verlag, 1997. Texts cited by number.
*CML*¹	G. R. Driver. *Canaanite Myths and Legends*. Edinburgh: T&T Clark, 1956.
*CML*²	J. C. L. Gibson. *Canaanite Myth and Legends*. 2nd ed. Edinburgh: T&T Clark, 1978.
COS	*The Context of Scripture*. Eds. W. W. Hallo and K. Lawson Younger. 3 vols. Leiden: Brill, 1997–2002.
CPA	Christian Palestinian Aramaic
CPA	J. L. Cunchillos and J. P. Vita. *Concordancia de Palabras Ugaríticas*. Madrid: Consejo Superior de Investigaciones Científicas; Zaragova: Institución el Católico, 1995.
DUL	*A Dictionary of the Ugaritic Language in the Alphabetic Tradition*. Translated by W. G. E. Watson. 2 vols. (continuous pagination between the two volumes). Handbuch der Orientalistik 67. Leiden: Brill, 2003.
JPA	Jewish Palestinian Aramaic
KTU	M. Dietrich, O. Loretz, and J. Sanmartín. *Die keilalphabetischen Texte aus Ugarit: Einschliesslich der keilalphabetischen Texte ausserhalb Ugarits*. Part 1: *Transkription*. AOAT 24/1. Kevelaer: Butzon & Bercker; Neukirchen-Vluyn: Neukirchener, 1976.

KU	H. L. Ginsberg. *Kitve 'Ugarit*. Jerusalem: Bialik Foundation, 1936.
Leslau	W. Leslau. *Comparative Dictionary of Ge'ez (Classical Ethiopic)*. Wiesbaden: Harrassowitz, 1987.
MLC	G. del Olmo Lete. *Mitos y leyendas de Canaan segun la Tradicion de Ugarit*. Institucion San Jeronimo para la Ciencia Biblica 1. Madrid: Ediciones Cristiandad, 1981.
NB	Neo-Babylonian
NJPS	The New Jewish Publication Society translation of the Bible
OB	Old Babylonian
PE	Philo of Byblos as cited in Eusebius, *Praeparatio Evangelium* (Attridge and Oden 1981).
RIH	Ras ibn Hani (excavation number)
RSP III	*Ras Shamra Parallels III: The Texts from Ugarit and the Hebrew Bible*. Edited by S. Rummel. AnOr 51. Rome: Pontifical Biblical Institute, 1981.
SB	Standard Babylonian
SPUMB	J. C. de Moor. *The Seasonal Pattern in the Ugaritic Myth of Ba'lu: According to the Version of Ilimilku*. AOAT 16. Kevelaer: Butzon & Bercker; Neukirchen-Vluyn: Neukirchener, 1971.
TDOT	*Theological Dictionary of the Old Testament*
Thespis	T. H. Gaster. *Thespis: Ritual, Myth, and Drama in the Ancient Near East*. Revised ed. New York: Norton, 1977.
TO 1	A. Caquot, M. Sznycer, and A. Herdner. *Textes ougaritiques I: Mythes et légendes*. LAPO 7. Paris: Cerf, 1974.
TO 2	A. Caquot, J. M. de Tarragon, and J. L. Cunchillos. *Textes ougaritiques II: Textes religieux, rituels, correspondance*. LAPO 14. Paris: Cerf, 1989.
UBC 1	M. S. Smith. *The Ugaritic Baal Cycle, Vol. 1: Introduction, with Text, Translation and Commentary of KTU 1.1–1.2*. VTSup 55. Leiden: Brill, 1994.
UG	J. Tropper. *Ugaritische Grammatik*. AOAT 273. Münster: Ugarit-Verlag, 2000.
UNP	*Ugaritic Narrative Poetry*. Edited by S. B. Parker. SBLWAW 9. Atlanta: Scholars Press, 1997.
WSRP	West Semitic Research Project of the University of Southern California (Professor Bruce Zuckerman, director)

ACKNOWLEDGMENTS

This work on CAT 1.23 began as part of my effort to think about the third major section of the Ugaritic Baal Cycle (1.4 VIII–1.6 VI), specifically as a study in the contrasting ways that Death appears in these two texts. I completed an initial draft of this study of 1.23 at the Pontifical Biblical Institute late in the spring term of 2004, where I was the Catholic Biblical Association Visiting Professor. My thanks go to the PBI and the Catholic Biblical Association for supporting me with this professorship. I am also very grateful to my family for sharing this adventure in Italy with me.

I am also grateful to my home institution, New York University, for granting me a term of sabbatical leave. My colleague, Daniel Fleming, read an early draft of this work and offered extensive comments that proved very helpful. Dr. Beate Pongratz-Leisten of Princeton University provided several thought-provoking comments to chapters 1, 4 and 5. She also gave me a copy of an unpublished essay of hers (Pongratz-Leisten forthcoming). I am also very grateful to these two scholars, who aided me further in theoretical matters pertaining to myth and ritual as textual categories. I also wish to thank Professor Jo Ann Hackett for her help with chapter 1 and Professor Martti Nissinen for his aid with chapter 4. Professor Jack Sasson sent me a copy of an essay of his (Sasson 2002), and for this I thank him. I also wish to thank Professor Christopher Foley for providing me with a copy of his 1980 McMaster University dissertation on KTU/CAT 1.23.

I owe a special debt to Professor Bruce Zuckerman, Director of the West Semitic Research Project of the University of California, for his help in nailing down readings of letters disputed in the secondary literature. The two of us went over these readings for several enlightening and enjoyable hours on 23–24 October 2004, and I am grateful to Professor Zuckerman for taking his own time to review each of the readings with me. The work of Professor Zuckerman and his team is helping to revolutionize the study of West Semitic epigraphy, and I am thankful to Professor Zuckerman for putting his resources at my disposal. I am grateful also for the generous hospitality provided by his wife Liz and him during my visit.

I had the pleasure of presenting the main points of this work in the Ugaritic classes of Professors William Schniedewind of the University of California at Los Angeles, Dennis Pardee of the University of Chicago, and Richard Averbeck of

Trinity International University. I am grateful for the reactions in their seminars and for their hospitality. In the spring term of 2005, my Ugaritic class at New York University devoted four sessions to this text, and I was able to rethink and clarify a number of points as a result of discussions with the students in the course. They also made a number of valuable suggestions. Two of the students in the Ugaritic course, Sara Milstein and Cory Peacock, also read parts of the manuscript and offered helpful comments, as did my daughter Rachel Smith, now a first-year undergraduate at NYU.

Finally, I wish to thank the SBLRBS for welcoming this work into the series. I am particularly grateful to Professor Susan Ackerman, the series editor, for her help with the manuscript in general and for her several constructive suggestions. I also thank Bob Buller, Billie Jean Collins, and Kathie Klein for their great help in preparing the manuscript for publication. Saul Olyan also offered a number of corrections, which I appreciate.

A number of the aforementioned faculty and students made some fine observations, which are cited in this work. I thank them for these points, though I hasten to add that they are in no way responsible for the defects in this book; I alone am responsible.

It is appropriate to dedicate this book to my teachers, Frank Moore Cross and Marvin H. Pope, as they sparred for years over the interpretation of the mythic narrative in 1.23.30–76. Midstream in their exchanges two decades ago, at the Ugaritic Studies group at the 1975 Society of Biblical Literature meeting, Marvin Pope closed his presentation on 1.23 with these remarks (Pope in M. S. Smith 1998b:664): "At this point, I cannot discourse on the meaning of the text as a whole, but hope that these few comments may serve to stimulate further creative controversy and progress toward understanding of this provocative document." I aim toward interpreting the text as a whole, and although at the end of this study I find it impossible to resolve a number of matters, I would echo Pope's words; I, too, hope that this study advances the understanding of 1.23. In producing this study, I was aided by the scholarly examples set by Pope and Cross and by the memory of their goodly help to me often coming to mind.

6 December 2005
Department of Hebrew and Judaic Studies
New York University

Since its initial publication (Virolleaud 1933), the work today often called "The Birth of the Beautiful Gods" (CAT/KTU 1.23 = RS 2.002 = UT 52 = *CTA* 23) has fascinated students of the Ugaritic texts. For its combination of ritual and mythic material, it is unique in the Ugaritic corpus. At the same time, the overall understanding of 1.23 has eluded scholars. Research on the text continued steadily up to 1980, but since that time there has been no fresh in-depth examination of this text. In view of new information and tools available in the field of Ugaritic studies, it seems timely to return to this classic of the Ugaritic corpus. Moreover, advances in the study of myth and ritual in the fields of anthropology and ritual studies have yet to be applied to this text. This study represents my effort to take advantage of these advances.

Several regnant assumptions have, to my mind, blocked progress in the understanding of the text. For decades, the text has been regarded as presenting a set of rituals (lines 1–29) and a myth (lines 30–76). Due in part to the "myth and ritual" approach taken to this text (described in chapters 1 and 4), elements that appear in either lines 1–29 or lines 30–76 have been thought to be operative in some sense in both sections. The results of this study indicate that matters that appear in 1–29 but not in lines 30–76 need not be assumed to underlie the latter. By the same token, themes that appear in lines 30–76 but not in lines 1–29 need not be presupposed in the former. The most dramatic instance of this reasoning has been the mistaken attribution of the theme of "sacred marriage." Based on the alleged recognition of this theme in the myth of lines 30–59, it has been imputed in turn to the rituals of lines 1–29. However, this line of interpretation is badly misplaced. At this point in the history of the study of this text, it might be thought that the "myth and ritual" approach and the sacred marriage theory that it fostered would no longer require refutation. However, there remain enough proponents of the "myth and ritual" approach to 1.23 that a more sustained critique is warranted. In short, the material not shared by both the rituals and the myths is not extraneous but is expressive of further sensibilities about the feast involved or about the nature of reality surrounding it. After study of the text, it is evident that several myths and mythic elements are not restricted to the material of lines 30–76; they are also embedded in the ritual material in lines 1–29, in particular a mythology of Death in lines 8–11, a mythology of the huntress goddess in line 16, and a mythic understanding of the Goodly Gods embedded in their title in lines 23–24. It is therefore necessary to speak of the myths and rituals of this text.

The question that arises from this observation concerns the relationship between the multiplicity of the text's rituals and mythic components. It is evident that both the rituals and myths share an overall trajectory or major theme centered on the Goodly Gods and the feast in which they take part. This theme envelops the ritual section in lines 1–29, specifically in lines 1–7 and 23–27, and it is the end-point of the longer mythic narrative in lines 30–76, in particular in lines 64–76. This observation has important implications for how the text should be understood. In his *editio princeps*, Virolleaud (1933) called the text "la naissance des dieux gracieux et beaux," and abbreviated its title as ŠŠ, standing for the two gods, Shahar and Shalim. Many scholars afterwards called the text "Shahar and Shalim," perhaps based in part on the assumption that these two astral gods are also the destructive *'ilm n'mm*. This long-held view can now be shown to be incorrect. Recognizing the central part played by the *'ilm n'mm*, other scholars have referred to this text as "The Birth of the Beautiful Gods." While this label represented an improvement over "Shahar and Shalim," it had the unfortunate effect of focusing on the longer narrative in lines 30–76 at the expense of the ritual materials in lines 1–29, and in fact it seized upon only one aspect of that longer narrative, specifically the deities' births. In view of the observation about the central place of the feast of the goodly gods in both the rituals and longer mythic narrative, it is evident that the text should be called "The Feast of the Goodly Gods." (The reason for the choice of "goodly" over "beautiful" is explained in the philological notes to line 1 in chapter 2 on pages 33–34; it is unlikely that these gods are "beautiful" in any conventional sense.)

Accordingly, the issue that looms over any study of this text involves understanding it as a whole. Studies have been particularly strong in the area of philology, and understanding of the motifs in the mythic narrative in lines 30–76 has improved over time. However, a basic syntax of its ritual elements, not to mention a sense of their relations to the longer mythic narrative, has remained a major desideratum of this text. Indeed, a broader sense of the text has rarely been forwarded since the older studies of W. F. Albright and Theodore Gaster and the more recent work of Paolo Xella. As Xella's groundbreaking 1973 study shows, the oppositional terms for the environment, "sown" (*mdr'*) versus "outback"[1] (*mdbr*),

---

1. This translation for *mdbr* holds a number of advantages. Despite being unusual for at least American English, it avoids the image of the sort of sandy terrain that the common translation "desert" conjures up in the minds of many in the United States. The translation "outback" also conveys the periphery associated with this term in Ugaritic. The translation also retains a sense of etymology of the root of *mdbr* (**dbr*, "to be behind"; cf. *děbîr*, "hindmost chamber," BDB 184).

issue in a larger code of symbolic meanings. In both the rituals and the myths, this code includes not only the environment, as Xella nicely demonstrated, but also corresponding oppositions in the nature of the deities as well as the components of the feast.

Complementing the overall presentation of the feast, the elements in the rituals and myths that do not explicitly express this theme nonetheless fit within its wider framework. This text contains multiple mythologies of death and destruction, as well as references or allusions to other mythologies. Sometimes these mythologies seem to work at cross-purposes. However, in the larger picture that I have attempted to sketch, these various mythological components work to create a canvas larger and more imaginative than what scholarship has usually painted. These elements that diverge from the central theme in the end contribute to it, in both the rituals and the myths.

Part 1 opens this study by addressing preliminary matters. Chapter 1 addresses some of the terms of engagement significant for this study and then moves into a brief history of scholarship and interpretive premises. These are followed by a presentation of text and translation, with basic publication information, a justification for the structure of the textual layout, and a list of the cast of characters involved in the text. The text, as given below, largely follows CAT and T. J. Lewis in *UNP* 208–14 (see also the notes in *CTA*, pp. 98–101). The latter edition was based on the photographic materials of the West Semitic Research Project of the University of Southern California, directed by Professor Bruce Zuckerman. I have benefited from my close study of these photographs also in conjunction with Professor Zuckerman, and the readings that emerged from this collaboration are cited in the discussions.

The translation is my own, but I have been aided by the older translations of Albright and Ginsberg, the later works of Caquot et al., Gibson, and del Olmo Lete, as well as the more recent translations of Lewis, Pardee, and Wyatt. Central to the translation is the recognition that the text, even the ritual material, is highly poetic, marked especially by bicola and tricola. The larger understanding underlying the translation is based on the examination that follows in part 2.

Part 2 constitutes a short commentary on the philological details of the text. There are two primary criteria deployed for understanding the words: their immediate poetic contexts (as well as the larger context of shared motifs and type-scenes); and the use of the same words and phrases elsewhere in the Ugaritic texts. These sometimes provide the keys to unlocking the meaning of various clauses and cola within this text. Some close parallels outside of the Ugaritic corpus also provide a number of important clues as to the meaning of some subsections. Philological study further afield remains a significant component of study, especially where the Ugaritic evidence is inconclusive. As usual with Ugaritic texts, many details cannot be resolved, despite the many etymologies offered in earlier studies (especially in the 1970s). Chapter 2 addresses the nine sections of lines 1–29, while chapter 3 handles the single, long narrative of lines 30–76. These chapters structure the philogical discussion section-by-section, as delineated toward the end of chapter 1 (in the section entitled, "The Structure of the Translation"). In their analysis, chapters 2 and 3 combine epigraphy, philology, literary analysis of motifs and type-scenes, and the identification of parallels within the Ugaritic corpus and elsewhere for various sorts of cultural information pertinent to the text.

The analysis cites a representative, though hardly exhaustive, listing of scholarly views concerning the vocabulary and grammar of this text. Indeed, it should be mentioned that chapters 2 and 3 do not identify all proposals made by scholars.[2] Instead, the main proposals (as I see them), along with the philological and literary support for each, are provided in the notes. The references and notes, especially the citations of secondary literature, are designed to be representative and not exhaustive. I have used the social-science format for citation of secondary literature in order to avoid the plethora of footnotes that would otherwise be needed. (The exception to this practice is the use of abbreviations, which are listed above.) In addition, I would point out that I have not discussed many reconstructions that have been proposed for the lacunas. In general, those without clear parallels remain largely hypothetical, and reconstructions without such clear parallels generate a weak basis for interpreting the text. Many of the various proposals of reconstructions can be found in Foley (1980), Trujillo (1973), Tsumura (1973), and *MLC*.

Part 3 moves to the larger questions surrounding the overall interpretation of the text. Based on the discussion in chapters 2 and 3, chapter 4 broaches this question primarily from a literary perspective, by examining the correspondences between lines 1–29 and lines 30–76. In view of the important role that the idea of "sacred marriage" has played in interpreting the text, I have decided to focus on this question in chapter 4, as the argument for this view has often proceeded from assumptions about the correlations between the two major sections of the text. With an eye to the mistaken attribution of sacred marriage in this text, chapter 4 takes a closer look at the textual relations between the ritual sections of lines 1–29 and the mythic narrative of lines 30–76. On the one hand, the comparisons of these sections indicate what they share, which allows for a clearer understanding of what the text as a whole is concerned with. On the other hand, the comparisons issue in a negative finding: the basis for a "sacred marriage" is shown to be lacking.

---

2. See Foley 1980; Trujillo 1973; Tsumura 1973; Xella 1973; the survey of Clifford 1975; the listing of views in *MLC* 427–48; and for later views, see Wyatt 2002.

Based on the literary observations discussed in chapter 4, chapter 5 takes up the task of probing the meaning of the text in its larger cultural context. Chapter 5 undertakes a synthetic examination of the text by noting how the various genres and cultural codes intersect and to what end. In part, this chapter follows up the theoretical reflections by Xella (1973:78–106), expanded by work within the field of ancient Near Eastern studies (in particular, Livingstone 1986) and by theorists working on ritual (such as Bell 1992, 1997).

At this point, we turn to part 1 with introductory considerations followed by a presentation of the text and translation of CAT 1.23.

PART 1

INTRODUCTION AND TEXT

1

INTRODUCTION AND TEXT

The scribe of CAT 1.23 did not provide the text with a title or his own name, unlike what one finds in a number of other Ugaritic texts. As noted early on by Albright (1934:133), the scribe did include single scribal lines running across the obverse of the tablet, indicating that lines 1–29 constitute a series of discrete pieces. In contrast, lines 30–76 show no such lines and present a single unit. It has been assumed by commentators that 1.23 forms a single text rather than a scribal combination of two texts, one on each side of the tablet. The physical evidence of the tablet of 1.23 supports this view, as the writing continues from the bottom of the obverse (lines 1–29) over the bottom edge (lines 30–34), and directly continues on the reverse (lines 35–76).[1] So 1.23 is not simply a tablet containing two texts, one written on either side. Because both lines 1–29 and 30–76 focus on the meal for the so-called Goodly Gods (*'ilm n'mm*), the presupposition of a single text appears additionally reasonable. At the same time, this view raises the issue of the relationship between the two parts, beyond their shared theme. This question is one of the main concerns addressed in chapters 4 and 5 of this study.

The scribal features in this text provide further information important for understanding this text. First and foremost, the scribal lines present in lines 1–29 are consistent with scribal production of ritual texts. The lines of the sort found in 1.23.1–29 are quite common in Ugaritic ritual texts;[2] though hardly entirely absent from literary texts, scribal lines are considerably rarer in such texts. Scribal lines in both administrative and ritual texts represent demarca-

---

1. For other examples of continuous writing running from the bottom of a column, onto the lower edge, and to the top of the next column, see 1.4 III–IV, 1.6 III–IV, 1.14 III–IV, 1.19 II–III and 1.24.

2. Daniel Fleming (personal communication) informs me that scribal lines are characteristic of the ritual texts from Emar as well.

tions of sections for the users of the texts. Scribal lines occasionally appear in literary texts to mark off a colophon at the end of a text (1.6 VI 54–58) or to mark a direction to the text's user (1.4 V 42–43; cf. 1.4 VIII 47–48). Scribal lines in literary texts may interrupt, or follow the completion of, the narrative line of literary texts, in order to add further information, whether the identification of the scribe at the end of a text or scribal instructions directed to the text's user within the narrative. Yet even these uses of scribal lines in literary texts correspond to their usage in administrative and ritual texts. In this regard, *ṯb lmspr*, "to (re)turn to the text," appears in 1.4 V 42–43 and 1.40.35, both delimited by scribal lineation. So the general situation in texts elsewhere corresponds to the scribal lines in 1.23: scribal lines to demarcate ritual information in lines 1–29; and no scribal lines in lines 30–76 as expected of the narrative of literary texts.

In characterizing lines 1–29 as ritual, care is required. For, if 1.23.1–29 is a ritual as such, it is unlike any ritual text known at Ugarit. This first major section of 1.23 is better regarded not as a single "ritual text." It is certainly not a list of offerings that characterizes so many Ugaritic ritual texts. Instead, 1.23.1–29 contains a number of third-person instructions, the sort of which one finds in Ugaritic ritual texts added to mentions of offerings (e.g., 1.43.23, 24–26; 1.104.16–20; 1.106.15–17, 23–24, 32–33; cf. 1.115.8, 10). The musical instruction in line 12 (and the mention of figures who appear to be singers in lines 14 and 29) may be compared with the instruction for the singer in 1.106.15–17: "And a singer shall sing the song, several times, before the king" (*wšr yšr šr p'amt lpn mlk*; Pardee 2002:54, 55). There is additional ritual information included in 1.23.1–29 as found in Ugaritic ritual texts: lines 19–20 compare well with 1.41.51 (as commentators have long noted).[3] In addition, 1.23.1–29 contains second-person commands (line 6) and greetings (lines 7, 26), with named addressees; these are somewhat rare in the ritual corpus.[4]

The first-person invocations in lines 1–7 and 23–28 are also unusual for the ritual corpus,[5] and perhaps these mark the specific departure of the ritual action of lines 1–29. In addition, it is these very lines 1–7 and 28–29 within 1–29 that relate closely to lines 30–76. All in all, lines 1–29 mix ritual instructions (lines 12, 14–15, 29), ritual information (lines 19–20, 21–22) and ritual performance (lines

---

3. For references and discussion, see chapter 2, on p. 62 below, in the examination of lines 19–20. See also p. 12.

4. For examples of second-person direct address in ritual contexts, see 1.40.19–22, etc.;1.108.19–27; and 1.161.2–10. This sort of address differs from the relatively common second-person instructions in ritual texts, for example in 1.39.20; 1.104.16–20; 1.116.9; 1.126.22, 23; 1.132.2; 1.161.30; and 1.164.20. See also 1.119.26–36 and 1.124.5.

5. First-person statements are rarely attested in ritual contexts outside of the sacrificial cult (e.g., in the incantations of 1.169.18 and RS 90.2014.2); I have found none used in sacrificial cult.

1–7, 23–27), along with ritual actions with mythic content (lines 8–11, 13, 28) and recitations of mythic material (lines 16–18, 25–26).

Assuming 1.23 represents a single text, what might the ancient scribes have called it? In fact, the two units might have been given separate titles. Lines 1–29 look like the sort of ritual mentioned in 4.149.14–16, as noted by Trujillo (1973:193),[6] with its cultic devotion in the "sown" (unless this were the name of a town):

| ḫmš yn | five (jars of) wine |
| bdbḥ mlkt bmdrʿ | for the sacrifice of the queen in the sown |

Accordingly, a scribe might have entitled lines 1–29 *spr dbḥ mlk wmlkt bmdrʿ*, "the document (or record) of the sacrificial liturgy of the king and queen in the sown." In other words, we have royal ritual, as emphasized by a number of scholars (e.g., Foley 1980; Wyatt 1998:325), or what Bell (1997:129) calls "the king's cult."[7] In this text, this royal cult operates outside the setting of the temple.

In contrast to lines 1–29, lines 30–76 constitute a single narrative unit, a mythic narrative, with a single scribal line demarcating the preceding ritual material. Other texts that fall into this classification of mythic narrative include the Baal Cycle (1.1–1.6), Kirta (1.14–1.16), and Aqhat (1.17–1.19). Accordingly 1.23.30–76 might have had a title analogous to the Baal Cycle, (*lbʿl*), hence *lʾilm nʿmm*, "regarding the Goodly Gods."[8] This section lacks scribal lines, like many shorter mythic narratives.[9] However, as this study indicates, this text as a whole is more complex than the ritual specifics of lines 1–29 or the narrative of lines 30–76. Any title would have to account for fundamental commonalities between the two major sections as well as their fundamental differences.

This understanding of the text and its sections underlies the main title of this book. Some terms in the main title are emic in nature, that is, words that the ancients themselves use for their own works elsewhere. The first part of 1.23 is a royal work, with the king and queen (*mlk* and *mlkt*) as participants, and it involves a ritual liturgy (*dbḥ*) in the sown (*bmdrʿ*). Royal sponsorship extends to the second part as well, if only because of the royal sponsorship of its scribal production. Both lines 1–29 and 30–76 have a feast in the sown for the "Goodly

---

6. On this text, note the remarks of Clemens 2001:86 n. 401, 337–38, 341–42.

7. This feature is addressed more fully at various points in this study, in particular in chapter 5.

8. For a discussion of the translation "goodly" for *nʿmm*, see chapter 2, pp. 33–34, in the examination of line 1.

9. Longer myths have scribal lines for information that lies outside of the text's narrative line. On the whole, it would appear that scribal lines are more characteristic of ritual texts (in order to mark their various ritual parts) than literary texts. For further discussion, see below.

Gods" (*'ilm n'mm*) as their main point or goal. Beyond these labels, the Ugaritic texts do not provide emic terms that characterize the parts or purposes of a text like 1.23.

To characterize the parts of the text marked scribally by lines as well as the text's dynamics, modern commentators have resorted to etic terms. In particular, *ritual* and *myth* are the two terms at the center of the modern discussion of the text, and it is to the issues attending this discussion to which we now turn.

Throughout the twentieth century, interpreters characterized the parts as *ritual* and *myth*, terms that are used also in this study, but with the recognition of their problems. Each term carries a certain amount of baggage and problematic modern history. Indeed, both myth and ritual in their contemporary uses have been claimed to be modern inventions. In a 1981 study entitled *L'invention de la mythologie*, Marcel Detienne made the then-radical claim that myth in its modern usage is essentially an intellectual construct used to classify stories that ancient and modern cultures tell about themselves. Although the ancients used *muthos* for various sorts of traditional narratives (see Doty 2000:6–7, 99–100; Edmunds 1990:1–20), in the modern context *myth* has become a general term for narratives relating the nature of reality as understood in different cultures.[10] More precise and intellectually satisfying definitions are elusive, as what myth is said by scholars to be or do varies often according to their background, as nicely illustrated in the survey of Baeten (1996). Anthropologists have long viewed myths as expressions of cultural values and perceptions. Structuralist theorists such as Roland Barthes decode the various codes in myths. Depth psychologists such as Erich Neumann and James Hillman probe myths for their insights into the human psyche. And historians of religion such as Mircea Eliade see myths as expressions of sacred realities. Problems afflicting the definition of the term *myth* are well known and regularly rehearsed in discussions of the Bible and the ancient Near East.[11]

The term *ritual* suffers from a comparable difficulty. Catherine Bell (1997:21) remarks on ritual as a modern construct:

> The idea of ritual is itself a construction, that is, a category or tool of analysis built up from a sampling of ethnographic descriptions and the elevation of many untested assumptions; it has been pressed into service in an attempt to explain the roots of religion in human behavior in ways that are meaningful to Europeans and Americans of this [twentieth] century.

In her surveys, Bell (1992, 1997) contributes to the larger theoretical discussion, in particular by showing the many presuppositions underlying the use of

---

10. See the summary presentation by Eliade 1991.
11. For example, Xella 1976; M. S. Smith 1994a; Averbeck 2004. See also Bell 1997:3–22.

the term ritual. At the risk of engendering problems, ritual is provisionally used here in the sense of actions taken (including recitations), with accompanying understandings, in a circumscribed setting. Rituals constitute a series of symbolic actions, whereas myths are symbolic narratives, or discourses concerning deities (Walls 2001:4, following Paul Ricouer).

To avoid the problematic aspects of the term *myth*, one could use the term *narrative* instead, and this has gained a certain acceptance in the field (e.g., the title, *Ugaritic Narrative Poetry*, abbreviated in this study as *UNP*). At some points, I do employ the term *narrative*, yet there is a distinct advantage to retaining the term *myth* in the context of this study. Using the word *myth* (as well as the adjective *mythic*) provides a conceptual grid for the text as a whole: characterizing the longer narrative of lines 30–76 as myth connects directly to some of what I will call the mythic images and evocations in lines 1–29. The latter include expressions or phrases (including divine epithets) that suggest a sort of mythic understanding shared with the overall theme of lines 30–76. There is another disadvantage to drawing a strong contrast between ritual and narrative. Like myth, ritual may be cast in narrative terms. Because of these considerations, I have retained the traditional terms, *ritual* and *myth*, but not without some concerns.

As Bell (1997:80) observes, traditional dichotomies posed between ritual and myth run the risk of simplification, as they delineate too neatly between ritual as what is performed or done and myth as what is narrated or said. Indeed, contrary to this dichotomy, 1.23 contributes to the larger discussion of myth and ritual by displaying in a single text the multiplicity of myths and rituals, their recurring interpenetration, and their disjunction at various points. And the connections are not only between rituals and myths. As we will see, one mythic segment (line 16) also connects to another (lines 67–68). Despite these important complexities in CAT 1.23, the terms *ritual* and *myth* remain the terms commonly used by students of religious texts both modern and ancient, and such terms help us students of these texts to enter into our discussion of them. At the same time, the discussion that follows indicates the inadequacy of these etic terms. With rituals and myths deliberately cast in the plural, the title is designed to situate this study relative to prior studies of this subject that construed the text essentially as one of "myth and ritual" (in the singular). In the spirit of Bell's critique, this study also questions the assumption that 1.23 consists of two parts that neatly divide into a set of rituals and a myth.[12]

Before shifting to a discussion of the other terms in the title of this volume, I would mention one further aspect about the rituals and myths in CAT 1.23. In

---

12. See the following section for further discussion.

sophisticated ancient texts such as this, there is a rather complex representation of what the myths and rituals "are" or "do." This representation is not expressed in theoretical terms but is embedded in the performance of the various rituals and the presentation of the different myths. As noted in chapter 5, the ancients did not write works on their theory of myth or ritual. Instead, theory is embedded in praxis. Ancient rituals and myths operate with traditional cultural ideas about ritual and myth, or they may develop further theoretical understandings. In the case of CAT 1.23, its various rituals and myths manifest a ritual theory over and against what is attested elsewhere in Ugaritic texts. In this way, the ritual practice of 1.23.1–29 is also a text of ritual theory. Similarly, the myths provided in various forms, not only in lines 30–76 but also within lines 1–29, suggest a rather complex understanding of myth.

Like the terms *myths* and *rituals* used in the main title of this work, the terms in the subtitle of this work are etic. The dynamics moving the dominant ritual of lines 1–7 and 23–27 as well as the myth of lines 30–76 to the meal in the sown involve several constructions of binary oppositions, some clearly emic, others etic. These oppositions, addressed in chapter 5, are mediated by expressions of intersection that arguably are constructed in order to issue in cosmic reconciliation or integration.[13] Accordingly, to read this text is to negotiate between emic and etic terms, to recognize the similarities and differences between the ancient terms of textual production and the modern modes of interpretation.

A Brief History of Interpretation of CAT 1.23

CAT 1.23 has occasioned considerable discussion since its publication in 1933.[14] As the first translations with philological notes were elucidating the basic understanding of this text (see Albright 1934; Ginsberg 1935), there was a flurry of discussion over Virolleaud's and Dussaud's reconstruction of southern Levantine phenomena in the text. Their interpretations included place-names such as Ashdod (*'ašdd* as then read in line 65) and Qadesh (*qdš* in line 65), as well as the figures of Terah the moon-god (see *'itrḫ* in line 64) and Arabs (*'rbm* in lines 7 and 12) (see Virolleaud 1933; Dussaud 1933). This approach came in for quick criticism (e.g., Albright 1934:138–40; Barton 1934:66). In part, the reading of the text eliminated some of these features, such as Ashdod in line 65 reread as *'ašld*. Other words seminal to this approach also were interpreted differently (e.g., *qdš*

---

13. This point is discussed at considerable length in chapter 5.

14. For the history of scholarship through 1973, see Foley 1980:109–44; Trujillo 1973:7–17; Tsumura 1973:228–39; and Xella 1973:12–24; see also the sketch in *TO* 1.360–65, and the listing of views in *MLC* 437–39.

as a general term for holy place; *'itrḫ* as a verb of betrothal in line 64; and *'rbm* as officials of some sort). As a result, this approach largely subsided by the late 1930s, although it would occasionally resurface later (e.g., "Arabs" in de Moor 1987:119 n. 13).

In the mid-1930s, study focused on the astral deities in the text. In the hands of Nielsen, the astral deities in this text corresponded to astral deities in South Semitic religion, which was used to support the reconstruction of a primitive level of Semitic religion (Nielsen 1936:70–97). Some of the evidence was problematic. It became apparent that *'itrḫ* was not related to the moon-god, Terah. However, there was no denying the importance of the astral deities, Shapshu and Shahar and Shalim, in 1.23. Indeed, as Cutler and Macdonald would later observe (1982), this is not the Ugaritic mythology of Baal and Anat. Other scholars following Nielsen's line of research would pursue the putative astronomical understanding underlying the text or the symbolism of the astral figures named in the text. This focus on the text's astral figures addressed a significant though limited segment of the text, and this approach would return to vogue in the late 1990s.

At about the same time in the 1930s, research was also moving in a decidedly different direction. Early studies had noted the ritual instructions in lines 1–29. Barton (1934) proposed a spring ritual setting for the text. Based on the name of Shalim, Barton situated this ritual at Jerusalem.[15] Although this particular detail did not hold up, interest in the rituals of lines 1–29 understandably continued. Particularly dramatic was the discussion over the instructions for cooking a "kid in milk" thought to be in line 14, as it seemed to provide a Canaanite antecedent for the biblical law of Exod 23:19, 34:26, and Deut 14:21 against boiling a kid in its mother's milk (Ginsberg 1935:72).

In an early study in 1934 and then in a landmark essay published in 1946, Gaster pursued a ritually oriented approach. Influenced by the "myth and ritual" approach popular at the time in biblical and ancient Near Eastern studies in Scandinavia and England, Gaster, in his 1934 study, saw the text "as the libretto of a miracle-play," which was "the prototype of the great feast of Sol Invictus healed in Syria" performed in the fall (1934:156). This fall setting would be accepted by the bulk of commentors (see *TO* 1.361). In his longer 1946 study, Gaster's approach to 1.23 began with well-established parameters. He divided the text into lines 1–29 and 30–76 based on this understanding (Gaster 1946:49–50; his italics):

---

15. Cf. Shalem in Ps 84; see also Wyatt 1996:336 n. 198.

The most cursory inspection of the text reveals a strange and curious feature: it possesses *two* prologues (one at the beginning (ll. 1–7) and the other in the middle (ll. 23–27). For this there must be a reason, and a moment's further examination discloses it: *All that precedes the second prologue is ritualistic; all that follows it is dramatic.* We thus have before us a religious "manual" divided into two "chapters," the one dealing with the sacrificial and similar rites of a cultic ceremony, the other presenting the text of a traditional mummery or "miracle play."

This observation about the division of the text had already been made by Albright (1934:133) and other scholars, and it would remain a crucial observation (e.g., Foley 1980; Tsevat 1978:25*; Xella 1973). In addition, this division can be supported by recourse to the distribution of scribal lines (which Gaster ignored in both studies), as noted above.

It was a further interpretive step taken by Gaster that distinguished his approach. Ritual and drama were mapped onto the two major sections of the text (lines 1–29, especially lines 1–7 and 23–27, and lines 30–76), sometimes in a one-to-one relationship. As a result, elements in one major section could be used to illuminate components in the other major section. Furthermore, Gaster shopped freely around the ancient Near East, India, and the Greco-Roman world in search of putative parallels. The result was a richly imagined world that included sacred marriage (*hieros gamos*) as well as other stock features seemingly evident in many texts studied by the myth and ritual approach. In this later study, Gaster switched from a fall seasonal setting to one in the spring.

The overall approach appeared defensible in view of the ritual and mythic material, and a number of writers followed Gaster. For example, Gordon (1949:57) cited Gaster's view as though it were unproblematic. In the wake of Gaster's work, later exemplified by his well-known book *Thespis*, 1.23 was regarded as a major support for the myth and ritual approach applied to other Ugaritic texts such as the Baal Cycle (1.1–1.6). Here, it seemed, the text provided both the text of the ritual and the myth performed for it. Echoing Gaster, de Moor (1972:2.17) would later characterize the text as the "libretto of a cultic play" ("this is a legitimate assumption"), culminating in "a sacred marriage rite." Cross (1973:22) also labeled the text in this manner. De Moor (1972:2.18; 1987:117–18) would identify in this sacred marriage the king as Ilu, Athirat as the queen, and Anat as a high priestess (probably a princess, in his view). Lipiński (1986) largely follows suit. Falling in a line of myth and ritual readings, Foley (1980:4) characterizes the text as "a lectionary for a royal ritual which defined the relationship between royal figures and gods." Foley (1980:10, 12, 24, 56, 178) offers his own version of identifications of royal figures, including the Goodly Gods with the "princes," which was presupposed by his interpretation of *šrm* in line 22 and by his reconstruction of *š[rm]* in line 2.

Of contemporary authors, it is Wyatt (1996:216–68, 1998:324–25, 2004, 2005a, 2005b) whose approach echoes the perspective of Gaster. Like Gaster, he expresses great sympathy for seeing *hieros gamos* in this text, primarily as an expression of royal ideology. Referring to the theory of the text as a *hieros gamos*, Wyatt comments (1998:325; his italics):

> It is here that I think that the *royal* dimension is important. A mythic paradigm is established here which is used to convey basic notions about the concern for the chief deity for the created order, and the implicit identification of his offspring with kings becomes the means whereby royal duties are represented as actualizing the theological programme.

The case is premised on a series of speculations (see also Wyatt 1977:381). For example, Wyatt identifies the *'ilm n'mm* with Shahar and Shalim, themselves "hypostases" of Athtar (the Venus star). The former view has been maintained by a number of scholars. However, the latter has been judged rather problematic, as Athtar is attested as an independent deity in the Ugaritic corpus. Indeed, the basis for identifying Shahar and Shalim as "hypostases" of Athtar is unclear. Crucial for Wyatt's interpretation, it is unclear that any identification between the sets of divine births and human kings is involved at all (see the discussion below). This series of identifications is central to Wyatt's thesis, so that the king can be recognized in the figure of El and his royal children can be seen in El's sets of offspring. Wyatt (1996:227, 229, 284) also makes Athirat into a sun-goddess (variously labeled "avatars" or "hypostases"), even though Ugaritic attests to Shapshu as a sun-goddess, sometimes in the same text as Athirat (e.g., 1.6 I). While one might argue that at one time Athirat was such an astral figure, it is not clear that this remains explicitly the case in the Ugaritic corpus. More problematic than any single hypothesis in Wyatt's overall presentation is how the overall interpretation builds up a considerable series of speculations, one on top of another. This criticism, however, is not to discount the value of Wyatt's observations at various points.

Gaster's approach to 1.23 has appeared particularly problematic on internal grounds, as the text comprises not one but two or perhaps even three myths. As Gaster rightly noted, the dominant narrative consists of lines 30–76. As de Moor (1972:2.17) would note later, myth and ritual "merge in this very strange text and it is often difficult to make a proper distinction between the two." Working on the assumption that lines 1–29 may be characterized in general as a series of ritual pieces of various sorts, embedded within them are pieces of mythic material, presumably sung. This is clearest in line 16, as Cutler and Macdonald recognized (1982:34, especially n. 7), but arguably it also occurs in lines 8–11 (see Gulde 1998:304). Ignored by Gaster, these are evidently evocations of mythic narrative that parallel and complement the larger narrative in lines 30–76. In addition, within lines 1–29 there is at least one case of a "ritual acknowledg-ment" or observation where no ritual action as such seems to be taking place. In lines 25–26, Shapshu is acknowledged as doing something, but there is no ritual action indicated. (The same might apply as well to the description of Mot in lines 8–9, but this is a more difficult case.) In short, the myth and ritual approach was severely constrained by its theoretical horizons (as discussed further in chapter 4).

With the demise of the myth and ritual approach, 1.23 was addressed through other lenses. Structuralist and narratological studies, in particular those by Xella (1973), del Olmo Lete (*MLC* 429–37), and Hettema (1989–90), advanced the understanding of linkages between different parts of the text, in particular between lines 1–29 and 30–76, but without the theoretical assumptions of the myth and ritual approach. This alternative approach has been fruitful, especially in helping to show the lines of connection between different parts of the text. Welch (1974:433) proposed to see a chiastic structure across the whole of 1.23, a suggestion that has not met with acceptance. The stylistic study of W. G. E. Watson (1994:3–7) raises an important question about the many attestations of -*m* in the text, perhaps used for repetitions of, or focus on, various words.

Perhaps as a reaction to the myth and ritual approach, the narrative-ori-ented approach does not address sufficiently the question of the text's cultural context. Accordingly, other scholars have continued to pursue a seasonal set-ting to 1.23. For example, de Moor has long maintained a fall setting for the text based on the viticultural language attested in the text.[16] Gulde (1998:323–24) allows for a slightly earlier time frame. Pardee has affirmed the early fall setting of the text (1997b:275) with a rather precise argument:

> There is one specific feature and one of a more general nature that may serve to fix this ceremony in the cultic cycle. The specific feature is the mention of "dwellings of gods, eight …" in line 19 (*mṯbt 'ilm ṯmn*), for that phrase finds its closest parallel in a ritual text (RS 1.003:50–51 [KTU/CAT 1.41.50–51] …) where "dwellings (of the gods)" are distributed four by four on a roof, probably that of the temple of 'Ilu, on the first day of an unnamed month that follows the month named Ra'šu Yêni, "the beginning of the wine." Though most scholars have seen the text as referring to only one month and have assumed Ra'šu Yêni to have been the first month of the year, the structure of RS 1.003 and a host of other arguments indicate that Ra'šu Yêni was in all likelihood the last month of the year, the lunar month preceding the fall equinox, during which

---

16. See de Moor 1972:1.6–8, 2.17–24, *SPUMB* 79 n. 30, 1987:117–28. Cf. Dijkstra 1998:285, espe-cially n. 89.

the grape harvest and vinification would have begun, and that the ceremony indicated in RS 1.003.50–55 is that of the first month of the new year.

Thanks to this observation (as opposed to the more speculative arguments), it is possible to operate with this seasonal background as the context for 1.23.

As a possible corollary to the question of 1.23's seasonal setting, Schloen (1993) and Dijkstra (1998) have returned to Nielsen's emphasis on its astral dimensions. Schloen and Dijkstra depend on the often criticized presupposition that Shahar and Shalim are to be identified with the *'ilm n'mm*. Dijkstra's reading of some careful astronomical calculations against the text is speculative on other counts as well. For example, Dikjstra's approach relies explicitly on the identification of Dawn and Dusk with the morning and evening Venus star, but most commentators would relate the Venus star in its evening and morning manifestations to the deities Athtar and Athtart. As illustrated by this problematic identification, Dijkstra's astral approach relies on questionable assumptions. Despite such difficulties, there may be more to the theory than it seems, and to my mind it borders on the brilliant. If Shahar and Shalim could be identified with the Gemini of the month of June (as suggested in *TO* 1.362), then the second set of births might have fitted with the fall equinox. If so, the astral dimension of the text may indeed have worked with the seasonal backdrop.

In his observations about 1.23's astral dimensions, Schloen (1998) has suggested that the astral gods of 1.23 are mythical allomorphs of the monstrous bovine children of El in 1.12. As evidence for these allomorphs, Schloen insightfully noted the transformation of the fallen stars into bovids in *1 Enoch* 86. These texts for Schloen (1993:219) involve expressions of "household kinship rivalry." In particular, Schloen sees in 1.23.67–76 an expression of this kinship bond:

> As children of the patriarch, the kinship bond extends far enough that they demand entrance, seeking work and rations with their kin at harvest time when agricultural laborers are needed.

The gods do indeed demand entrance, in order to secure provisions. On the level of the mythological narrative, who is implicitly inside the sown already? Schloen is right to pose the issue in terms of kin (as does Wyatt 1996:223), but Dawn and Dusk differ in nature from the *'ilm n'mm*. There is a fundamental difference about these sets of offspring missed by Schloen and others who would identify them (e.g., Foley 1980:186). Theoretically, other texts cited by Schloen and Wyatt could suggest this sort of identification, but the parallels with 1.23 are assumed to reflect the same understanding of the divine figures. Instead, it is quite possible that 1.23 may contain an inversion of the traditional themes that these modern authors find in this text. This question particularly affects their identification of the *'ilm n'mm* as beneficial deities, a problematic view on a relatively straightforward reading of the text.

Like Yamm and Mot in the Baal Cycle, these deities are destructive and monstrous in character; in this respect they strongly differ from the beneficial deities in El's family. Following a typology developed by Franz Wiggermann (1992, 1996a, 1996b) for Mesopotamian literature, I have proposed that the divine society in the Ugaritic texts can be divided in broad terms between beneficial deities often represented anthropomorphically and divine enemies often represented as monstrous (M. S. Smith 2001:27–40). The beneficial gods at Ugarit at their core largely consist of the astral family of El. (In the Baal Cycle, this family stands in some tension with Baal and Anat.) Dawn and Dusk belong among the children of El's astral family. What is missed in the analyses of Wyatt and Schloen is that, unlike Dawn and Dusk, the *'ilm n'mm* are presented in 1.23.61–64 as destructive deities. Although these too are divine children in this text, it is clear that they are not recognized as regular members of the family, despite their affiliation with El. In fact, in 1.23 they are expelled by El. In contrast, it is the astral family that is at home in the sown, and the destructive *'ilm n'mm* reach this zone only by effort and permission. They are otherwise outsiders.

In view of these proposed interpretations, there have been various attempts to interpret the text's purpose and setting. As noted above, Gaster saw the text as a celebration of firstfruits. *TO* 1.363–65 stresses the importance of fertility in the text, a view also expressed by del Olmo Lete (*MLC* 438–39). Cutler and Macdonald (1982) suggested the text was designed to avert famine, against the sort of forces represented by the ravenous *'ilm n'mm*. In a similar vein, Dietrich and Loretz (1998) take the text essentially as an incantation, "Beschwörung gegen die Schädlichen Naturkrafte." Following suit, Gulde (1998) calls the text "die Beschwörung des *Agzrym bn ym*." This approach would seem to apply quite well to lines 8–11. Tsumura (1973:222–23, cited in 1999:236 n. 73) offers a more complex version of this approach:

> The main theme and purpose of the cult depicted in UT 52 is the fertility of the land through the birth of the Good Gods of fertility which assures food and drink for the community of Ugarit. Hence, its goal is the inauguration of a new seven year cycle of plenty in the land by means of banishing the destructive power by sympathetic magic, giving assurance of enough bread and wine to the new-born Gods of fertility, a "Heptad,"[17] in the act of drama and introducing into the ritual the heptad-theme in terms of the "traditional"

---

17. The difficulty with this particular element of Tsumura's understanding is addressed in chapter 3, pp. 115–16 n. 64.

sevenfold performances of liturgy and the motif of "good"-ness in keeping with the atmosphere of [the] entire rite. This cult was probably reenacted at the end or toward the end of the seven year cycle of famine.

Tsumura's points nicely address the several references to "seven" in the text, and surely he is correct in highlighting the importance of agricultural plenty. Moreover, there is in lines 8–11 a banishing of the destructive power. However, Tsumura's view hinges on taking the *'ilm n'mm* as nondestructive, which reads against the apparent meaning of lines 62–64 (see excursuses 1 [pp. 68–69] and 4 [pp. 105–9]). Indeed, as highlighted in *TO* and *MLC*, the text otherwise takes a rather complex view of the cosmic destructive powers. This is particularly evident in lines 52–76, which presents a conciliating end point for the potentially destructive *'ilm n'mm*. Unlike incantational texts where conflict against hostile powers is standard, the powers represented by the *'ilm n'mm* seem to be permitted into the zone of the participants. They are invited, not warded off magically, but included ritually in the celebration of the meal. Gaster's old instinct about relating this text to the offering of firstfruits may come close to the mark for this section, and accordingly, we might modify Tsumura's understanding by suggesting that Death is warded off in lines 8–11 in the ritual, but destructive powers are included in the feast at the end of the text. Such inclusion may represent a means of averting the power of such forces, but this mode of averting such power differs from incantations or elimination rituals.[18] In short, the text contains rather different views of, and approaches to, the cosmos's destructive powers. It is possible that Tsumura is correct in seeing a transition between seasons of famine and plenty. This might be viewed less as the literal setting; instead, the text might be taken as the expression of a wish for plenty and for the avoidance of famine, with seven years being a literary vehicle for expressing this hope.

From this history of interpretation, brief as it is, it is possible to gain a general appreciation of the structure and setting of this text as well as the relations between its different components. Following Gaster, one may see this text as a sort of firstfruits celebration of agricultural fertility. In contrast to his later word (1946), Gaster (1934) recognized the late summer/early autumn as the seasonal context for this text, a view that was seconded by others, such as de Moor (1972:2.17–24) and Pardee (1997). Indeed, it is precisely during what Fitzgerald (2002) has called "the fall interchange period" between the dry and rainy seasons that this text presents various rituals and narrative pieces. The approach

---

18. For elimination rituals, including Lev 16:7–22, see Loretz 1985:35–57; Janowski and Wilhelm 1993; Janowski, "Azazel," *DDD* 128–31; Wright 1987; Borowski 2002c:418, all with references to the pertinent literature. For further discussion, see chapter 5.

of Dijkstra and Schloen suggests the need for greater sensitivity to the astral expressions in, and perhaps behind, the text. With Pardee's calendrical reckoning, locating the text in the context of the month preceding the autumnal equinox may suggest an intersection of terrestrial seasonal time with cosmic astral time suggested by Dijkstra and Schloen.

Building on the structural observations of Xella and Hettema, it is possible to see in 1.23 several "mythologies of death" or, perhaps better put, various mythologies of death and life. These present and perform various reconciliations of death and life, as experienced in and through the natural world. This approach enjoys the virtue of accounting for the several intersections between the rituals and the narratives as well as the series of twin ritual actions and the double figures found in the narrative of lines 30–76. Opposition of space is crucial to the rituals (lines 3–4 on the one hand versus lines 13 and 28 on the other) and also in the narrative (especially lines 66–76). This opposition of space is reconciled by their intersection during "the fall interchange period," experienced on the terrestrial plane in the shift of weather patterns but also perhaps realized or read on the cosmic plain through the stars. The timing of the coming rains of the fall could have been correlated with the important astral event of the autumn equinox that would have made a combined reading of terrestrial and astral reality a particularly powerful one. In short, the text contains a plentitude of ritual actions and narrative recitations that provide a variety of perceptions about death, some negative, others less so. None of these is predicated on the traditional and perhaps more familiar model of conflict and combat known from the Baal Cycle. Instead, 1.23 celebrates both the destruction of death (lines 8–11) and the incorporation of powers of destruction into the realm of life (lines 68–76).

Interpretive Premises about Death and Destruction in 1.23

In view of the centrality of death and destruction in this text, it may be instructive at this point to lay out its perspectives on these themes. The Ugaritic texts offer a number of different and sometimes overlapping pictures of death, or what may be called "mythologies of Death." Some of these appear in narrative, some in the ritual elements. The mythology of Death in the Baal Cycle (KTU/CAT 1.4 VIII–1.6) offers a different model of what is found in KTU/CAT 1.23. The first is premised on cosmic conflict, expressed by the struggles between Death personified as the opponent of the warrior storm-god, Baal. In contrast, 1.23 offers no mythology with Baal, and there is no conflict between warriors serving as the model of relations between death and life. Instead, 1.23 offers an entirely different picture, or I should say, pictures of death and destruction, some played out in rituals, others embedded in narratives related contextually to these rituals. Indeed, what I wish to highlight is that 1.23 manifests a plurality of approaches to death and destruction. The pictures of death and destruction in 1.23 largely involve a series of oppositions that intersect in ritual and narrative; this intersection produces a momentary reconciliation or integration of some opposites of reality.

In the putatively ritual section of 1.23 (lines 1–29), it is the death of Death that permits the life of the harvest (lines 8–11). The metaphors of lines 8–11 depict Death's destruction in the language of the vine, pointing implicitly to the fuel for life that this destruction yields. Implicitly the feast celebrating life requires a harvest, the death and destruction, of the natural components consumed; there is no drinking of wine, or feast, without the destruction or death of the vine's fruit. With the elements of the feast coming from a process of the death of Death, life in a sense feeds on death; from death comes life.

In the narrative of lines 30–76, the early life of destructive forces is followed. Lines 30–54 form the backdrop to El's family, first in his acquiring wives and then in his siring his astral children. These lines provide the larger context for what follows. After an account of how the destructive forces are born into the world (lines 55–61), they begin to feed on life (lines 61–64). In response, they are expelled by El, the ultimate author of life and death. The constraint of these figures is expressed by their consignment to a realm like Death, the barren steppeland (lines 64–70). Yet, these destructive forces need life, and so they ask for a place within the realm of life, expressed by the cultivated land or sown (lines 70–76). The request is granted, and they enter for a ritual moment to share in the divine fare. This is a moment of cosmic reconciliation without conflict. The cosmic forces of destruction, perhaps analogous to Death, are allowed to share in the divine feast derived from the fruits that in a sense come from death's demise (cf. lines 8–11). The divine food to which they are granted access is a symbolic recognition of their own divine nature. Destruction, in the form of these Goodly Gods, is therefore not merely warded off or destroyed as with Death in lines 8–11; it is included, if only for a ritual moment, to share in the food and wine of the divine feast belonging to the beneficial, life-giving gods and goddesses (lines 1–7, 23–29; lines 70–76). Destruction, as with Death, then is intertwined with life; perhaps in a sense it is its twin reality. Both destruction and life suffer from each other, and they grow, thanks to the other; and both can be included at the same feast, the ritual celebration of reality. Both sides of reality are divine.

To arrive at this picture requires many detailed arguments and consideration of both smaller and larger issues in 1.23. There are two interpretive premises necessary for the picture that I have just given, and which is pursued further below. The first, following the vast majority of scholars (though hardly all), is that *mt* in line 8 is "Death." The second is that the *'ilm n'mm* represent destructive cosmic forces as known in other texts. (That Death is one of the *'ilm n'mm* is possible, though hardly necessary, and it is discussed in two excursuses.) Otherwise, the overall interpretation that I offer regarding 1.23 does not depend on my decisions about other major interpretive difficulties, which are addressed in chapters 2 and 3.

TEXT AND TRANSLATION

TEXT NUMBERS

RS 2.2002 = ŠŠ (Virolleaud 1933) = *UT* 52 (Gordon) = *CTA* 23 = KTU/CAT 1.23. Museum number: AO 17.189.

SITE LOCATION

Acropolis, House of the High Priest (= Library), Tranche C, point topographique 6 = 209 (Bordreuil and Pardee 1989:26; for a map of the House of the High Priest, with point numbers, see Bordreuil and Pardee 1989:25).

DIMENSIONS AND PHYSICAL CONDITION

195 x 128 x 30 mm. (Bordreuil and Pardee 1989:26). For a description of the physical condition, see *CTA*, p. 96.

TEXT EDITIONS

Virolleaud 1933; *CTA*; KTU; CAT; Lewis, *UNP* 208–14; Bordreuil and Pardee 2004:2.27–31.

PHOTOGRAPHS

Bordreuil and Pardee 2004:CD-ROM, no. 5; West Semitic Research unpublished photographs (see acknowledgements).

VOCALIZATION

Bordreuil and Pardee 2004:2.31–34.

TRANSLATIONS

Albright 1934:133–38; Bordreuil and Pardee 2004:2.27–31; Caquot, Sznycer, and Herdner, *TO* 1.357–79; Dietrich and Loretz 1998; *CML*[1] 120–25; Gaster 1934,

1946, *Thespis* 418–35; *CML*[2] 123–27; Ginsberg 1935:63–72, *KU* 77–86; Gordon 1949:57–62, 1966:94–98; Gulde 1998:295–302; Hettema 1989–90:82–86; Lewis, *UNP* 208–14; de Moor 1972:2.17–24, 1987:117–28; del Olmo Lete, *MLC* 440–48; Pardee 1997b:274–83; Trujilllo 1973; Tsumura 1973, 1999; Wyatt 1996:224–27, 1998:324–35, 2002:324–35; Xella 1973.

STUDIES

Albright 1934:133–38; Bordreuil and Pardee 2004:2.34–36; Caquot, Sznycer and Herdner, *TO* 1.353–79; Cross 1973:22–24; Dijkstra 1998; Gaster 1934, 1936, *Thespis* 406–35; *CML*[2] 28–30, 123–27; Ginsberg 1935; Gulde 1998; Haran 1978, 1985; Hettema 1989–90; Komoróczy 1971:79–80; Lipiński 1986; Milgrom 1985; de Moor 1972:2.17–24; del Olmo Lete, *MLC* 427–48; Pope 1955:38–40, 1979; Ratner and Zuckerman 1985, 1986; Schloen 1993; Segert 1986; Trujillo 1973; Tsevat 1978; Tsumura 1973, 1974, 1978a, 1999:228–37; W. G. E. Watson 1994; Wyatt 1996:224–35, 1998:324–35, 2002:324–35, 2004, 2005a, 2005b; Xella 1973.

PART 1, LINES 1–29: RITUAL ACTIONS AND NARRATIVE RECITATIONS

[The front of the tablet]
Section 1, lines 1–7: Invitation to the Feast

1	ʾiqrʾa ʾilm nʿ[mm]	Let me invite the Goo[dly] Gods,
2	wysmm bn šp[ ]	Indeed, the beautiful ones, sons of …
3	ytnm qrt lʿly[ ]	Those given offerings on high …
4	bmdbr špm yd [ ]r	In the outback, on the heights …
5	lrʾišhm wyš[ ]xm	to their heads and …
6	lḥm blḥm ʾay	Eat of every food,
	wšty bḥmr yn ʾay	And drink of every vintage wine.
7	šlm mlk šlm mlkt	Peace, O King! Peace, O Queen!
	ʿrbm wṯnnm	O enterers and guards!

Section 2, lines 8–11: Ritual Recitation about Mot

8	mt wšr yṯb	"Death-and-Ruler (Death the Ruler) sits,
	bdh ḫṭ ṯkl	In his (one) hand a staff of bereavement
8–9	bdh/ḫṭ ʾulmn	In his (other) hand a staff of widowhood.
9	yzbrnn zbrm gpn	The pruner prunes him (like) a vine,

| 10 | yṣmdnn ṣmdm gpn | The binder binds him (like) a vine, |
| 10–11 | yšql šdmth/km gpn | He is felled to the terrace like a vine." |

Section 3, line 12: Recitation and Response Indicators

| 12 | šb'd yrgm 'l 'd | Seven times it is recited over the dais (?), |
| | w'rbm t'nyn | And the enterers respond: |

Section 4, lines 13–15: Words of Song with Ritual

| 13 | wšd šd 'ilm | "And the field is the field of El/the gods, |
| | šd 'aṯrt wrḥm<y> | Field of Athirat and Rahm<ay>." |

14	'l 'išt šb'd	On the fire seven times
	ǵzrm g ṭb	The boys with a good voice:
	gd bḥlb	Coriander in milk,
	'annḫ bḥm'at	Mint in curd.

| 15 | w'l 'agn šb'dm | And on the basin seven times: |
| | dǵtt | Incense. |

Section 5, lines 16–18: Song

| 16 | tlkm rḥmy wtṣd [ ] | "Rahmay goes hunting ..." |

| 17 | tḫgrn ǵzr n'm [ ] | The handsome guys are girded ...
Or: She is/They (the goddesses) are girded
with goodly might (?) ... |

| 18 | wšm 'rbm yr[ ] | And the names of the enterers ...
Or: and the name, the enterers ... |

Section 6, lines 19–20: Divine Dwellings

| 19 | mṯbt 'ilm ṯmn | The divine dwellings are eight, |
| 19–20 | ṯ[ ]/p'amt šb' | .[..] seven times. |

Section 7, lines 21–22: Dressing of Singers

| 21 | 'iqn'u šmt | Blue, red, |
| 22 | ṯn šrm | crimson of/are the singers
(or: of/are the two singers). |

Section 8, lines 23–27: Invitation Reiterated

| 23 | 'iqr'an 'ilm n'mm | Let me invite the Goodly Gods, |
| | ['agzr ym bn] ym | [Ravenous pair a day old] day-old [boys], |

24	ynqm b'ap zd 'at̲rt	Who suck the nipple(s) of Athirat's breast(s)
		…
25	špš mṣprt dlthm	Shapshu braids their branches (?),
25–26	[ ]/wġnbm	[…] and grapes.
26	šlm ʿrbm wtnnm	Peace, O enterers and guards,
27	hlkm bdbḥ nʿmt	Who process with goodly sacrifice.

Section 9, lines 28–29: Song Reiterated

28	šd {šd} 'ilm	"The field is {the field} of El/the gods,
	šd 'at̲rt wrḥmy	Field of Athirat and Rahmay."
29	xxxxx.xxb	

Part 2, Lines 30–76: Divine Narrative

Section I, El and His Wives: Lines 30–49

Subsection A, Lines 30–39a: El and the *mšt'ltm*
Lines 30–35a: *mšt'ltm* at the sea
[The bottom edge]

30	[ ]l[ ]y[ ]'i gp ym	… to the seashore
	wyṣġd gp thm	And he marches to the shore of the Deep.
31	[ ]x[ ] 'il mšt'ltm	El […] the two servers (?),
	mšt'ltm lr'iš 'agn	Servers (?) from the top of the pot.
32	hlh tšpl hlh trm	See her, she's low; see her, she's high.
	hlh tṣḥ 'ad 'ad	See her, she cries: "Daddy, Daddy!"
33	whlh tṣḥ 'um 'um	And see her, she cries: "Mommy, Mommy!"
	t'irkm yd 'il kym	El's penis lengthens like the sea,
34	wyd 'il kmdb	Indeed, El's penis, like the flood.
	'ark yd 'il kym	El's penis lengthens like the sea,
35	wyd 'il kmdb	Indeed, El's penis, like the flood.

[The back of the tablet]
Lines 35b–39a: *mšt'ltm* in the house

35	yqḥ 'il mšt'ltm	El takes the two servers (?),
36	mšt'ltm lr'iš 'agn	Servers (?) from the top of the pot.
	yqḥ yš<t> bbth	He takes, se<t>s (them) in his house.

37	ʾil ḫth nḫt	As for El, his staff descends (?),
	ʾil ymnn mṭ ydh	As for El, his love-shaft droops (?).
37–38	yšʾu/yr šmmh	He lifts (his hand), he shoots skyward,
38	yr bšmm ʿṣr	He shoots in the sky a bird,
38–39	yḫrṭ yšt/lpḥm	He plucks, sets (it) on the coals;
	ʾil ʾaṯtm kypt	El indeed entices the two females.

Subsection B, Lines 39b–49a: El Secures His Wives
Lines 39b–42: First Condition Expressed

39	hm ʾaṯtm tṣḥn	If the two females cry:
40	ymt mt	"O man, man!
	nḥtm ḫṭk	Your staff droops,
	mmnnm mṭ ydk	Your love-staff sinks!
41	h[l] ʿṣr	Lo[ok] a bird
	tḫrr lʾišt	You're roasting on the fire,
	ṣḥrrt lpḥmm	Browning on the coals."
42	ʾa[ṯ]tm ʾaṯt ʾil	(Then) the two fe[mal]es will be wives of El,
	ʾaṯt ʾil wʿlmh	Wives of El, and his forever.

Lines 42–46b: Second Condition Expressed

42–43	whm/ʾaṯtm tṣḥn	But if the two females cry:
43	y ʾad ʾad	"O Daddy, Daddy!
	nḥtm ḫṭk	Your staff droops,
44	mmnnm mṭ ydk	Your love-staff sinks!
	hl ʿṣr	Look a bird
	tḫrr lʾišt	You're roasting on the fire,
45	wṣḥrrt lpḥmm	Browning on the coals."
	btm bt ʾil	(Then) the two females will be daughters of El,
45–46	bt ʾil/wʿlmh	Daughters of El, and his forever.

Lines 46b–49a: First Condition Realized

| 46 | whn ʾaṯtm tṣḥn | And see, the two females cry: |
| | ymt mt | "O man, man! |

47	nḥtm ḫṭk	Your staff droops,
	mmnnm mṭ ydk	Your love-staff sinks!
	hl ʿṣr	Look a bird
48	tḥrr l'išt	You're roasting on the fire,
	wṣḥr<r>t lpḥmm	Brow<n>ing on the coals."
	'aṯtm 'aṯ[t 'il]	(So) the two females are wiv[es of El],
49	'aṯt 'il w'lmh	Wives of El, and his forever.

Section II, Births of the Pairs: Lines 49b–64

Subsection A, Lines 49b–59: Dawn and Dusk
Lines 49b–52a: Sexual Relations and Birth

49	yhbr špthm yšq	He bends down, kisses their lips,
50	hn špthm mtqtm	See how sweet their lips are,
	mtqtm klrmn[m]	Sweet as pomegranate[s].
51	bm nšq whr	As he kisses, there's conception,
	bḥbq ḥmḥmt	As he embraces, there's passion.
51–52	tqt[nṣn w]/tldn	The two cr[ouch and] give birth
	šḥr wšlm	to Dawn and Dusk.

Lines 52b–54: The Birth Announcement

52	rgm l'il ybl	Word to El was brought:
52–53	'aṯ[ty]/'il ylt	"El's [two wi]ves have given birth."
53	mh ylt	"What have they born?"
	yldy šḥr wšl[m]	"A newborn pair, Dawn and Dus[k]."
54	š'u ʿdb lšpš rbt	"Make an offering to Lady Sun,
	wlkbkbm knm	And to the stationary stars."

Subsection B, Lines 55–64: The Goodly Gods
Lines 55–59a: Sexual Relations and Birth

55	yhbr špthm yšq	He bends down, kisses their lips,
	hn špthm mtqt[m]	See how swee[t] their lips are,
	<mtqtm klrmnm>	<Sweet as pomegranates.>

| 56 | bm nšq whr | As he kisses, there's conception, |
| | bḥbq ḥ[m]ḥmt | As he embraces, there's pa[s]sion. |

| 56–57 | ytbn/yspr lḥmš | He sits, counts to five, |
| 57 | lṣ[...]šr pḫr | For ... [...] the assembly sings (?). |

| 57–58 | kl'at/tqtnṣn wtldn | The two crouch and give birth, |
| 58 | tld ['i]lm n'mm | Give birth to the Goodly [G]ods, |

| 58–59 | 'agzr ym/bn ym | Day-old devourers, one-day-old boys, |
| 59 | ynqm b'ap dd | Who suck the nipple of the breast. |

Lines 59b–61a: The Birth Announcement

| 59 | rgm l'il ybl | Word to El was brought: |

| 60 | 'atty 'il ylt | "El's two wives have given birth." |

| | mh ylt | "What have they borne?" |

| | 'ilmy n'mm | "Twin (?) Goodly Gods, |

| 61 | 'agzr ym bn ym | Day-old devourers, one-day-old boys, |
| | ynqm b'ap dd | Who suck the nipple of the breast." |

Lines 61b–64a: Aftermath of Birth, The Appetite of the Goodly Gods

| 61–62 | št špt/l'arṣ | They set a lip to earth, |
| 62 | špt lšmm | A lip to heaven. |

	wy'rb bphm	Then enter their mouths
	'ṣr šmm	Fowl of the sky,
63	wdg bym	And fish from the sea.

	wndd gzr l<g>zr	As they move, bite upon <bi>te
63–64	y'db 'uymn/'ušm'al	They stuff—on both their right and left—
	bphm wl tšb'n	Into their mouths, but they are unsated.

Section III, The Goodly Gods in the Outback and the Sown: Lines 64b–76

Subsection A, Lines 64b–68: Their Consignment to the Outback (*mdbr*)

| 64 | y 'att 'itrḫ | "O wives I have espoused, |
| 65 | y bn 'ašld | O sons I have begotten: |

| | š'u ʿdb tk mdbr qdš | Make an offering amid holy outback, |
| 66 | ṯm tgrgr l'abnm wlʿṣm | There sojourn mid rocks and brush." |

| 66–67 | šbʿ šnt/tmt | For seven years complete, |
| 67 | ṯmn nqpt ʿd | Eight cycles duration, |

| 67–68 | 'ilm nʿmm ttlkn/šd | The Goodly Gods roam about the steppe, |
| 68 | tṣdn p'at mdbr | They hunt to the edge of the outback. |

Subsection B, Lines 68b–76: Their Admission into the Sown (*mdrʿ*)

| 68–69 | wngš hm nǵr/mdrʿ | The two approach the Guard of the sown, |
| | wṣḥ hm ʿm nǵr mdrʿ | And the two cry to the Guard of the sown: |

| 69–70 | y nǵr/nǵr ptḥ | "O Guard, Guard, open!" |

| 70 | wptḥ hw prṣ bʿdhm | And he himself opens a breach for them. |
| 71 | wʿrb hm | And the two enter: |

| | hm ['iṯ ṯmt (?) l]ḥm | "If [there is there (?) f]ood, |
| 71–72 | wtn/wnlḥm | Give that we may eat! |

| 72 | hm 'iṯ [ṯmt (?) yn], | If there is [there (?) wine ...], |
| | [w]tn wnšt | Give that we may drink!" |

| 73 | wʿn hm nǵr mdrʿ | And the Guard of the sown answers them: |

| | ['iṯ lḥm...]xt | "[There is food for the one who ... (?)] ..., |
| 74 | 'iṯ yn dʿrb btk [...] | There is wine for whoever enters ...[...]" |

75	mǵ hw	... he himself approaches,
	lhn lg ynh[...]	He serves a measure of his wine ...
76	wḥbrh ml'a yn[...]	And his companion fills (it [?]) with wine ...

THE STRUCTURE OF THE TRANSLATION AND THE CAST OF CHARACTERS

It is necessary at the outset to explain the reasons for the division of the
text and translation as laid out above. As noted early on by Albright (1934:133),
the sections of the first section, lines 1–29, are delineated by scribal lines,
which serve as the basis for its division. This stands in contrast with lines 30–
76, which has no scribal lines and therefore appears to be a narrative whole.
For lines 1–29, the difficulty is not their delineation into sections, but in dem-
onstrating that they represent a larger whole with structurally identifiable

parts. Lines 1–29, in fact, contain significant internal repetitions indicating a measure of coherence. More specifically, the invocation of lines 1–7 repeated in lines 23–27 and the reference to the divine field of line 13 repeated in line 28 indicate that lines 1–29 should be read as some sort of ritual whole. (Determining what sort of ritual whole will occupy a good deal of the discussion in this book.)

For lines 30–76, no scribal lines provide an indication for divisions. So speaking generally, lines 30–76 constitute a single whole. At the same time, there are internal indicators, mostly various sets of repetitions, that suggest literary sections within lines 30–76. The correspondences between the sexual relations, births, and birth announcements for the two sets of newborns help to indicate the overall structure of the narrative of part 2. From the correspondences between the births in the middle of the narrative, it is evident that lines 49–61 constitute a paired set of correspondences. Accordingly, lines 30–49 would thus represent an initial section, and lines 61b–76 a third major section. From the parallels, it is evident that the additional description of the Goodly Gods' ravenous appetite in lines 61–64 at the time of their birth belongs to the rendering of their birth in the second section, which provides the motivation for the third section of lines 64–76.

Within the first section of lines 30–49, there is a set of correspondences that suggest the delineation of subsections. Within the larger section of lines 30–49, there is the question of the organization of lines 30–39. The double mention of *mšt'ltm* (lines 31 and 35–36) would suggest subdividing lines 30–39 into lines 30–35 and 36–39a. Lines 39b–49 show a series of parallel structures that also allows for delineation. It is clear that lines 39b–42 correspond to lines 42–46, and that these sections in turn correspond to the narrative outcome in lines 46–49. Accordingly, three subsections are evident within lines 39b–49.

Within the third section of lines 64–76, there is a contrast between the outback (or steppe), on the one hand, and, on the other hand, the sown. Based on this opposition, it may be suggested that lines 64–68 (the outback) and lines 68–76 (the sown) constitute the subsections of the third major section in lines 64–76.

At a lower level of narrative, one detail in the third section echoes an element in the second, and that is the command of El to provide an offering: in the second section this is commanded in line 54, and in the third section this is ordered in line 65.

Based on the preceding observations, the following schema represents my understanding of the narrative's overall structure:

Section I. El and His Wives: Lines 30–49
Subsection A, Lines 30–39a: El and the *mšt'ltm*
Lines 30–35: *mšt'ltm* at the sea

Lines 35–39a: *mšt'ltm* in the house

Subsection B, Lines 39b–49: El Secures His Wives
    Lines 39b–42: First Condition Expressed
    Lines 42–46a: Second Condition Expressed
    Lines 46b–49a: First Condition Realized

Section II. Births of the Pairs: Lines 49–64a
    Subsection A, Lines 49b–59: Sexual Relations and Birth
        Dawn and Dusk   Goodly Gods
        Lines 49b–52a   Lines 55–59a

    Subsection B, Lines 52b–64a: Birth Announcement and Offering
        Dawn and Dusk   Goodly Gods
        Lines 52–53 + 54   Lines 59b–61 (+ 65–66)
                           +

                        Aftermath of Birth,
                        The Appetite of the Goodly Gods
                        Lines 61–64a

Section III. The Goodly Gods in the Outback and the Sown: Lines 64b–76
    Subsection A, Lines 64b–68a: Their Consignment to the Outback (*mdbr*)
    Subsection B, Lines 68b–76: Their Admission into the Sown (*mdr'*)

The organization of the following text, translation, and notes in chapters 2 and 3 follows this delineation of lines 1–76.

For the sake of convenience, I provide the cast of characters for the two major sections:

Section I: The Rituals (lines 1–29)
    Humans
    "I" (line 1)
    King (line 7)
    Queen (line 7)
    Royal attendants (lines 7, 12, 26–27)
    Singers (lines 14, 29)

    Divinities
    The unnamed Goodly Gods (lines 1–2)

Mt w-Šr, the god of Death (line 8)
Athirat wa-Rahmay (lines 13, 28)
Rahmay (line 16), presumably the same figure as Athirat wa-
Rahmay, or at least one of these two figures
Athirat (line 24), presumably the same figure as Athirat wa-
Rahmay, or at least one of these two figures
Shapshu, the sun-goddess (line 25)

Section II: The Narrative (lines 30–76)
El (line 30 [partially reconstructed], 31, 33–35, 37, 39, 42, 45, 49, 52,
59)
The two unnamed females (lines 31–58)
Dawn and Dusk (lines 52, 53)
Shapshu (line 54)
The stars (line 54)
The unnamed Goodly Gods (lines 58–76)
The unnamed Guard of the sown (lines 68–76)
The unnamed companion of the Guard (line 76)

PART 2

COMMENTARY

2
LINES 1–29: RITUAL ACTIONS AND NARRATIVE RECITATIONS

SECTION 1, LINES 1–7: RITUAL INVITATION

1	ʾiqrʾa ʾilm nʿ[mm …]	Let me invite the Goo[dly] Gods, …
2	wysmm bn šp[m …]	Indeed, the beautiful ones, sons of …
3	ytnm qrt lʿly[ ] …	Those given offerings on high …
4	bmdbr špm yd [ ]r …	In the outback, on the heights …
5	lrʾišhm wyš[ ]xm …	to their heads and …
6	lḥm blḥm ʾay	Eat of every food,
	wšty bḥmr yn ʾay	And drink of every vintage wine.
7	šlm mlk šlm mlkt	Peace, O King! Peace, O Queen!
	ʿrbm wt̠nnm	O enterers and guards!

Lines 1–2

Strictly speaking, the opening verb *ʾiqrʾa* is not a hymnic invocation to the unnamed gods (Gulde 1998:304), as the proper term for a hymn is **šyr* (cf. *ʾa*[*š*]*r* in 1.24.1 and *ʾašr* in 1.24.38). Nor is it simply an invocation (cf. **qrʾ bšm*; so Gaster 1946:57; see Lewis, *UNP* 208). The key to this verb, and indeed to the entire first section, is the recognition that it represents an invitation to a feast, as noted by Trujillo (1973:19, 35, 46–47).[1] In support of this view, Pardee (1997b:276 n. 1) cites CAT 1.161.4–9, 11–12. Parallels, with the verb used in the

---

1. This approach is broached but not pursued by Tsumura 1973:19, 179. For the volitive verb form here and in line 23 with an energic *–n*, see Rainey 1971:165; Tsumura 1973:19; *SPUMB* 168–69; *UG* 455, 499, 725.

context of a meal, appear in 1.21 II 2–3, 10–11 and 22 II 3–4, 9–10 and 18–20. In these contexts, El calls (*qr'//*ṣwḥ) the Rephaim to a feast in his house. In addition, one may note the noun qr'at in 1.116.2, which DUL (708) takes as "banquet, festival." Pardee (2002:94, 116 n. 151) renders this noun as a "gathering" for a sacrifice and compares the verbal forms in 1.161. Overall, the context of the feast and the human parties mentioned in 1.23.6–7 suggest that *qr' may convey invitation.

Lichtenstein (1968:25; 1977:25–30) has studied the topos of the feast in detail and observes the sequence of preparation, invitation, and service of food and drink in numerous Mesopotamian, Ugaritic, and Israelite texts (see also Clifford 1983, and below). This pattern is evident in 1.4 VI 38–59: preparations for the feast (lines 38–43); invitation to the participants to the banquet (lines 44–46); and the feast of food and wine (lines 47–55). 1.15 IV 15–28 contains the sequence of preparations, followed by the summons to guests, while 1.3 I shows the sequence of preparation, food, and drink. Proverbs 9:1–6 also manifests the same basic sequence of events led by the figure of Wisdom, who prepares her feast, issues her invitation, and includes food and wine (Lichtenstein 1968:21–22, esp. n. 102). For Prov 9 the pursuit of Wisdom is implicitly likened to the rich fare of the feast that even a divine can enjoy, as in 1.4 VII 38–59.

Lichtenstein (1968) compares the pattern of preparation plus invitation in a number of other ancient Near Eastern texts. In the Hittite myth of Illuyanka (ANET 125–26), the goddess Inaras prepares a lavish feast and issues a personal invitation to her unsuspecting victim. In Enuma Elish III:7–9, Anshar issues an invitation to the divine council (ANET 64): "Let all the gods proceed hither, Let them hold converse, sit down to a banquet, Let them eat festive food, partake of wine." In the Akkadian myth of Nergal and Ereshkigal (ANET 103–4), the god sends a messenger to fetch the portion of Ereshkigal, queen of the underworld, who cannot ascend to the prepared feast.

In these myths, a divine figure issues the summons to the guests. In the ritual of 1.23.1, the first-person figure remains unnamed. In view of the human agents named in line 7,[2] it may be inferred that a human party proffers the invitation in line 1. If correct, then it would appear to be a ritual specialist who mediates between the gods of line 1 and the human parties mentioned in line 7. Later in lines 14 and 29, singers (less likely, princes) are mentioned, and in lines 26–27 offerings are acknowledged. Accordingly, the setting seems to be a feast for gods, with the king, queen, and attendants present and accompanied by song and offering. Therefore, the first-person figure would theoretically seem to be a

---

2. I am unaware of any Ugaritic text that uses mlk and mlkt for a divine pair.

priest. It is noteworthy that if this first-person figure were indeed a priest, it is one who operates in this text outside of temple practice.

A further speculation about the conceptualization of this figure may be suggested, based on three correspondences between lines 1–7 and the final section of the narrative in lines 65–76. The first correspondence involves the locations mentioned in lines 2–3 and the *mdbr* in lines 65, 68; the second the mention of food and drink in lines 6 and 71–76; and the third the references to the Goodly Gods in lines 1 and 67. With correspondences in setting, consumables, and gods, we may suppose a further correspondence between the first-person figure behind line 1 and the "Guard of the sown" in lines 68–69 and 73 (see also lines 69–70). In short, the priest behind line 1 who invites the gods to eat and drink wine in line 6 structurally corresponds to the "Guard of the sown" who allows the Goodly Gods to enter and partake of the food and wine produced by the sown.

The terms for the gods, *nʿmm//ysmm*, are aesthetic, as in CAT 1.96.2–3: *wnʿm ʾaḥh/kysmsm*, "Indeed, her brother's loveliness, handsome as he is" (Smith, *UNP* 225). The first noun also applies to Baal's mountain (1.3 III 31; cf. BH *yĕpēh nôp*, "beautiful of height," Ps 48:3; *miklal-yōpî*, "utterly beautiful," Ps 50:2). According to Pardee (1997b:276 n. 5), Ugaritc *nʿm* is "the primary adjective for expressing goodness, *ṭb* the secondary one, that is, the distribution is just the opposite of the one in biblical Hebrew." At the same time, it is also evident that "goodness" in these instances is aesthetic. They indicate that the word may denote good appearance (see Ginsberg 1935:46). Foley (1980:21) stresses the use of this term for the gods as a sign of their royal character. However, other words not used with royal figures exclusively appear here as well, and so it would seem that royalty is not necessarily the primary association of the term in this context. This is indicated further by the characterization of the gods as *ysmm* (cf. Arabic *wasama*, "to be pretty," and *wasîm*, "pretty," cited in *UT* 19.1119). 1.4 IV 13–15 presents Athirat's servant hoisting her onto the animal's "beautiful back" (*ysmsmt bmt*; a variant of the same phrase without –*t* in 1.19 II 11). On the aesthetics in this context, Pardee (1997a:259 n. 149) observes: "It is debatable whether the donkey was beautiful in its own right, but it certainly was when its trappings were of gold and silver. The Ugaritic expression consists of a substantivized adjective preceding the nouns in question: *ysmsmt bmt pḥl*, lit. "the most beautiful (part[s] of) the thorax of the male equid." Perhaps the donkey was thought to be beautiful in its own right.

Selecting a proper translation for *nʿmm* in this text is difficult. The usual translations appear inadequate for one reason or another. "Beautiful" and "attractive" seem a bit strong (and lengthy), while "gracious" refers in common English more to manner than physical appearance. "Good," though philologically acceptable, may convey in English a moral connotation; such a sense is absent from this text. Perhaps closer to the mark is "goodly," which, according to *Merriam-Webster's Collegiate Dictionary* (10th edition, 2002), denotes both attractiveness and considerable size. The gods' attractiveness may derive from the idea of them as newborns in line 60, or it is possible that an antiphrastic expression may be involved. Tsumura (1973:190) noted (but rejected) the comparison of *n'mm* with *n'my*, used as a term for the underworld (1.6 II 19–20), where Mot overpowers Baal. In excursus 4, I maintain that *'ilm n'mm* are destructive forces (arguably similar to Mot). The considerable size of the *'ilm n'mm* is evident in lines 61–64. It may be mistaken to interpret an epithet in terms of the narrative, especially at such considerable distance from this opening invocation. However, this title for the gods also appears in the narrative section of lines 30–76; so perhaps this is not a real difficulty. In sum, "goodly" etymologically and contextually is at least as suitable as the other proposals. As for the "Goodly Gods" and their character, further discussion is reserved for excursuses 1 and 4, which are located in the discussion below where more of their features are presented in the text.

The reading *šp*[*m*] is generally preferred to an alternative sometimes seen in the literature, *šr*[*m*]. The latter reading, suggested by Virolleaud in his *editio princeps*, may have been driven by *bn šrm* in line 22 (see *CTA*, p. 98 n. 2). This reconstruction was followed by Tsumura (1973:21–25; 1999:228, 234), who would see singers here. Foley (1980:22–24) likewise follows this reading, but he interprets the word as "princes" here and in line 22. Foley's further proposal (1980:178) that the "Goodly Gods" are to be identified as royal figures depends on this reading. However, a close examination of magnified WSRP photographic material shows that while *p* can fit the contours of the remaining wedges, the reading *r* cannot be sustained. In the undamaged area of the sign, there is clearly room for the head of the lower middle horizontal wedge of *r*. However, there is no sign of such a wedge. In addition, the break of damage cuts horizontally without showing any head of *r* but fits the pattern of the horizontal lower wedge of *p*. Therefore, the reading of Virolleaud followed by Tsumura cannot be sustained. Efforts to interpret and/or reconstruct the end of line 2 are discussed at some length by Foley (1980); I prescind from any additional reconstruction.

Lines 3–4

Lines 3–4 are difficult. The clearest elements are the locations, mostly outside of the urban setting of Ugarit for the invocation of the Goodly Gods. *Mdbr*, "outback," in line 4 is the clearest, and *špm* seems to follow suit. In his *editio princeps* of this text, Virolleaud (1933:137) compared *šĕpāyîm bammidbār* in Jer 4:11. Tsumura (1973:27) and Xella (1973:44) mention the same combination of locales in Jer 12:12. Both biblical passages are cited by *TO* (1.369 n. b). In these verses, the locations denote a landscape without sustenance. The most up-to-date Ugaritic dictionary (*DUL* 835; see Xella 1973:44) prefers for *špm* "dune," hence "in the desert of dunes," based on Syriac *šapyō* and Arabic *safiyy*. I agree with Pardee (1997b:276 n. 8) that the *mdbr* would seem not so much a desert with dunes but an ecological zone lacking in water.

The end of line 3, *l ʿly*[ ] could also refer to such a locale. Citing BH *ʿăliyyâ*, Virolleaud (1932:137) was led to understand *qrt* as "town" (so too *TO* 1.369). At the same time, it is to be noted that the preposition *l-* here differs from the *b-* that opens line 4 and its places. Ginsberg (1935:46) renders: "Glory be given unto the Exalted Ones." The effort to see *ʿly*[ ] as an allusion to "the gods most high" (so Lewis, *UNP* 208) may well be correct. Somewhat like Ginsberg's rendering for the initial line, Lewis translates lines 3–4 as follows:

> Render glory to the gods most high,
> In the desert, the windswept heights.

There is poetry in this proposal, and especially with line 4, it works well thematically with lines 1–2. The verb *ytnm* in line 3 could yield the sense attributed to it by Lewis (*UNP* 203, evidently presupposing **wqr*; so too Ginsberg 1935:46; Gaster 1946:58; *DUL* 713, with further references), which sounds also biblical (cf. Ps 68:35: "Ascribe strength to God" [*tĕnû ʿōz lē(ʾ)lōhîm*; cf. Ps 29:2: *hābû lyhwh kābôd šĕmô*]). However, the imperative of this verb is *tn*. Therefore, another verbal form is involved, such as a jussive with mimation ("let one give ..."). Trujillo (1973:61) has construed *ytnm* as passive, with *qrt* as the subject: "Let a meal be given." Or, the final *–m* could point to the plural of a participial form. Pardee (1997b:276) assumes a participial form and understands the gods as those "who have provided a city on high." These gods seem, however, to have little if anything to do with settled life (cf. Pardee 1997b:276 n. 7). Pardee is right to see the gods as the antecedent to the participle,[3] but it may be passive (see Xella 1973:41–42). Foley (1980:10; 1987:72 n. 47) renders the clause as passive: "Let a city be given to [those most high .../on high (?)]." However, this translation ignores the lack of agreement in gender between the subject (feminine *qrt*) and the prefix verb (with its masculine *y–* and not feminine *t–*), a problem recognized by W. G. E. Watson (1994:4).[4]

The sense of the use of *ytnm* also depends on the larger context of lines 3–4. The locations in lines 3–4 suggest deities not customarily called upon in

---

3. For a participle following nouns in this text, see lines 26–27.
4. For further discussion of the options, see Wyatt 1998:323–26 nn. 2 and 3.

cities, temples, or the like, as most deities are in the many sacrificial texts from Ugarit. For two sets of places in an incantational context, see 1.169.3–4, 7–8; the latter includes *bmrmt*, "on the heights." These Goodly Gods are never mentioned in such sacrifices, and it would appear that they belong outside of the regular regimen of cultic observance. Therefore it would seem that these deities differ in category from the recipients of cultic devotion in Ugarit's temples. In light of this observation, it appears preferable to follow Trujillo (1973:61) in relating *qrt* to **qry* (*DUL* 714–15; *UBC* 1.203 n. 158), used in the D-stem for the presentation of offerings.[5] According to Leslau (445, 797), South Arabic *qrw* means "to offer a sacrifice," while **qry* in the West Semitic languages refers to an invitation to a feast. If correct, then the gods are to receive offerings in the peripheral region. Given this meaning, *ytnm* in line 3 may have a sacrificial connotation (cf. the etymologically related noun for offering, *ytnt*, 1.127.5; cf. 1.14 III 31, V 42, VI 12). I would agree with Pardee's rendering "on high" for *l'ly*[ ] in line 3 and view the places mentioned in line 4 as specifications of this phrase.

Line 5

Line 5 provides only one clear expression, literally "to their heads" (cf. "on their heads," Lewis, *UNP* 208).

Line 6

Line 6 presents an invitation to feast. This sort of double offering of food and drink also heads up the invitation in 1.4 IV 35–38: "eat, indeed drink" (*lḥm hm štym*). The terms in line 6, except the final element, also appear in the context of Baal's feast in 1.3 I (see especially line 5, *wyšlḥmnh*, and line 16, *ḥmr*). De Moor (*SPUMB* 75) compares the expressions *ḥmr yn* in 1.23.6 and *yayin ḥāmar* in Ps 75:9. He asserts that *ḥmr* is "the new wine which is still in the process of fermentation ... available very soon after the pressing of grapes in September." It is possible that the expression is to be reconstructed as well in 1.17 VI 3 (Wright 2001:100–101). De Moor also notes *ḥmr yn* in a Persian period Phoenician inscription from Shiqmona (Cross 1968 = Cross 2003:286–89).[6] Loretz (1993) largely follows de Moor in understanding *ḥmr* as new wine. Grabbe (1976:61) suggests that *ḥmr* simply means wine, and this conclusion is supported by evidence at Emar, where *ḥamru* is a gloss for wine, not a special type of wine.[7]

---

5. So Trujillo 1973:50; *MLC* 440, 658; Wyatt 1998:325 n. 3.

6. The phrase *ḥmr yyn* appears in Arad ostracon 2.5 (Pardee 1978:298). In the Arad inscription, it has been taken as a kind of grade of wine kept in a different sized container, a "*ḥomer* of wine" (see Pardee 1978:298; *DNWSI* 1.384), which makes sense in view of the amounts of goods otherwise listed. A measure is, however, not involved in 1.23.6 or Ps 75:9, or apparently in the inscription from Shiqmona.

7. See Fleming 1992:143 nn. 238, 239; Westenholz 2000:62; Pentiuc 2001:55–56.

At the same time, this leaves unanswered how one would understand *ḫmr yn* here. Translating "gärendem Wein," Tropper (*UG* 851) characterizes *ḫmr yn* as an epexegetical genitive. Lloyd (1990:181) disputes this general approach, in seeing *ḫmr* as a container; no philological argumentation is offered in support of this alternative. It is difficult to know how specific the sense of *ḫmr* is in the context of this feast, but given the usages elsewhere in Ugaritic and Hebrew (see Zamora 2000:306–14, 512), fermentation or at least some part of the process related to wine-making appears plausible.[8] In Lam 1:20 and 2:11 the root refers to the churned innards of a person in lamentation. Cross (2003:287 n. 13) captures the problem in his remarks: "The precise force of the expression escapes us. Perhaps it means 'well fermented wine', i.e., 'vintage wine'." In sum, some aspect of wine-making, perhaps fermentation, remains the proposal that enjoys the greatest support.

The particle *'ay* used at the end of each poetic line here suggests "any" thing that can be offered (Lloyd 1990:180). The particle appears in the name of the first weapon made by Kothar for Baal, *'aymr*, in 1.2 IV 19–20 (Xella 1973:45). Its name means "may he expel any/all."[9] Cognates include the Akkadian indefinite pronoun *ayyu* (*UT* 19.142; Trujillo 1973:69). This proposal represents the current consensus view (*DUL* 133), and it is accepted here.

As a second proposal, Cutler and Macdonald (1982) as well as Tsumura (1973:27–28; 1999:229, cf. Tsumura 1978b) take the particle as a negative, against the other Ugaritic attestations of the word. The view may be driven by an interpretation of the text as a ritual to avert famine (as it seems particularly in the case of Cutler and Macdonald), as an abundance of food and drink would militate against this interpretation. Indeed, there is no famine in sight, either in line 6 or in lines 73–76. Tsumura prefers to see here an "abstinence from eating and drinking," since in his view the destruction of the god Death is "prerequisite for bringing the abundance of food and drink" (1973:28; 1999:233). This approach presupposes a particular understanding of the ritual actions. Though the view is understandable, the immediate context of the invitation militates against this approach. It reads against the theme of the invitation where *'ay* would signal an invitation to a bounteous banquet of any and all food. As noted in the cases above, the invitation to the feast does not offer an abstinence from food and drink, but the opposite.

A third view of Ugaritic *'ay* in this context has been offered by Clifford (1983:28). He compares the particle to BH *hôy* in Isa 55:1–2, which he translates

---

8. See Ben Sira 34:30, and 37:27 in the margin of ms B, and in ms D, so *CDH* 3:258; see also Lipiński 1970:84–85.

9. See the discussions in *DUL* 64; *UBC* 1.343; *UG* 172, 244; see also Wyatt 1998:326 n. 5.

as a particle of greeting, "ho!" The genre of invitation to the feast would seem to favor this interpretation. However, Clifford's proposal does not take into account the use of Ugaritic *'ay* where it seems to mean "all" or "any" (1.2 IV 19, noted above). Moreover, the two occurrences of Ugaritic *'ay* that Clifford would render "ho!" (the other attestation being CAT 1.17 VI 3–4, largely reconstructed) may be rendered "all" or "any" in reference to the plenty of a feast offered by the speaker. Disassociating Ugaritic *'ay* and BH *hôy* enjoys the further advantage of not requiring a phonological irregularity between cognates, although in this instance such an irregularity is possible. Despite these caveats, the contribution reflected in Clifford's overall comparison is to be recognized.

Line 7

Line 7 invokes a new set of agents after the Goodly Gods of lines 1–2. The address begins with the king and the queen and proceeds to what seems to be cultic personnel (*'rbm wtnnm*), mentioned in a liturgical context in line 12.[10] Many scholars compare *'rbm* to priestly personnel known in Akkadian as *ēreb bîti*.[11] In addition, the royal circle includes officials called *tnnm* (*DUL* 922–23). Many commentators understand them as military personnel, based primarily on comparison with Akkadian *šanan(n)u*, attested at Ras Shamra and Alalakh (*CAD* Š/1:366).[12] Wyatt (1998:326 n. 8) also notes *tnn* in 1.14 II 38, which suits "archer" or the like. Cutler and Macdonald reject the military view of *tnnm* as inappropriate to the context of 1.23 (1982:39). However, there is no intrinsic problem with Rainey's view that these are military personnel who "seem to have played some role in a religious drama about the birth of the gods." Pardee's translation, "those who stand guard," is eminently plausible. Echoing the general translation of Driver (*CML*[1] 121), Lewis perhaps wisely prescinds from too much specificity with his translation "ministrants and marshals." At the same time, it is to be noted *'rbm* is not a cultic title elsewhere (Pardee 1997b:276 n. 12), and so the use of the expression only in this context suggests a meaning suitable to it. Below I will probe the suitability of its basic meaning "to enter," the sense that Pardee (1997b:276) adopts in his translation. Later, in lines 26–27, these figures are those who "process with goodly sacrifice" (*hlkm bdbh n'mt*).

The remaining question about line 7 involves the precise force of *šlm*. Lewis (*UNP* 208) renders as a greeting "Hail," while Tsumura (1999:229) suggests "peace," and Tropper (*UG* 728) "Heil." The translations of Lewis and Tropper are

---

10. Gaster 1946:58–59; Xella 1973:149–56; *DUL* 181.

11. Gaster 1946:56; *TO* 1.370 n. e; de Moor 1972:2.19 n. 69, with further proponents listed; Wyatt 1998:326 n. 7.

12. See de Moor 1972:19 n. 70, citing Rainey 1965:22. Note also Tsumura 1973:30–31; W. G. E. Watson 2000:571–72; *UG* 676.

particularly clever, as they capture the function of the word as a greeting and its expression of well-being (as in the largely defunct American English expression "hail and hearty"). As this is the first reference to the parties, their entry into the text by a greeting makes contextual sense. A number of commentators (e.g., Tsumura 1999:236) compare CAT 1.161.31–34, which offers wishes for well-being also fronting *šlm* before each party named. A comparable expression of wishes for "peace" may be involved in line 7. Disputing this view, Pardee (1997b:276) translates: "Give well-being." Following the imperatives to the gods in line 6, these also would be imperatives to the gods, as it is divinities who give *šlm* to people (Pardee 1997b:276 n. 11). It is possible, however, that the ritual welcomes the royal party into the picture following the first-person invitation to the gods. In the context, both the gods and the royal party are welcomed into the ritual setting.[13] Tropper (*UG* 727–28) compares 1.161.31–34 and lists both under the rubric of "Nominalsätze mit volitivischer Nuance." In view of the context, this understanding seems reasonable. A comparable epistolary use of BH *šlm* appears in Arad 16 and 21 (see Zevit 2001:395).

The section as a whole presents a ritual invitation of offering to *'ilm n'mm*. The figures initially invited to the offering come from outside the common setting of shrines or temples. As observed by Trujillo (1973:65), the description of line 4 suggests that these gods are invited to come from the *mdbr*. The human participants involved in the offering belong to the royal court, specifically the king and queen along with their attendants. The ritual here seems to take place at a point that lies between the *mdbr* of the *'ilm* of lines 1–4 and the urban home of the royal parties named in line 7. If the later lines 62–76 serve as any indicator, this location would be what is there characterized as the "sown" (*mdr'*). As noted in the introductory chapter, a general parallel for this sort of offering is provided by CAT 4.149.14–16 (Trujillo 1973:193), with its cultic devotion in the "sown" (unless this is the name of a town):

ḥmš yn	five (jars of) wine
bdbḥ mlkt bmdr'	for the sacrifice of the queen in the sown

While offerings seem to be characteristic of temple cult, both this text and 1.23.1–7 provide indication of offerings made in the sown. Furthermore, it is worth noting that the queen is mentioned as a cultic participant in both 1.23.7 and 4.149.14–16, hardly the norm in Ugaritic ritual texts.

---

13. The topic perhaps deserves further examination in light of parallels. Note one hymn from Ebla: "the Annuna gods have, O Enlil, founded it (= the city), the great gods have said (to you? to it = to the city?) 'hail!'" See Krecher 1992:293.

Section 2, lines 8–11: Ritual Recitation about Mot

8	mt wšr yt̠b	"Death-and-Ruler (Death the Ruler) sits,
	bdh ḫt ̠tkl	In his hand a staff of bereavement,
8–9	bdh/ḫt ʾulmn	In his had a staff of widowhood.
9	yzbrnn zbrm gpn	The pruner prunes him (like) a vine,
10	yṣmdnn ṣmdm gpn	The binder binds him (like) a vine,
10–11	yšql šdmth/km gpn	He is felled to the terrace like a vine."

Lines 8–9

The binomial name does not involve two figures, in view of the singular pronominal suffixes in line 8 on *bdh* (< **bi-yadi*; see *UG* 774–75). Virolleaud (1932), Ginsberg (1935:48), Gibson (*CML²* 28 n. 1, 123), *TO* (1.370 n. g), and other scholars identified the figure as Mot (see further the discussion below), with *šr* taken as the second element in Mot's binomial name, like the names of Kothar wa-Hasis, the craftsman-god, and Nikkal wa-Ib in 1.24 (Lewis, *UNP* 207). The word *šr* in line 22 occurs with the apparent meaning of "singer" or "prince" (Akkadian *šarru*; cf. BH *śar*). In keeping with the context here is the sense of "king, prince, ruler," as he sits (perhaps enthroned; van Zijl 1972:219; or less likely constrained, so Kosmala 1964:149). It is also befitting to attribute staffs in hand to a ruler. This meaning for *šr* also suits the context of the word in 1.12 II 51–52 as well as 1.123.3 (Pardee 2000b:698). Another suggestion is "dissolution" (*CML¹* 121 n. 121, 148, 161) or "evil" (de Moor 1987:120 n. 15; 1990:244; Foley 1987:71; Tsumura 1973:31–32; 1999:229), based on BH *śārā*, "to contend," Arabic *šariya*, "to grow angry," and *šarā* "to do evil," and Aramaic/Syriac *śry*, "to have a bad odor" (so Leslau 536). For the variations, see Pardee 1997b:276–77 n. 13. Ugaritic parallels supporting this approach are lacking.

Since the figure is said to be sitting or enthroned in the initial line of the tricolon of lines 8–9, the description seems to be anthropomorphic. It is for this reason that the two instances of *bdh* are rendered "in his hand," and not simply "in his power" (though surely this meaning is philologically possible). Moreover, the staffs in the god's two hands presuppose an anthropomorphic picture of hands and not only an abstraction of power (this is supported also by the iconographic parallel noted below). The figure described is evidently one whose power is destructive (lines 8–9) and whose power is metaphorically pruned back, tied, and felled (lines 9–11). From the nouns, it is evident that this is a figure of human destruction: "childlessness"//"widowhood" (Virolleaud 1932 citing Isa 47:8, as noted by Albright 1934:133 n. 172a; so too Driver, *CML¹* 121 n. 7). This is not a positive picture of the figure involved, but it is one that admirably fits "Death," as early commentators noted. Cutler and Macdonald (1982:40) follow suit: "There is no reason why *mt* should not mean simply 'death' here." Lewis (*UNP* 207) characterizes this identification as the main one today: "If there is a consensus…, it would be to see a reference to Mot, the god of Death."

An alternative proposal that El and not Mot is the figure involved goes back to Aistleitner (1953) and has been followed by Wyatt (1992b; reiterated in 2002:326–27 n. 10; see also 1976:421), as well as Dijkstra (1998:286–87). Both see a picture of El's circumcision here. This change in direction is inspired in part by the use of *mt* in lines 40 and 47 with reference to El. Wyatt (1992b:426) proposes the following (with the text references to 1.23 supplied in square brackets):

> While we are insufficiently informed about Canaanite circumcision rites and their symbolism…, I submit that the association of ideas between circumcision and fruit-production in Israel and Judah, as attested in the Bible, is probably not an innovation, but part of the traditional metaphorical furniture of the West Semitic languages, and suggests the possibility that the pruning imagery of the passage cited above [1.23.9–11] is also a figure for circumcision, and that El himself is to be understood as undergoing the rite in preparation for his subsequent marriage [narrated in lines 30f.].

Dijkstra sees here "the primal circumcision of El representing here the ideal husband prepared for manhood." Pardee (1997b:277 n. 13) partially follows this approach, in suggesting that *mt* means a generic man (cf. Akkadian *mutu*; BH *mĕtîm*/*mĕtê*), perhaps as a positive reference to a figure such as El. This view is unlikely to win much support, if only because it favors reading the word with a homograph attested at considerable remove, in lines 40 and 46, with too little concern for the clues in the word's immediate setting in line 8. In particular, El certainly is not a god with staffs of destruction. At the same time, Pardee's proposal nicely draws attention to the two staffs of Mot and El, which perhaps serve as foils from a thematic perspective: the staff of Mot brings death, while the staff of El brings life.

That *mt* is "Death" and not simply "man" receives further confirmation from an Aramaic incantation bowl published by Montgomery (1913:127–28, no. 3 and pl. 4). Montgomery (1934:63–64) had mentioned these bowls in general terms in his discussion of the *'ilm n'mm*, but the crucial comparison to 1.23.8–9 was made by Tsumura (1973:32–33, 183; 1974), noted by Gibson (*CML*² 28 n. 1), and discussed further by Fleming (1991:148–49). There is one particular bowl showing the Angel of Death with a weapon in each hand; the accompanying text describes his work as taking away children and spouse. This is the best parallel to the picture of Death in lines 8–9. The staffs in 1.23.8–9 are related further by Fleming (1991:148–49) to Emar 256:5–6, which refer to disinheritance as the breaking of a man's two staffs. Fleming writes: "In Mesopotamia generally, where we have the most extensive evidence, the *ḫaṭṭu* appears to symbolize a person's life and identity, so that its breaking strips him of both." Gaster (1946:59) had seen sexual double entendre here, with pruning suggesting emasculation, a vinestalk suggesting the penis, and pruned vine being the slain god. Although Gaster's suppositions exceed the evidence (for criticism, see Cutler and Macdonald 1982:41), the destruction of the figure in question is taking place; it is an act of violence rendered in viticultural terms.

Wyatt (1977) is critical of the approach taken by Tsumura, Gibson, and Fleming: "it is precisely the external evidence which justifies the interpretation of the colon as referring to two staffs." Wyatt himself is assuming that a single staff is involved based on his own external evidence of passages where two objects, animals or goddesses are really one, in Wyatt's words, "duplicated to fulfill poetic requirements." One of his parade cases involves the weapons made by Kothar in 1.2 IV. However, this passage in the view of most, if not all, interpreters presents two weapons, not one. So just as there are two weapons and not one in 1.2 IV, so there seem to be two staffs and not one in 1.23.8–9. In short, the parallel cited by Tsumura, Gibson, and Fleming remains germane.

The power of Death is indicated by CAT 2.10 (Lipiński 1983; Pardee 1987), which mentions pestilence as "like death" or perhaps "like Mot." Following the introductory identification of speaker and addressee in lines 1–3 and greetings in line 4, the body of the letter in lines 5–6 takes up the matter of the pestilence. In lines 11–13, the speaker describes the severity of pestilence:

w.yd/'ilm.	For the hand of the gods
p.kmtm/ʿz.mʾid	(is) here, like death/Mot, exceedingly strong.[14]

In this letter, the power of death, perhaps personified as Mot, is manifest as pestilence on the terrestrial level. Such pestilence may be situated stereotypically in the context of the late summer heat (Jer 9:20; cf. 8:13, 20; 9:9), when the scorching sun may afflict crops, animals, and humans. Jeremiah 9:20 is particularly pertinent, as it mentions the power of Death over the young child. Pestilence and the power of Death were experienced in the power of the scirocco (Hos 13:14–15; see M. S. Smith 1990:53; and the discussion in lines 9–11).

Pardee (1997b:277 n. 15) makes an astute observation in suggesting that *tkl* here may be a wordplay on *'uṯkl*, used in 1.41.1 for a "bunch of grapes," in view of the viticultural imagery here. The same may be said for **zmr* in 1.23.8–9 and 1.41.51 (cited below at lines 19–20), as mentioned also by Pardee (1997b:279 n.

---

14. See Lipiński 1983:124; Marcus 1974:406; Pardee 1987.

32). The implicit message evoked by such wordplay may be that the power of Death wanes at the time of the first cuttings of grapes.

Lines 9–11

The roots of the verbs in this tricolon are generally well understood (see the survey in Dietrich and Loretz 2000:185–86). The verb *zbr* (Leslau 631, *DUL* 999; *UG* 156) is cognate with BH *zmr* and Arabic and Ethiopic *zabara*, "cut, prune." Leslau explains the difference of bilabials as "alternance." Tropper (*UG* 156) explains in more detail: "Der Lautwandel *m > /b/ ist hier dissimilatorisch motiviert (vgl. dialektal-ar. *zbr* 'schneiteln' [Dozy I, 578–79])." Ethiopic *mazbara* is used for destruction, according to Leslau (377), a sense not far removed from its meaning in line 9. The root *ṣmd* in line 10 means "to tie" or "to bind," in keeping with the vine tending. The third verb is generally taken as the C-stem of middle weak *ql, "to be low" (*UG* 593, 605, 651). The first two verbs bear the third masculine singular pronominal suffix, arguably doing double-duty for the third verb, *yšql*, "he fell," as suggested by Gibson (*CML*² 123), among others, and followed below. The alternative is to take the verb as passive, specifically as the result of the first two verbs.[15] Grammatically, this approach holds the advantage of not requiring the carry-over of the object-suffix from the first two verbs to the third verb.

As an alternative for this view of the third verb, Dietrich and Loretz (2000:187–88, 191) propose to read *yšqṣ* (< *qṣṣ) for *yšql* based on the photo in *CTA* (plate XXXII). Accordingly, they translate the third line: "er wird beschneiden seine Pflanzung wie einen Rebstock." In the high-definition photographic WSRP material, the reading is in fact clear, when the letter is compared to *l* in line 12. In both cases, the middle vertical wedge shows the head and a vestigial tail. So the reading *l* is indicated. Following the sign is a further vertical wedge (the head and tail are clear), which is to be understood as a word-divider.

There is another epigraphic observation worth making in lines 11–12. The writing in line 11 curves up at the end of the line in order to fit the final three letters, as is clear in Virolleaud's copy (*CTA*, figure 67) and the WSRP photographs. It is as if the scribe was trying to squeeze in the last word of the line. This is not exceptional, as a similar curving upward in order to fit the end of the line appears in line 14. In both instances, the scribe was apparently trying to fit in the last signs of the line. However, there is a difference with the situation in lines 11–12 and lines 14–15. Line 12 contains two words, *km gpn*, and then has plenty of space. The scribe could have written the last word in line 11 at the beginning of line 12. In contrast, with line 14 the scribe turns the writing

---

15. I wish to thank my student Stephen Russell for pointing out this possibility to me.

upward, as what is written in line 15 goes to almost the end of the line. As is clear in Virolleaud's drawing, there is no space on line 15 for the material in line 14. The question is why the scribe did not write the final word in line 11 at the beginning of line 12, where he had plenty of room. It might be inferred that as the scribe was writing line 11, he did not realize that *km gpn* was to follow; thus he may have thought that he could finish the section with line 11 by squeezing in the last three signs. Then after he finished writing line 11, the scribe read the next part, which turned out to be the rest of the section that contained two more words, *km gpn*. He was forced to start a new line for only these two words. Bruce Zuckerman (personal communication) has made a further observation about the epigraphy in lines 11–12. The scribe may not have been listening to the text being dictated to him as he copied it, as it seems unlikely that someone dictating the text would have separated off the two words. Instead, it appears likelier that the scribe was reading off a prior copy and thought that the section ended with what he was writing on line 11.

The subjects in the first two lines are usually taken to be *zbrm//ṣmdm*. Dissenters from this view include Trujillo (1973:80) and Tsumura (1973:33–36; 1999:229). They take these nouns as cognate accusatives in construct to *gpn*, which means "vine."[16] There are two further questions about *zbrm//ṣmdm*. The first is whether they are singular or plural. Most scholars render them in the plural (e.g., Trujillo 1973:80; Tsumura 1973:33–36; 1999:229), but the verbal forms that they govern are ostensibly singular: *y–* is used for the third masculine singular, while *t–* is used for the third masculine plural (see Dobrusin 1981; *UG* 455, 458, 459). The second issue is whether the nouns stand in construct to *gpn* in both lines, which is how many critics take these plural nouns ("vine-pruners" //"vine-binders," as in Lewis, *UNP* 208). An apparent difficulty with this view is that *zbrm* and *ṣmdm* are ostensibly not in construct, if they are plural nouns. To avoid this problem, Tropper (*UG* 436, 479, 828) argues that *–m* on both nouns is enclitic and not part of these nominal forms, a view supported by the singular forms of the verbs. If the nouns are not in construct, then it would follow that *gpn* in the first two lines could be a metaphor, parallel to the simile with *kgpn* in the third line. According to del Olmo Lete,[17] the comparative *k–* in the third line may do double-duty in the first two lines.[18] Accordingly, del Olmo Lete's proposal is plausible.

---

16. See Kühne 1974:164–65. In 1.4 IV 4–7//9–12, the word is used metaphorically for ropes or the like, as in Gen 49:11; see Greenfield 1964:527 n. 2.

17. *MLC* 441; see also Zamora 1999:71, as well as W. G. E. Watson 1994:4.

18. A good example of this sort of double-duty, from a posterior line to an anterior one, in this case involving the subject, is in 1.12 I 25, cited on p. 98.

One difficult term in the tricolon is *šdmth*. The majority view seems to be "terraces" (*DUL* 810), in view of 2 Kgs 23:4, as understood by L. E. Stager.[19] For support, Stager also compares Deut 32:32 and Isa 16:8, where *gpn* is parallel to *šdmt* (already noted by a number of commentators, such as Gaster 1946:56). Stager himself observes that *šdmt* is used not always specifically for viticulture but more generally for agriculture (Hab 3:17, where the produce is food). Leslau (486) compares Ethiopic *sedemā, sedāmā, sədemā, sademot, sadimot,* "cereal spoiled by fog, kind of grass that grows in a field of wheat, fields," with the further comment, "transcription of Heb *šədemā*, pl. *šedemōt*, 'special kind of tilled land, terrace' through Gk. *sadmenōth*."

The rendering "terrace" has been considered unsuitable to the context (Wyatt 1992a). To obviate this difficulty, Driver (*CML*[1] 121), Xella (1973:36), and *TO* (1.370 n. j) render "vineyard." Similarly, in his discussion, Stager (1982:116) uses the expression "terraced vineyards," while Segert (1986:218) calls them "vineyard terraces." In Stager's view, the terraces are the location for the vineyard. The phrase, *šdmt bgp*[*n*], in CAT 1.2 I 43, is often cited in this connection. This phrase would suggest that an exact parallel with *gpn* is not required. Instead, *šdmt* may belong to the same constellation as *gpn* such that *šdmt* may be syntactically connected to *gpn* by the preposition *b*–. Accordingly, it may be reasoned that both nouns belong to the same larger arena of experience rather than being precise synonyms. The same point may apply to *śdmt* in the biblical verses. In Isa 16:8, *gpn* as the B-word specifies what is cultivated on the *śdmt*, the A-word. This usage differs in Deut 32:32: *gpn* as the A-word may set the word-field for *śdmt*, the B-word. In sum, it is acceptable to take the word as "terrace" or even "vineyard" in these instances.

Another approach has been taken by Wyatt (1992a; 2002:327 n. 12), who sees a plant "shoot" felled by the pruners. W. G. E. Watson (1994:4) follows Wyatt's translation, and Lewis (*UNP* 206) renders similarly "his tendrils." The contexts in Deut 32:32 and Isa 16:8 would work with this proposal, where the word is parallel to *gpn* (although as noted above precise synonyms may not be involved). The etymology proposed by Wyatt is problematic, however. He takes the word as a causative formation of the root *dm* "meaning that part of the plant which produces (causes to grow? ...) the juice." Here the problem is that *dm* means "blood," and it refers to juice metaphorically when it is further qualified by another noun. In 1.4 III 44, wine (*yn*) is called "[blo]od of trees" ([*d*]*m* *ʿṣm*), or less literally "[blo]od of the grapevines" (Ginsberg 1982:101 n. 131). This image is attested in comparable form of the "blood of grape(s)," for example in Gen 49:11 (*bayyayin*//*ûbĕdam-ʿănābîm*) and Deut 32:14 (*wĕdam ʿēnāb tišteh-*

ḥāmer).[20] The expression *dm ʿnb* occurs also in Ben Sira 39:26 [manuscript B]. In the Tyrian legend of the invention of wine cited by Achilles Tatius II:2,[21] Dionysus the god of the vine said that wine "is harvest water, the blood of the grape (*haima botrous*)."[22] The further problem with Wyatt's proposal is that the root is unknown in the C-stem formation.

Pardee (1997b:277 n. 17; so too Gulde 1998:295, 305–7), noting the lack of a firm etymology for *šdmt*, breathes new life into an old suggestion made by Lehmann (1953) that it is a compound word. Citing this proposal, Tsumura (1973:34–35; cf. 1999:229) simply translates "field" and sees a sort of wordplay with the name of Death, which is an attractive possibility. At the same time, Tsumura's discussion does not account for the ending –*mt* of the noun. In favor of the literal rendering, "field of Death," Pardee offers some arguments. Pardee translates *mt* in line 8 as "field-of-a-man," based on his argument for *mt* in line 8 as man rather than "Death." As noted above, the context in lines 8–11 militates against this understanding, despite Pardee's observation that *mt* has this meaning in lines 40//46. Gulde's main point in this direction lies in her comparison of this term with *šd ʾilm* and *šd ʾatrt* in line 13; accordingly, a divine name or at least reference to divinity also should be seen in *šdmt*. Gulde's point is clever and appealing, but it ultimately falters on the problem that Pardee himself notes for his view: the BH counterpart to Ugaritic *šdmt* is *šdmt* (Deut 32:32 and Isa 16:8), while BH "field" is spelled *śādeh*. Although Tsumura (1973:35) recognized this difficulty, he does not explain it.

What most, if not all, commentators seem to agree on is the relevance of Deut 32:32 and Isa 16:8. In the context of 1.23.8–11, a metaphorical understanding envisioning Mot's limbs would make suitable sense, on the basis of the parallelism of the word. Here comparison with Deut 32:32 and Isa 16:8 would be appealing. The question is which limb is involved. Wyatt (1992b; 2002:326–27 n. 11) believes that lines 8–11 allude to some ritual action performed before the *hieros gamos* that takes place between El and his two wives down in lines 30–61. Inspired by the biblical characterization of young trees as "uncircumcised" in Lev 19:23, Wyatt (1992b:426) remarks:

> The pruning imagery of the passage cited above is also a figure for circumcision, that El himself is to be understood as undergoing the rite in preparation for his subsequent marriage.

---

20. So *CML*[2] 58, which also cites 1 Macc 6:34. For further discussion, see *SPUMB* 146–47; Fisher 1969:66–67; cf. Akkadian *damu* in *CAD* D:79.

21. Gaselee 1917:60–61; cf. *Thespis* 180.

22. Further parallels are provided in Lipiński 1970:86–87, and de Moor and van der Lugt 1974:14; see also Zamora 2000:599–601.

Wyatt's theory, followed by Pardee (1997b:277 n. 13) and Dijkstra (1998:286–87), may take some support from Pope's comparison drawn from a Ndembu ritual. Citing Victor Turner's study, *Revelation and Divination of Ndembu Ritual*, Pope (in M. S. Smith 1998b:663) noted "the root ritual of the Ndembu of Zambia in the ceremonial wounding and slaying of the god Kavula. The chopping of the root represents the killing of the god and also foreshadows the symbolic death of the candidates." In this approach to this section of CAT 1.23, there would be a ritual analogy between the fate of the god and the transition of the males to adulthood as envisioned by Wyatt and Pope.

Wyatt's particular interpretation first of all requires that these lines have El as their focus (and not Mot). As noted above, the association of El with destruction seems unsuitable. Wyatt's approach also does not explain the verb, *yšql*, which looks like a term for killing. In the symbolic view of Wyatt, this may be only the destruction represented by the cut skin. However, there is no indication that this is the meaning of the verb. At the same time, Pope's parallel would vitiate this criticism, insofar as the "killing" here would be symbolic for cutting. As a further issue, parallels work if the texts compared really are parallels. Pope (in M. S. Smith 1998b:663) cited John 15:1–8 along with the Ndembu ritual; these two comparisons with 1.23.8–11 point in quite different directions. I would take a more mundane view that is related in a general way to Wyatt's rather imaginative interpretation. It is my guess that Mot's limbs may be the image evoked, whether implicitly the limbs fall "to the terrace" or explicitly they fell "his tendrils." Either way, Death's limbs are pruned and he himself is felled as a result. In this connection, we might return to the image of "the hand of Death," described as a power to be feared (CAT 2.10, quoted above). This "hand" is perhaps included in what is pruned of Mot. A final point: for the vine in biblical images of divine judgment, Albright (1934:138 n. 173) compared Isa 63:1–6 and Rev 14, especially verses 14–20. Although these passages do not bear directly on 1.23 but on other Ugaritic texts (see Good 1982), they highlight the larger viticultural context of this section of 1.23 (also found in lines 26 and 72–76).

Without any intervening textual indicators, the text moves from lines 1–7, with its explicit ritual context, to lines 8–11, with its unmarked context. The latter section initially depicts the god of Death, sitting (or enthroned) with his two staffs of destruction. Then the section presents him pruned like the vegetation of the late summer crop of grapevines. The picture of Death suffering violence may be ironic, as the god is thought to be responsible for destruction. One may compare the process of the destruction of Death in 1.6 II (so de Moor 1990:243–44), which in turn generates the return of life in the form of the god Baal (see P. L. Watson 1972). In contrast to 1.6 II where the agricultural imagery evokes the springtime grain harvest (Livingstone 1986:163), the comparable imagery and vocabulary of 1.23 in this section suggests a time when the power of Mot is waning. With its imagery of vine-pruning in the summer, 1.23 reflects the approaching season of the grape harvest, in short, the transition in late summer/early fall from the dry season to the rainy season (*SPUMB* 79). Gaster would locate the text in the spring, based in part on the Gezer Calendar (*ANET* 320; *COS* 2.85:222; *KAI* 182). Gaster (1946:72) notes that according to the calendar, pruning begins in the month of June, and therefore the events should be located in the spring (see Kosmala 1964).[23] However, June is hardly the spring. Moreover, the Gezer Calendar refers to the two months of pruning (roughly June–July), preceding the month of summer-fruit (roughly August) and the double-month of ingathering (roughly September–October). In short, the rubric may evoke the waning power of Mot in the mid-summer, as the fruit waxes in strength (see lines 25–26). As the inverse image to this presentation of Mot, Gulde (1998:305) quite rightly cites the strength of Mot (*byd mt*) in the Baal Cycle (1.3 V 17–18//1.4 VIII 21–24//1.6 II 24–25).

A central question is whether this section is a ritual action or a sung or recited narrative. It should be ritual in view of its place within lines 1–29, which are shot through with ritual indicators. However, just as line 16 is a narrative piece embedded within the larger ritual context of the section of lines 16–18, lines 8–11 could be narrative and not ritual action (see Gulde 1998:304, 308 n. 45). Still, the opening of line 12, *šbʿd yrgm*, could refer back to lines 8–11 as what is to be recited "seven times." For this reason, it is reasonable to regard lines 8–11 as a ritual recitation (one sort of ritual action) performed within the context of the ritual that opens in lines 1–7. It may be an incantation, as Trujillo (1973:80, 83) argued.

For those who assume a ritual action here, they see a ritual pruning of the vine symbolizing the vanquishing of Mot (Gaster 1934:157). For de Moor (1987:120 n. 15; 1990:244), there may be involved a sort of ritual effigy of Death, represented "as a kind of scarecrow" shorn of its limbs like the vegetation of the summer pruning. Trujillo (1973:87–89) entertains the possibility of a statue of Mot ritually involved here, and he compares punishment of figurines in a number of Mesopotamian ritual texts (such as Maqlu). If 1.23.8–11 constitutes recited narrative, it includes a picture (perhaps a mythology) of Death stripped of its life. If the word *ʿd* in line 12 were to be understood as a dais or a pedestal on which some sort of ritual item standing for Death was placed, then it might be thought that lines 8–11 were both sung and acted out. A final question is the actual subject of lines 9–11. Whether an indefinite "he" or "pruner"//"binder" is the subject, the identity of this figure remains otherwise unspecified, much like

---

23. For evidence of a spring setting for the text, Gaster also cites the kid in its mother's milk in line 14, but this view has long been shown to be unlikely (see discussion of lines 13–15 below).

the "I" of line 1 (see the discussion of this line). In either case, the lines express a sense of Death's power waning in the late summer, as the vine mentioned three times in lines 8–11 increases with life later in the text.

SECTION 3, LINE 12: RECITATION AND RESPONSE INDICATORS

12   šb'd yrgm 'l 'd   Seven times it is recited over the dais (?),
        w'rbm t'nyn   And the enterers respond:

The older history of interpretation of this line has been surveyed by Wilson (1991). Pardee (1997b:278) renders the verb as third-person plural, but in view of the argument of Dobrusin (1981) that the plural of the prefix indicative in Ugaritic is *t-*, it would seem better to render the verb in the passive voice as a singular referring to the content of what is recited in lines 8–11.[24] It is difficult, if not impossible, to know who is performing the recitation of line 12a; this stands in contrast to the situation in line 12b, where the 'rbm is the explicit subject of the verb. In view of the combination of 'rbm wtnnm in line 7, it might be guessed that the implicit subject of the passive verb in line 12a are the tnnm.

The prepositional phrase in the first line is the main difficulty in this section. Pardee (1975:369) probes the prepositional possibilities: "Seven times they recite (it) to/about/against the 'd." Among early commentators, Gaster (1947) and Driver (CML¹ 121, 141) suggested "on the lute," based on Arabic 'ēd (see Trujillo 1973:102; Xella 1973:52; also Lewis, UNP 208). Wilson (1991:49) criticizes the translation "lute," based on other occurrences of 'd. In 1.16 VI 22, the word evidently refers to a space and not an instrument: ytb krt l'dh, "Kirta sat/returned to his 'd" (cf. "to his prime," in Greenstein, UNP 40). The word apparently refers to a place in the house of Baal of Ugarit in 1.119.9: b 'd bt b'l 'u(!)grt.

De Moor (1972:2.18) renders "dais" (see also Wyatt 2002:327). Pardee (1997b:278) proposes "next to" or "above" ("if the architecture permitted it") "the 'D-room.'" Retaining the basic sense of *rgm found elsewhere, DUL (147) translates: "seven times it is recited in front of the throne." Wilson (1991) offers further cognates and a reconstruction for this sort of situation. He compares Greek edos, "seat, abode, temple" as well as BH 'ēd, "witness," erected as an altar in Josh 22:27, 34 as a representation of the deity's presence. He also considers whether the word is related to Sumerian ID, in particular in KAR 214, which lists temple courts, including [ki]-[s]a-al ID ap-su-u. Based on this reference as

---

24. For the verb and parallels in the passive voice, see UG 513, 867; for the numeral, see UG 150, 204, 378.

well as others, Wilson (1991:51) would hypothesize that "when entering the temple, one had to go up to the ziggurat terrace (which would help to explain the preposition 'l in *CTA* 23:12 if we assume that the 'd there was also elevated), then undergo purification before entering the cella." Unfortunately, Wilson does not provide a translation of 1.23.12 based on his interpretation of the situation ("seven times it is to be recited up at the room"?). It is unclear what sort of ritual space is actually involved in this text, which seems to take place in the sown and not in a conventional temple location. It is also to be recognized that the text makes no mention of a purification ritual. Finally, it seems unlikely that all of the etymological possibilities cited by Wilson are related to one another. At the same time, the contextual evidence afforded by the Ugaritic data might favor Wilson's general approach.

One final suggestion should be noted. Tsumura (1973:38–39; 1999:229) takes the interpretation of 'd in a very different direction. Citing an oral suggestion made by C. H. Gordon, Tsumura proposes "according to habit," as found in Arabic. Tsumura suggests that this is a sort of ritual expression. This appears plausible, although this usage, to the best of my knowledge, does not occur elsewhere in Ugaritic ritual.

The recitation of line 12a seems to be the content of lines 8–11, while the response mentioned in line 12b seems to be the content of line 13. In both instances, a sung recitation is evidently presupposed (cf. 1.106.15–17: "And a singer shall sing the song, several times, before the king" (*wšr yšr šr p'amt lpn mlk*; Pardee 2002:54, 55). The sevenfold recitation of 1.23.12 has been compared to the incantation performed twelve times in 1.100 by Trujillo (1973:84–85), who also notes death as an issue in both texts (see "the tree of death" in 1.100.64–69). Trujillo further suggests that the other ritual actions take place during this recitation in 1.23.12. Sevenfold actions are attested in ritual texts from Ras Shamra: sevenfold offerings made in 1.43.7, 8 and in 1.110.11; a sevenfold procession mentioned in 1.43.26; and a sevenfold royal "ascension" (**'ly*) in 1.112.7, what Pardee (2002:101 n. 21) calls a "cyclical procession" to a sanctuary. As Tsumura (1973:222–23, cited in 1999:236 n. 73) rightly stresses, sevenfold components mark the ritual of 1.23 in particular (lines 12, 20, 29; cf. line 66). If seven marks completion or fullness, then such sevenfold actions themselves generate ritual completion or fullness. In any case, it seems reasonable to suppose that other ritual actions may have taken place during such sevenfold ritual processes. In the case of 1.23, the speech and actions represented in lines 1–29 could overlap in ritual time.

Section 4, Lines 13–15: Words of Song with Ritual

13   wšd šd 'ilm   "And the field (is) the field of El/the gods,

	šd ʾaṯrt wrḥm<y>	Field of Athirat and Rahm<ay>."
14	ʿl ʾišt šbʿd	On the fire seven times
	ġzrm g ṭb	The boys with a good voice:
	gd bḥlb	Coriander in milk,
	ʾannḫ bḥmʾat	Mint in curd.
15	wʿl ʾagn šbʿdm	And on the basin seven times:
	dġṯt	Incense.

Line 13

Tsumura (1999:229) takes the initial noun as a *casus pendens*, but Tropper (*UG* 854) represents the consensus in taking the clause as a nominal sentence. He provides other examples of nominal sentences in which the noun used as the subject is also the predicate's noun in construct; these include 1.23.42 below. In either case, the initial noun is not in construct with a following noun, and therefore is singular and not plural; the other mentions of "field" logically follow suit.

The word ʾilm could refer to El with mimation (see *MLC* 441; W. G. E. Watson 1994:5) or to gods in general, or to the Goodly Gods invoked in line 1 (so de Moor 1972:2.18, 1987:120, 122: "the two gods"), or even to "divine" as a superlative (Wyatt 2002:327 n. 15). The pairing of El and Athirat wa-Rahmay makes excellent sense, although the other views are possible. De Moor (1987:120 n. 18) also compares a line in a hymn to Inanna (Kramer 1969:81). Trujillo (1973:104) suggests that the "field" is for her husband, El in this case: "the ceremonial ploughing would be a symbol of El's intercourse with the two goddesses." Xella (1973:53) suggests an alternative translation for šd ʾilm, "the divine breast."

On the assumption that line 13 refers to the field of beneficial deities, we may suppose that the line provides information bearing on the fall festival, a view that comports with other ritual lines in this text. Accordingly, the field represents another way to refer to the sown where the rituals take place. Such a setting works well for the harvest of the summer fruit, as it is in the field where this harvest comes to pass. Biblical examples of the fall festival in the field (e.g., Judg 9:27; 21:20) follow suit. At the same time, it is to be noted that the field is also the site of the other sorts of offering, for example the one consisting of a kid and a meal offering made by Manoah and his wife in Judg 13:9, 19. So the offering in the field may have been a general practice at the social level of families and clans. If so, 1.23 appropriates this sort of practice, extends royal sacrificial praxis over this space out from the traditional site of royal ritual, namely, the temple and palace, and thereby expresses monarchic hegemony over the wider society.

Line 14

The term *ǵzrm* refers to personnel who may serve in a number of capacities (Xella 1973:138–49, esp. 145). As P. D. Miller (1970:160) notes, *ǵzrm* here "may refer to a type of cultic personnel though difficulties in translation do not allow such certainty about the meaning." Unless *g ṭb* is accusative and not genitive, the form *ǵzrm* is either a singular or plural construct, in which case, the *–m* is not morphological but enclitic. The specification of the figure(s) with "good voice" (*ǵzrm g ṭb*; cf. *ǵzr ṭb ql* in 1.3 I 20) suggests singing is the capacity by which the personnel is recognized in this larger setting, although in the immediate context here this same personnel also participates in conducting part of the sacrificial ritual.

As argued in *TO* (1.371 n. p), the word *gd* is generally regarded as coriander or the like (*DUL* 294; Cohen 1996:136–37), based on BH *gad* (Exod 16:31; Num 11:7) and Arabic *gadiyy* (Lane 394). Exodus 16:31 refers to manna as *kězeraʿ gad*, "similar to coriander seed" (Borowski 2002a:98). *Kisibirru*, thought to be coriander, figures in Old Babylonian meat broth recipes (Yale Babylonian Collection cuisine tablet A, lines 7, 63, 69, 72; so rendered with a question-mark by Bottéro 1995:31, 53, 56, 57, 206; 2004:26, 28, 29). Akkadian *kisibirru/kisibirrîtu* is widely attested in other sources (*CAD K*:420–21). According to Thompson (1949:66), Aramaic *kusbarta* is cognate (Jastrow 623); if so, post-BH *kusbar* would be related as well. From the textual sources, coriander was evidently widely in use. According to Borowski (2002a:98 n. 12, with secondary literature), coriander is attested archaeologically from the tomb of Tutankamun and Late Assyrian Nimrud. An annual umbelliferous plant with divided leaves and pink or white flowers, coriander (*coriandrum sativum*) is native to the Levant (Jørgensen et al. 1980:110–11). Today the seeds are said to "have a hot, harsh flavor," as opposed to the milder leaves, which are sold as cilantro or Chinese parsley (Skelley 1994:81).

For decades, the phrase *gd bḥlb* was understood as a "kid in milk," based on a brilliant comparison by Ginsberg (1935:65 n. 4 and 72 Postscript) made with Exod 23:19, 34:26, and Deut 14:21. Ginsberg suggested that 1.23 represented a Canaanite ritual practice presupposed by the biblical prohibitions. The comparison seemed to provide a ritual basis for understanding the biblical injunctions to justify the separation of dairy and meat products: since the "Canaanites" combined such food products as reconstructed for 1.23.14, the Israelites should not do likewise. This interpretation was influential, as it led Gaster (1946:50, 61–62) to situate the text in the springtime rather than in the fall. This view was widely accepted by other scholars as well.[25] However, by the late 1970s, it was becoming clear that 1.23.14 could not sustain this interpretation. No longer could *gd*

---

25. For example, Driver, *CML*[1] 121 n. 12; de Moor 1972:2.76; Tsumura 1973:43.

be a "kid," since in this context "kid" would be spelled *gdy*, as it is in 1.79.4 and 4.150.3 (see also 4.423.23; *DUL* 295). The reading of the line showed a number of other difficulties.[26] In the end, there was no "kid in its milk."[27]

There has been some dissent from the new consensus. Despite their own negative answer to the question as to whether line 14 contains "a kid in milk," Ratner and Zuckerman (1986:52) would hold out for the possibility. Although strictly speaking this reading of *gd bḥlb* in line 14 is to be rejected, there remains the possibility of "a dairy and meat meal" in the text, though perhaps only at an implicit level of sections 4 (lines 13–15) and 5 (lines 16–18); to indicate why, it is necessary to look first at the rest of this section.

The word *ḥlb* has long been assumed to mean "milk" or the like, cognate with BH *ḥālāb*. For this word in Exod 23:19, 34:26, and Deut 14:21, Heckl (2001) and Sasson (2002, 2003) have rejected the view that the word is "milk," and instead suggest revocalizing the word as *ḥēleb*, animal "fat." In a brilliant piece of cultural history, Sasson accepts that BH *ḥlb* can mean either "milk" or "fat," depending on the context, and he suggests that in the prohibitions in Exod 23:19, 34:26, and Deut 14:21, the meaning is "fat." He notes also that whatever the precise meaning of these prohibitions, they are not cultic in nature since sacrificial food was burned (not boiled). In the end, Sasson sees the prohibition not as cultic but as "a gnomic observation couched as a legal formulation": cooking a young animal in its mother's fat would require the killing of the young with its breeder. In short, the biblical injunctions for Sasson reflect a sage observation about managing flocks. For Sasson (2002), the textual interpretation in favor of the homonymous "milk" rather than "fat" in these verses was a secondary development designed to sharpen distinctions between Jewish ritual practices from those of their neighbors. Sasson also notes the discussion of Knauf (1988), who cites the combination of dairy and meat in Gen 18 and in an episode in Sinuhe (*ANET* 20; *COS* 1.38:79). Sasson suggests that the Sinuhe reference may be ironic, in that the eating of flesh and drinking milk may be a way of caricaturing

---

26. For the rereading, see CTA p. 98; Ratner and Zuckerman 1985, 1986; see also the critical remarks made by Loewenstamm 1973:209 and Trujillo 1973:107–8.

27. For the larger discussion, see Haran 1978, 1985; Milgrom 1985; Ratner and Zuckerman 1985, 1986; Tigay 1996:369 n. 29; Pardee 1997b:278–79 n. 26; for further reviews, see Keel 1980; Heckl 2001; and Sasson 2002. For all his considerable theoretical sophistication and his claims to attend to culture in his approach, Kunin (2004:37, 45, 70–71) favorably discusses this old view, without any recognition that it has been seriously undermined and without any actual mention of the textual basis in 1.23.14 formerly thought to support the proposal. Moreover, Kunin's discussion omits biblical texts besides the biblical prohibitions that combine dairy and meat products (mentioned below). The further discussion of the matter by Kunin (2004:73, 95–96) shows no real interest in the cultural setting of the prohibition within ancient Israel; instead, the discussion leaps to an entirely abstract neo-structuralist mapping that pays some more attention to postbiblical issues.

those considered to be uncivilized nomads. Following up Sasson's proposal, Guillaume (2002) has further suggested that BH *ḥlb* is specifically rennet.

On the whole, Sasson's reinterpretation is illuminating and in several respects persuasive. At first glance, it is unclear how the overall proposal fits with the ritual contexts of Exod 23:19 and 34:26, which places the injunctions after the command: "The first-fruits of your land you shall bring to the house of the LORD your God." Unless one were to posit that the two clauses are to be disassociated, the biblical contexts sound cultic. How the apparent ritual context is to be reconciled with Heckl and Sasson's proposal that the injunctions are not ritualistic remains to be worked out. It is possible that the verses were added secondarily to their present contexts. Indeed, their formulations do show a certain self-contained character; they lack integration into their contexts. Even so, one might ask then why these verses were connected to their contexts in the minds of those who added them. There is a way to answer this objection: redactors connected these prohibitions to their current contexts because in their time the prohibitions were related thematically to offerings. Sasson's approach has nicely anticipated this difficulty in that the verses could have been added to such contexts following the reinterpretation of *ḥlb*, "fat," as "milk." In sum, there is no difficulty that Sasson's insightful proposal regarding the biblical prohibitions cannot surmount. It is not clear that this is also true of Deut 32:14, which Sasson mentions but does not really explain (see below). The issues surrounding the biblical evidence are complex, and an extended discussion of them lies beyond the scope of this work. As suggested below, this old comparison, thought for over two decades to be irrelevant, remains significant for studying 1.23, as it highlights the potential of alimentary categories for understanding the *dbḥ* in 1.23.

As for 1.23.14, Sasson rightly claims that this line is not yet fully understood. He suggests that in any case it has been shown to be irrelevant to the biblical injunctions: "as a result of a closer inspection of the original, it has become obvious that the passage had been biblicized and can scarcely be rendered as it had been, thus removing the evidence for the alleged parallel." On this point, Sasson stands in the company of Haran, Milgrom, Ratner and Zuckerman, and the other authorities cited above. Sasson's study raises the interesting question as to whether or not Ugaritic *ḥlb* here is a dairy or an animal product. Sasson discusses the use of fat to sauté meats and vegetables. Generally speaking, one might see in line 14 a combination of ingredients for treating the food for the *dbḥ* to which the *'ilm n'mm* are invited in lines 23–24 and 26–27. At the same time, within line 14 there is a certain internal parallelism, which if correctly perceived, would suggest that the two terms in question, *ḥlb* and *ḥm'at*, belong to the same word-field. Since the latter would seem to be a dairy product, the former would appear to follow suit. Furthermore, the use of Ugaritic *ḥlb* in 1.15 II 26 likewise points to milk from the breasts of the goddess, and the attestations in the administrative texts comport with this view (4.272.2, 5; 4.707.20). It may be noted further that fat is absent from Ugaritic ritual, according to Pardee (2000a:326). In contrast, Mesopotamian recipes ca. 1600 include meat broths with milk (*šizbu*) and other ingredients (Yale Babylonian Collection cuisine tablet A, lines 31–32, 40–44; Bottéro 1995:44, 46, 219–20; 2004:27–28; for milk generally in the Mesopotamian diet, see Bottéro 2004:88–89). Meals could include both meats and dairy products, as exemplified in the second-millennium Sumerian myth known as the Marriage of Sud (Civil 1983; Bottéro 2004:100–101). In view of these sources, it would appear that the meat and dairy meal is eminently plausible for 1.23. The discussion as it pertains to 1.23 further involves the word *ʾannḫ* in line 14.

The Ugaritic *hapax legomenon* *ʾannḫ* is quite difficult. The current consensus is expressed in *DUL* (81), which cites Akkadian *ananiḫu, naniḫu* (*CAD A/II*: 111 and *AHw* 50) and Syriac *nōnḫō* (*LS* 131) in the putative meaning "mint" (*mentha*). Akkadian *naniḫu* appears in an NB list of plants in a royal garden (*CAD A/II*:111). An SB text provides an equivalence of Akkadian *ananiḫu* with *urnû*, itself understood as "mint" with a question mark by von Soden (*AHw* 1432). Tsumura (1973: 43) as well as Ratner and Zuckerman (1986:40–42) consider the evidence rather weak for indicating the precise nature of the Ugaritic word. As a result, other proposals for some sort of animal (*DUL* 81) have been forwarded. However, a number of considerations militate in favor of seeing some sort of herb here. Syntactically, *ʾannḫ* seems to belong to the same class as *gd*, and contextually, it seems to be some element that goes "in" (*b–*) *ḥmʾat*. Despite the demurrals of Tsumura and Ratner and Zuckerman, *ʾannḫ*, to judge from the syntax and context, would fit with the proposed meaning "mint" or the like. At the same time, the identification is hardly secure, and other words have been entertained as terms for mint; compare for example, Akkadian *nīnû*. In the Yale Babylonian Collection cuisine tablet A (lines 22, 43, etc.), *nīnû* is added to meat broths along with several other ingredients. It is translated as "mint" with a question mark by Bottéro (1995:38, 39, 46, 212; 2004:69).[28] However, this may be "bishop's weed" (cf. Thompson 1949:67–69, 77). As these terms show, it is very difficult to be sure of the identification of such herbs in any given context. For the purposes of this discussion, it is assumed, given what is known, that *ʾannḫ* refers to mint.

Thought also to be mint, Greek *hēdyosmon* (meaning "sweet-smelling") appears in a list of herbs in parallel sayings in Matt 23:23 and Luke 11:42 (Jør-

---

28. See also *CAD N*:241. Note also Ugaritic *nnʾi*, in *DUL* 633. Cf. Jewish Aramaic *ninyāʾ*, "bishop's weed," so Jastrow 905; and JPA, CPA, and Syriac *nnʿ*, "mint," listed in Sokoloff, *A Dictionary of Palestinian Jewish Aramaic*, 352.

gensen et al. 1980:143–44). Modern sources report mint used in milk. Mint evidently helps to prevent milk from curdling or turning sour, and it is also used in cooking meat (Touissant-Samat 1992:533), just as we find in Mesopotamian cuisine. In 1.23, mint might serve to flavor the sauce for the meat (inferred from line 16, discussed below), unless cooking in a pot is what is imagined (cf. line 31; 1.4 II 8–9; the Mesopotamian meat broth recipes in Bottéro 1995, 2004; 1 Sam 2:12–17).

The Ugaritic *hapax legomenon ḥmʾat* is a dairy product, thought to be butter (ghee) or curds.[29] Like 1.23.14, Gen 18:8 includes *ḥemʾâ wĕḥālāb*. Also comparable is Deut 32:14: *ḥemʾat bāqār wăḥalēb ṣōʾn ʿim-ḥēleb kārîm*. As in 1.23.14 and Gen 18:8, *ḥemʾat* and *ḥalēb* in this text are dairy products, mentioned along with "the fat of lambs," *ʿim-ḥēleb kārîm*.[30] In Judg 5:25, *ḥālāb* and *ḥemʾâ* are parallel terms for liquids offered in a bowl. Proverbs 30:33 suggests a more specific relationship between *ḥemʾâ* and *ḥālāb*: "the churning of milk produces butter" (*mîṣ ḥālāb yôṣîʾ ḥemʾâ*).[31] Whatever the precise sense of the words, the four biblical passages linking *ḥemʾâ* and *ḥālāb* (Gen 18:8; Deut 32:14; Judg 5:25; Prov 30:33) suggest that both are dairy products. The same would appear to apply in the juxtaposition of the same two parallel nouns in 1.23.14. In conclusion, the contextual clues and biblical parallels favor the view that *ḥlb* in line 14 is a dairy product.

The relations of these alimentary components to meat vary. In Gen 18:8, an animal is explicitly mentioned: *ben-bāqār* is presented with *ḥemʾâ wĕḥālāb*. In Deut 32:14, reference to animal fat is followed by reference to animals for the meal (*ʾêlîm*, etc.). In 1.23.14, the animal of the feast is not mentioned at all, but it is suggested by the larger context, specifically by the characterization of the food in line 6, by the ritual recitation about the hunt in line 16, and by the reference to *dbḥ* in line 26. Deuteronomy 32:14 bears further on 1.23.14 in two respects. First, it adds another component of the feast known also from 1.23, namely, the wine characterized as *ḥāmer* (see *ḥmr yn* in 1.23.6). Second, the food elements in Deut 32:14 and 1.23.14 are not part of cultic celebrations limited to the customary zone of shrines and temples (cf. Deut 32:13). In view of these shared features, Deut 32:14 seems to be the biblical passage most approximate to the milieu of 1.23.

---

29. Cf. Job 10:10, with its reference to the production of cheese (*gĕbînâ*) by the congealing (**qpʾ*) evidently of milk (*ḥālāb*), which is mentioned in the parallel A-line.

30. The Punic Marseilles tariff (*KAI* 69:14) mentions milk and fat in the sacrificial context of a *mnḥ[t]* offering (*wʾl ḥlb wʾl ḥlb*).

31. This rendering of *mîṣ* follows Clifford (1999:268), who cites medieval commentators to this effect as well as Akkadian *māṣu*, "to churn milk." Clifford also notes the wordplay of *ḥemʾâ* with *ḥemâ*, "wrath," in this context.

To summarize, the elements of *gd* and *'annḥ* in 1.23.14 seem to be herbs in *ḥlb* and *ḥm'at*. In view of these two terms together and given *ḥm'at*, it would seem that *ḥlb* would follow suit as a dairy product. The components in line 14 seem to belong to a larger meal. To anticipate the discussion of line 16, the meal combines the explicit dairy and nondairy ingredients in line 14 with the meat implied by the reference to the hunt in line 16. In the end, CAT 1.23 may show a combined dairy and meat meal. Though not for all the reasons that he gave, perhaps Ginsberg was right after all. We will return to this question in chapter 5.

Line 15

The word *'agn* was clarified in the *editio princeps* of Virolleaud (1933:15), which cites Exod 24:6 and Akkadian *agan(n)u* for "basin." Later commentators have noted Phoenician, Hebrew, and Aramaic *'gn*, "crater, open bowl, basin" (*DNWSI* 1.9–10; cf. Phoenician *'gn* "amphora," Greenstein 1976:50, 54; "jar," Pardee 1997b:280 n. 45). Gordon (*UT* 19.65), Pope (1955: 80), and Tsumura (1973:43) instead took the term as "fire," based on putative Indo-European cognates (Sanskrit *agni*, Latin *ignis*). It would seem, however, that Ugaritic *'agn* is something that is physically fashioned. CAT 6.70.1 refers to *'agn z p'l* PN, "basin which PN made" (see *DUL* 26; and the discussion at line 31). Commentators on Ugaritic *dġtt* have long followed the comparison of Hoffner (1964) with Hittite *duḥḥuiš*, incense or the like. Lewis (*UNP* 208) translates "incense." *DUL* (268), citing Hoffner, renders "perfumes." Wright (2001:202) stays with "incense."

The ritual actions in lines 14–15 suggest cooked food. Accordingly, the ritual actions have moved from the invitation of lines 1–7 to the topic of the field of the goddess in line 13 to cooking in lines 14–15. One may see here cooking taking place in the field of El and Athirat, the region of the sown "field," to which the *'ilm n'mm* invoked in lines 1 and 27–28 will be invited ritually. There is another possibility, though contextually it lacks evidence. In view of the reference to the goddess in line 16, it could be that line 13, as well as the content in line 28, ought to be associated with line 16 as three allusions to a narrative about the goddess on the hunt. The *šd* is the locale for the hunt in other texts, so it may help to explain the reference to the goddess and the *šd* together in line 13. In this case, *šd* would refer to "open country," referring to the periphery as in CAT 1.6 II 20 (cf. 1.5 VI 6, 29).

Line 13, it would seem, is a line to be spoken, but there is a disagreement about whether lines 14–15 are entirely ritual or partially a spoken rubric. Ratner and Zuckerman (1986:45) oppose the standard view that all of line 14 is ritual and put the last four words, in line 15, in quotation marks, but these look like ritual action. In either case, the section mentions elements of the fall feast in the field.

All in all, the ingredients in line 14 do not look like a meal or an entire sacrificial offering on par with the invitation in line 6. What we have here is the "coriander in milk (animal) fat, mint in curd" that figures in the larger meal of food and wine evoked in lines 6 and 27. To anticipate the discussion of the next section (lines 16–18), line 16 may figure in this overall picture of food: the goddess goes off to hunt and presumably returns with the game to be used as an offering, to be given to the gods invited to eat and drink in the first section (lines 1–7). Thus, behind this mythological allusion in line 16 is the securing of meat for the offering. If this is true, the fourth and fifth sections (lines 13–15 and 16–18) presuppose a combination of a meat and milk meal.

The implications for understanding the larger context of 1.23 as well as the biblical verses that Ginsberg cites in comparison are taken up in chapter 5. At this point, it may be noted that the meat of the Ugaritic text is undomesticated, while the elements of the biblical verses seem to derive from domesticated species (the milk or [animal] fat of the mother with its young). Accordingly, the biblical verses show a different alignment of categories. 1.23 combines domesticated and undomesticated components in the sown between the outback where game is found and the home of the urban royalty sponsoring the ritual. Whether or not BH *ḥlb* in the biblical verses is "milk" or "(animal) fat," the biblical prohibitions differentiate between elements derived from domesticated sources, perhaps befitting the domesticated setting of "the house of the Lord your God." The significance of this observation is discussed in chapter 5.

Section 5, Lines 16–18: Song

16	*tlkm rḥmy wtṣd* [ ]	"Rahmay goes hunting ..."
17	*tḫgrn ǵzr nˁm* [ ]	The handsome guys are girded .../ Or: She is/They (the goddesses) are girded with goodly might (?) ...
18	*wšm ˁrbm yr*[ ]	And the name of the enterers ... Or: and the name, the enterers ...

For the reconstruction of line 16, del Olmo Lete (*MLC* 442), followed by W. G. E. Watson (1986:347), suggests *tlkm rḥmy tṣd* [*aṯrt*], based on line 13//28. Tropper (*UG* 829) lists the enclitic *–m* on the first word as the single example where it occurs at the beginning of a new textual unit. The song of line 16, with the reference to the goddess Rahmay, might relate to "and the field of Athirat and Rahmay" in line 13 (also line 28). If correct, there is a song referenced through these sections devoted to the goddess going on the hunt to her field. If not, we still have the goddess on the hunt, which is here narrated and presumably sung. If indeed this is Athirat in line 16, we need not imagine her as the elderly matriarch of the pantheon but as a relatively young goddess like the deities who hunt in other texts. To anticipate the discussion of El in lines 30 and following, he is not necessarily the elderly patriarch as he appears in other texts such as the Baal Cycle; instead, he is acting in his procreative role, in other words, relatively younger than his presentation in the other texts. The text of 1.23 offers a glimpse of the divine parents when the cosmos was still young (*CML*[1] 28 n. 1; Cutler and Macdonald 1982:34).

The description of the goddess in line 16 as hunter resembles 1.114.23: "Anat and Athtart hunt" (*'nt w'ttrt tṣdn*; see also 1.22 I 10). The combination of verbs is known in 1.12 I 34 for Baal (Parker, *UNP* 189): "Baal roams about hunting" (*b'l ytlk wyṣd*). The only difference with respect to the verbs involves the Gt-stem of the first verb. At the same time, it may be noted that it is paralleled in the narrative in 1.23.67–68 (see below); hence the mythic piece here connects to another myth.

Other texts describe the hunting goddesses. In the difficult 1.92, Athtart seems to hunt (*'ttrt wṣwd*[, in line 2), and to do so, she goes into the outback (*tlk bmdbr*, in line 3). An unpublished text from the 1998 season, RIH 98:2, is a hymn to Astarte (lines 1–2), which mentions the "quiver and the bow" (*'utpt wqšt*) in line 30; it would appear that these belong to the goddess (Pardee forthcoming). Anat is likewise associated proverbially with the hunt in 1.22 I 11, "as when Anat sets out to hunt" (*km tdd 'nt ṣd*). The association of Anat with the hunt probably underlies the narrative link between the hunt at the end of 1.17 V, in line 39, and the encounter that ensues between the goddess and Aqhat in 1.17 VI. (It may also explain the label "*marzeah* of Anat" in CAT 4.642.2, 4–8.)

As in 1.12 I, 1.10 II describes Baal out hunting. In this text he is equipped with his bow and arrows, and the goal of his travel is said to abound in bulls (lines 6–9). For comparison we may note also "the hunt of Adad" (*ṣa-du ša* [d]*Iškur*) in Emar 466:90 (Arnaud 1986:422, 424). Like 1.114, this text includes the hunt in the context of the *marzeah* (McLaughlin 2001:33). This comparison leads to the question as to whether the hunt in its religious usage was a feature associated with the activity of the *marzeah* in the second millennium at Emar and Ugarit. Drinking is more prominent in the *marzeah* texts surveyed by McLaughlin (2001), but the eating evidently included the game of the hunt, at least in some instances. We may ask whether the hunt in this setting of the *marzeah* is an upper-class sort of activity that expresses an old cultural ideal. Finally, we may note the iconographic evidence for the hunt, depicted on a gold cup from Ugarit (AO 17208); it depicts a hunt, with wild goats and bovines (see Caubet 2002:219–22; Borowski 2002b: 293–94). As these sources illustrate, the "religion of the hunt" is a well-attested feature in the Ugaritic texts. Mesopotamian, Israelite, and Punic sources also attest to the sacrifice of hunted game (M. S. Smith forthcoming).

Given how much focus has been given to noting correspondences between myth and ritual in this text, the complexity of interpretation involves not only noting pieces of myth embedded in different ways within lines 1–29 but also in acknowledging their conjunctions with the mythic narrative in lines 30–76. Thematically, it might be understood that the hunt in the ritual section of 1.23 inversely parallels the hunt in the narrative section: the goddess goes out to the steppe to hunt and to return to the sown with her game, while the 'ilm n'mm hunt out in the steppe and then move into the sown where they find their food. The bicolon of lines 67–68, especially in terms of the locale of the action, finds a close parallel in 1.12 I 34 (Parker, *UNP* 289): "he prowls the edge of the wilderness" (*yḥ p'at mdbr*). It is evident that the hunt by the goddess is not a theme only of narratives but also of ritual texts. In this connection, we may note the hunt of Athtart in Emar 446.19–20, evidently in the late summer (see Fleming 2000:145–46). The relationship of the ritual to the narrative is complex, then, as the ritual in itself seems to evoke a different narrative of divine hunting parallel to the hunt of the Goodly Gods. We might also see this recitation as evoking the sacrificial meal to which lines 14–15 are preliminary alimentary preparations (items to be served with the meat of the hunt). Or, perhaps we should see here a song about the goddess that follows the food and drink. In a number of banquet texts, notably 1.3 I, 1.17 VI, and 1.108.1–5, music follows food and drink.

Line 17 may hang together as a single line, as rendered above, or it is possible that the end of line 16 goes with the first word of line 17, while the last two words of line 17 go with whatever is in the lacuna at the end of the line (so *CML*[2] 124). How the incipit in line 16 fits together ritually with the following lines 17–18 is unclear. On the face of it, line 17 mentions cultic servants dressed for ritual. However, it is possible that they prepare themselves for a ritual action. What action might this be? Gaster (1946), followed by Trujillo (1973:119–20), suggests a ritual procession of statues. While possible, there is no particular contextual indication for this ritual action.

It is to be noted that, like the Goodly Gods ('ilm n'mm), the *ǵzrm* are called n'm. These same figures may be identified further as the 'rbm in line 18, with the term name (*šm*) perhaps used here to express commission, a use for the noun best known from 1.2 IV 11//19, where Kothar pronounces names over the weapons that express their function. 1.23, however, involves a naming scene with a figure and not things. Closer in this regard is the naming scene in 1.1 IV 14–15 where El designates Yamm as his heir:

šm bny yw 'ilt	"The name of my son is Yw, O goddess."
wp'r šm ym	And he pronounces the name of Yamm.

As in 1.23.18, "name" in this context may stand in construct to the party designated. However, given the difficult state of 1.1 IV, perhaps not too much stock should be put into this comparison; still it is suggestive for the function of the name. One final naming incident also involves persons rather than things. In 1.12 I, El sends off the divine female servants into the wilderness to give birth; in lines 25–29 he speaks regarding their offspring (see Parker, *UNP* 189):

ḫl ld ʾaklm	"Labor, give birth to the Eaters
tbrkk	—May they (the gods) bless you!
wld ʿqqm	Give birth to the Tearers
ʾilm ypʿr šmthm	—May El pronounce their names!"

Without getting into the problem of the first three lines, the fourth and last line is the same as Kothar's commission to the weapons in 1.2 IV 11//18 and is suggestive of their identity. This approach might be pursued in other texts where conflict and naming play a crucial role in identity. Other examples with conflict, naming, and blessing are 1.12 I and Gen 32.

In view of the importance placed on the name in these passages, the ʿrbm in line 18 are perhaps in some sense designated for the task designated by the root *ʿrb. Viewed in these terms, the role of ʿrbm that these figures play may be related to their mentions in lines 7 and 26. If the references to the ʿrbm in lines 7, 18, and 26 were interpreted *in tandem*, then perhaps they perform what their name seems to literally mean, namely, "those who enter." If such a reasoning were to hold, then the officials indeed "do" in a sense what the Goodly Gods do in line 71: wʿrb hm, "they enter." The gods are told later in line 72 by the Guard of the sown that "there is wine for those who have entered" (ʾiṯ yn d ʿrb). We may sound a cautionary note because the approach seems to run afoul of the etymological fallacy of confusing the meaning of a word with the general sense of the root. However, this approach may be grounded instead in another aspect of the text. Along with the ṯnnm, the ʿrbm in line 26 "proceed with goodly sacrifice(s)." Similarly, in lines 72–73 the Goodly Gods proceed into the sown for wine, and for food as well, if line 73 can be reconstructed on the basis of parallelism and with help from lines 71–72. If one were to read the officials' role in line 26 as ritual providers, then one might wish to speculate further that ritually they provide the food analogically to what mythically the Goodly Gods receive in lines 67–68. The matter may be more complex. As noted above, the "myth" of this ritual action in lines 16–18 belongs to the goddess, and the offering of line 26 may only parallel in some sense the story of the Goodly Gods in lines 67–76. Accordingly, the text contains two hunting mythic narratives, one coupled with the ritual (lines 16–18) and another (line 26) paralleled in the longer narrative (see line 68). Clearly, this text offers no simple correspondence of ritual and myth.

SECTION 6, LINES 19–20: DIVINE DWELLINGS

19	mṯbt ʾilm ṯmn	The divine dwellings are eight,
19–20	ṯ[ ]/pʾamt šbʿ	.[..] seven times.

Given the lacuna, it is difficult to know what is going on exactly. On the face of it, Lewis (*UNP* 209) offers a reasonable rendering:

> The gods' thrones are eight,
> Th[eir thrones] are seven in a row.

The word *mṯbt* appears in ritual contexts for divine abodes (cf. 1.3 IV 48–53//1.3 V 39–44//1.4 IV 52–57; see also 1.16 V 24; 1.53.5, noted by Pardee 1997b:275); so Lewis has correctly identified the basic topic of this section. His approach assumes parallelism of "eight"//"seven" (as found in numerous translations). However, usually numbers in parallelism are ascending, not descending. For this reason, it seems unlikely, despite the effort of W. G. E. Watson (1993b:438), to posit chiasm here with the numbers in lines 56–57 and 66–67. Watson's view further presupposes a reconstruction of the counting months of pregnancy of lines 56–57 (apparently at line 51, though he does not clarify). Instead of seeing descending numerical parallelism here, *TO* (1.372 n. t) and Trujilllo (1973:123) considered taking *ṯmn* as the locative adverb with nunation.[32] However, the key to this section and in particular to the number "eight" is to be found in CAT 1.41.50–51, as noted by several scholars.[33] As noted by these scholars, this context uses *mṯbt* in the ritual setting of 1.23.19–20. Pardee (2002:62, 65) translates the relevant lines:

> At that time, the king [will offer a sac]rifice to PRGL-ṢQRN on the roof, where there will be dwellings (*mṯbt*) of branches (ʾ*azmr*), fo[ur] on one side, four on the other: a ram as a burnt-offer[ing].

The number eight in this text matches the number of dwellings in 1.23.19 (Pardee 1997b:279). Pardee also cites 1.53.5 in this connection, where the expression *mṯbt ʾilm* appears in another, albeit damaged and unclear, ritual context. A further reference perhaps occurs in another ritual, CAT 1.104. In their con-

---

32. *DUL* 913, citing CAT 2.30.9: *w ṯmn ʿm* [ʾ*u*]*my*, "and there with my mother..."; 2.41.20–21: *wʾuḫy/yʿmsn ṯmn*, "and may my brother load it there"; CAT 9.433.10 (as cited in the *DUL* entry): *wṯmn mnm šlm*, "and there whatever peace...."

33. See Gaster 1946:65; de Moor 1972:2.2181, *SPUMB* 78–80; Xella 1973:57; Pardee 1997b:275; Dijkstra 1998:280–83.

cordance, Cunchillos and Vita (1995:1394) read in 1.104.21 *wmbt.ʾilm ṯm*[*n*][34] and emend to *wmṯbt.ʾilm ṯm*[*n*]. If the emendation were to be accepted (as by de Moor 1987:121–22 n. 25; *UG* 832), it would provide a further witness to the divine dwellings as eight in number. Dijkstra (1998:283) understands the *mṯbt ʾilm* as referring to "certain stars or constellations." Most commentators prefer to see in these dwellings temporary shelters for the statues of the gods to be present during the ritual (see de Moor 1987:118; note also Trujillo 1973:123).

For *pʾamt šbʿ* Lewis suggests "seven in a row." Pardee instead regards the phrase as a number of repetitions for a speech act (as elsewhere in the text). The word *pʾamt* occurs with the meaning "times,"[35] but not "row." In the ritual text 1.41, line 53 contains the same phrase, *pʾamt šbʿ*. 1.41 (especially line 51, with its reference to *mṯbt*) is further relevant, as it is situated at the same time of year as 1.23 (Pardee 1997b:275). The offering of the fall firstfruits to the gods in their dwellings is arguably the setting shared by these two texts. It may also shed light on lines 8–11, for the language of **ʾazmr* (1.41.51) is realized ritually as the word for branches used for the divine dwellings. The celebration of autumnal first fruits is thematically Death's pruning (**zmr*). As a final observation about 1.23.19–20, these two lines enjoy sonant parallelism[36] in *mṯbt* and *pʾamt*.

Section 7, lines 21–22: Dressing of Singers

21	ʾiqnʾu šmt	Blue, red,
22	ṯn šrm	crimson of/are the singers
		(or: of/are the two singers).

Some older commentators take this section as a single verbal clause (e.g., *CML*[1] 121; see also Xella 1973:58; cf. *TO* 1.372 n. u): "I am zealous for the names/of the royal ones." In favor of this view, Driver (*CML*[1] 121 n. 15) cites Ezek 39:25: "and I will be zealous for my holy name" (*wĕqinnēʾtî lĕšēm qodšî*)." This view has not met with acceptance (see de Moor 1972:2.21), in part from a lack of parallels in Ugaritic material.

---

34. In the edition of CAT, 1.104.21 is read: *wm.bt.ʾilm ṯm*[*n*].

35. *DUL* 659, citing examples in 1.39.20; 1.41.43, 52; 1.43.7; 1.162.20; 1.73.15.

36. Berlin's treatment of sound pairs has advanced the understanding of sonant parallelism, and her definition of a sound pair (1985:104; her italics) is followed here: "*the repetition in parallel words or lines of the same or similar consonants in any order within close proximity.*" Observations regarding various links between cola in this commentary are based more specifically on three criteria used by Berlin to delimit sonant parallelism (Berlin 1985:105): (1) "at least two sets of consonants must be involved"; (2) "the sets must be in close proximity, within a word or adjacent words in both lines"; and (3) "'same or similar consonant' means the identical phoneme, an allophone..., or two phonemes which are articulated similarly."

From the mention of *'iqn'u*, one might see lapis and other types of stones here (Trujilllo 1973:128–30; van Soldt 1990:343). In this case, it might be guessed that the line involves images of the gods, perhaps those housed in the dwellings mentioned in the preceding section, in lines 19–20. In that case, *šrm* here might be "princes," although such a usage for cult statues is unknown.

An evidently superior alternative is to take these lines as the colors of the clothing worn by the singers.[37] They apparently acquire clothing (*ḫpn*) in the somewhat broken 4.609 II 17 (*DUL* 400). CAT 4.168.2–3 describe a requisition of garments for singers: *tltm lm'it š'rt/lšr 'ttrt*, "130 (shekels of?) wool for the singers of Athtart" (see *DUL* 799). The preceding section of this text, in line 1, shows the same combination of colors arguably attested in 1.23.21: *ḫpn d 'iqn'i w šmt l 'iyb'l*, "a cloak of blue and red for PN." CAT 4.182.4–6 lists garments in a series of colors: *'all lbnm*, *'all šmt*, and *'all 'iqn'i* (see also lines 16–17; for discussion, see van Soldt 1990:342–44). From his studies of these terms in Akkadian and Ugaritic texts from Ras Shamra dealing with color garments, van Soldt (1990:343) derives the following equations: *takiltu* = *'iqn'u*, "blue," and *tabarru* = *šmt*, "red." The word *tn* could be the number "two" or yet another color. The numeral *tn* appears several times before a noun in the plural (e.g., 4.102.5, 8, 23, 4.123.20, 4.141 III 12, 13), but it is also used as a color for clothing (e.g., 4.146.8; *DUL* 922). The overall syntax apparently involves a nominal clause or sentence, given the nominative case ending on *'iqn'u*. The colors of the garments would signal high status, perhaps even royal or high cultic (priestly?) associations.

Section 8, lines 23–27: Invitation Reiterated

23	'iqr'an 'ilm n'mm	Let me invite the Goodly Gods,
	['agzr ym bn] ym	[Ravenous pair a day old], day-old [boys],
24	ynqm b'ap zd 'atrt [...]	Who suck the nipple(s) of Athirat's breast(s)
		...
25	špš mṣprt dlthm	Shapshu braids their branches (?),
25–26	[ ]/wġnbm	[...] and grapes.
26	šlm 'rbm wtnnm	Peace, O enterers and guards,
27	hlkm bdbḥ n'mt	Who process with goodly sacrifice.

---

37. For example, Tsumura 1973:51–52; 1999:229; *MLC* 442; *DUL* 922. Trujillo (1973:131) suggests "bracelets" (with cognates).

Lines 23–24

The invocation here, reconstructed on the basis of the parallels in lines 58–59 and 61, recalls the opening line of the text (for the initial verbal form, see Rainey 1971:165). The word *'agzr* is an elative form of *gzr*, "to be ravenous, gluttonous" (Pope 1979:707; see also citations in *DUL* 29, citing BH *gzr*). Alternative views of *'agzr ym* have been proposed based on suppositions about the nature of these deities. *TO* (1.359) sees *'agzr ym* and *bn ym* as maritime expressions: "ceux qui fendent la mer" and "enfants de la mer," respectively (see also Tsumura 1973:55). Lipiński (1986:210), followed by Gulde (1998:314 and n. 56; see also W. G. E. Watson 2000:567), explains the word as Hurrian *a-ga-aš-ša-ri* and glossed by *bn ym*, "sons of the sea." The word *gzr* appears later in the text in line 63 in reference to the same gods, and so recourse to a Hurrian loan, with the added explanation of its being glossed by a comparable Ugaritic phrase, is not compelling. It seems unlikely that in the same text the word is both Ugaritic in itself and a Hurrian gloss.

Pardee views *'agzr* in reference to Shahar and Shalim (whom he identifies with the *'ilm n'mm*), who "divide" (**gzr*) the day (*ym*).[38] It seems preferable to hew close to the actual use of **gzr* in lines 63–64. Ever since Albright, a variety of commentators have compared Isa 9:19 (with **gzr//*'kl*).[39] The phrase *bn ym* is plausibly rendered either "sons of the sea" (Virolleaud 1933:142) or "sons of a day" (i.e., "one-day-old" infants). Many commentators prefer the latter since the Goodly Gods are newborns. Others observe that they seem to be born near the sea. The word *bn* is used for a newborn in 1.24.7 (often compared to Isa 7:14; Marcus, *UNP* 218 n. 1), if the reconstruction *b[n]* is correct: *hl ġlmt tld b[n]*, "behold, the young woman will give birth to a so[n]." In the history of discussion, *bn ym* has been related to the expression in 1.4 VII 15–16 with the same consonants, but it is unclear whether the two are related (see the cautionary remarks in *SPUMB* 161).

The gods sired by El are variously called "suckers of the nipple(s) of the breast(s) of Athirat" (*yr.q n b'ap zd 'atrt*) in 1.23.24 (cf. lines 59, 61, and the discussion of these lines in the next chapter). In view of lines 59 and 61, *zd* may be singular and not plural. Kirta's son, YṢB, is said to be one who "sucks the milk of A[thi]rat, draws the breast of Adolescent [Anat], the wet nurses [of the gods]"

---

38. For further consideration of Pardee's thesis, see excursus 1 below.

39. Albright 1938:37; de Moor 1972:2.21 n. 84; Trujillo 1973:133–34, 187; Xella 1973:59; see also Tsumura 1973:54, who rejects the comparison. See the discussion of lines 61 and 63–64 in the following chapter. Since the epithet occurs in that context as well, it is unclear why connecting *'agzr* there with the attested word *gzr* also in that larger context is unwarranted, as Tsumura (1973:54) seems to think. For further discussion of Isa 9:19 in connection to **gzr*, see the discussion of line 63 in the following chapter, pp. 114–15.

(1.15 II 26–27). An ivory panel from a royal bed excavated from Ugarit depicts a female giving suck to two figures (Pope 1977:pl. XI), perhaps a portrayal of the divine nursing of the king.[40] Accordingly, many commentators see a royal theme behind this motif.

Line 25

The form *mṣprt* remains a most intractable word. Not surprisingly, Gulde (1998:296) accepts an older reading of *myprt* going back to Bauer (see the listing in *CTA*, p. 99 n. 4; *CML²* 124) and translates: "lässt wachsen die Rebschösse." In the judgment of *CTA* (p. 99 n. 4), ṣ "semble, épigraphiquement, plus probable qu-un *y*." Herdner's judgment is to be preferred in light of the WSRP high-definition photographic material. Though the size of the letter is about right for *y*, the middle and lower heads of the wedges of *y* should be at least somewhat visible. In particular, on the right-hand side of what would be *y*, especially the bottom right wedge would appear in what is a clear area. The *y* from lines 8 and 9 also show wider space between the two sets of vertical wedges, compared to the wedges of the letter under discussion here in line 25. In contrast, ṣ fits the visible wedges and their spacing. For the reading *mṣprt*, the following proposals have been forwarded (see W. G. E. Watson 1993a:53 n. 56; *DUL* 587):

1. "She who arranges, repairs or takes care (of someone)," in *DUL* 587, citing Arabic *ḍafara*, *ḍāfara*, (Lane 1795–96), ESA *ḏfr*, Ethiopic *ḍafara*. Yet it is to be noted that the meaning of these forms is "to braid" and the like (see Leslau 148). Based on these cognates, translators render, "Shapshu nurses/aids their weakness"; so *MLC* 442, 537, 615; Hettema 1989–90:83; see also Pardee 1997b:279 n. 37. It is to be noted that the meaning of the putative South Semitic cognates is more concrete than that posited for the Ugaritic form. For further discussion, see below.

2. "Le soleil fait rougir leur treille [ ]," in *TO* 1.373 and n. w; *CML¹* 123: "Shapshu makes their tendrils abound with...." From this approach, W. G. E. Watson (1993a:53 n. 56) entertains a similar possibility: "Shapshu trims their 'hair' (i. e., their tendrils)." Watson cites Akkadian *ṣepēru* "to strand (hair and linen); to trim, decorate" and D-stem *ṣuppuru*, "to pare (vegetables and nails)," for example, "may her spells 'trim' her as (one trims the vegetable)," in Maqlu V 31 (*CAD* Ṣ:133). It is unclear how the sun-goddess would be understood as trimming vegetation.

3. "May pale Shapshu lead them"; so *CML²* 124, 151. The translation appears to be largely derived from a perception of the context.

---

40. For these and other parallels, see W. G. E. Watson 1979. For further arguments, see Walls 1992:153–54; Lapinkivi 2004:129–30, 141–42 n. 652.

4. "[The puppies] of Shapshu/the watch-dog at their door," so de Moor 1987:122. There is little in the context to support this view.

Of these proposals for the verb, the first perhaps fits best, especially with one of the current interpretations of *dlthm*. This noun has been taken in context to mean: "(may DN take care of) their weakness" (*DUL* 271) < **dll*, "to be poor." Since the *–hm* suffix on *dlthm* has the gods as its antecedent, *dlthm* as well as the preceding words in the line refers to the gods.

Suitable to the context is the comparison of Gaster (1946:57) with BH **dālît*, "branch" (Jer 11:6, Ezek 17:6–7; 19:11; 31:7, 9, 12).[41] Gaster's approach seems to work in the larger context with the fruit mentioned in the next line. Tsumura (1973:57) suggests that the proper form of branches in this context would be **dlyt-*, not *dlt-*, since the root of this plural noun is third weak. However, it is possible that the form reflects the collapse of a diphthong. Accordingly, a verb suggesting the benefit of Shapshu's power on vegetation such as "help" or "aid" or the like could work here. In this case, Shapshu tends for the vine presumably by her shining rays (cf. Lewis, *UNP* 209: "Shapshu shines [?] on their branches"). The problem is the lack of etymological evidence for this meaning as such. One might prefer an understanding based the basic meaning of the cognates cited for the first proposal, "to braid." The idea would be that Shapshu is said to braid their branches, perhaps as an expression of their growth.

But whose branches are these? The difficulty of the translation is the *–hm* suffix on *dlthm*, which would appear to have the *'ilm n'mm* as its antecedent. Therefore, *dlthm* and the preceding verb should refer to some action on the part of Shapshu that is beneficial or at least appropriate to these gods. The first interpretation is therefore superior, although it remains somewhat unconvincing. One remaining issue involves the form of *mṣprt*. It might be a D-stem participle functioning as the main verb of the clause. However, predicate participles are evidently rare in Ugaritic.[42] So one might suppose that this is a nominal clause, to be translated along the following lines: "Shapshu is the one who braids their branches."

The beginning and end of this section parallel the beginning and end of the first section, in lines 1–7. The major difference with the parallelism of line 7//lines 26–27 is that the latter lines add a reference to the bringing of sacrifice. Accordingly, it may be speculated that the sacrificial actions mentioned in the fourth section, between the first and eighth sections, represent the content of the sacrifice in the eighth section. The major difference between sections 1

---

41. Xella (1973:60) cites Akkadian *dallitu*, "vigna," but this word is not listed in the *CAD* or *AHw*.

42. See *qr'it* in 1.100.2 versus *tqr'u* in the same syntactic slot in the rest of the text. For discussion of predicative participles, see M. S. Smith 1999.

and 8 involves their middle lines. Both refer to consumables, food and wine in line 6 and grapes in line 26. We may speculate that in view of the other parallels between lines 1–7 and lines 23–27 these consumables are parallel. If so, then it is these consumables that are the content of the offering (or part of it) mentioned in line 27.

This section also raises a question about the nature of ritual in this text. As with the second section of 1.23 (lines 8–11), this one contains material that involves no particular ritual instruction as such. To be more specific, the invocation of lines 23–24 and the greeting in lines 26–27 are intelligible as ritual actions, but the mention of Shapshu in lines 25–26 involves no comparable ritual action. As ritual, it would seem to involve a statement on the part of the first-person speaker ("I") of line 23 that Shapshu is performing some action at this point in the ritual, but this is not ritual action in the customary sense. Nor is it said to be recited. Accordingly, the ritual purpose is obscure. It might be thought that the sense of what constitutes ritual action may include observations made by ritual participants and perhaps not simply actions that they take. Even so, the purpose remains unclear.

EXCURSUS 1: THE IDENTITY OF THE ʾILM NʿMM (PART 1)

A major question involves the identity of these gods, who are also the main subject of the narrative in 1.23.52–76. Since the narrative section describes them, further considerations of their identity are taken up in the discussion of their initial appearance in that narrative section, specifically at line 58. At this point, an initial consideration is addressed as it arises in the reconstructed material of lines 23–24. Pardee offers elegant reasoning (1997b:279) in identifying the ʾilm nʿmm with Shahar and Shalim, as it bears on the understanding of the title [ʾagzr ym bn] ym reconstructed in line 23 (based on lines 58–59 and 61).

Pardee translates the title, "who delimit the day, sons of a (single) day." He comments (1997b:279 n. 35):

> If one accepts that the "gracious gods" are Šaḥru-wa-Šalimu, then an interpretation reflecting their character appears most plausible, i.e., gzr, "to cut," denotes the separation of night from day ... i.e. cutting the day into two parts, while bn ym, literally "sons of a day," indicates that the two gods exercise their function within a single day.

Pardee's interpretation is quite appealing (see similarly, Dijkstra 1998:271 n. 31). However, there are four considerations militating against his identification of the gods:

1. Dawn and Dusk are not conceived of in terms of zones of steppe and sown (see lines 64–76), in contrast with the Goodly Gods. This contrast of zones is

noted by Pardee (1997b:283 n. 67), but he does not indicate how it fits into a mythology of Dawn-and-Dusk.

2. The births of Dawn and Dusk (lines 52–54), with no counting of months and with an offering to the sun-goddess, are also presented differently from the birth of the Goodly Gods (line 56).

3. It does not seem that Dawn and Dusk were understood as ravenous of birds and fish (lines 62–63). Pardee (1997b:282 n. 63) does try to explain the birds and fish as expressing a sort of horizontal axis of east (= sky) and west (= sea), but he himself notes that birds for sky is hardly limited to the east.

4. There is a further consideration of the text's larger setting, about which Pardee otherwise makes many pertinent and helpful observations. The text concerns the early fall period, a time when the mythology of Death makes compelling sense; however, no such mythology for Dawn-and-Dusk is known (cf. Dijkstra 1998).

Pardee's rendering of *'agzr* also disassociates the meaning of the word from the meaning of the word *gzr*, which the *'ilm n'mm* display in lines 63–64. This is less crucial than the four considerations above, as the text could use the same root in two different ways. However, in view of the four considerations, it would seem that in fact **gzr* may well be used in a similar way in both the title *'agzr ym* and in *gzr l<g>zr* in lines 63–64. In sum, the identification of Dawn and Dusk as the Goodly Gods, while explaining some features, falters on a number of grounds. The major alternative is to view the Goodly Gods as destructive powers, a possibility that is discussed further in the next chapter.

SECTION 9, LINES 28–29: SONG REITERATED

| 28 | šd {šd} 'ilm | "The field is {the field} of El/the gods, |
| | šd 'aṯrt wrḥmy | Field of Athirat and Rahmay." |

| 29 | xxxxx.xxb | |

Line 29

The line is clearly a third to a quarter in length, compared to lines 28 and 30. The reading of this line is most difficult, as shown by the disparity among views. Gulde (1998:297, 309) reads *'ilm yṯb* for the line, thereby following the lead of *CTA* ([----].y[ṯ]b) and CAT ('il[m].yṯb). This approach would evidently tie in with the material in line 19. In contrast, Lewis (*UNP* 209) reads: [š]b'd ǵ[zr]m.g. ṯb xxx. This set of readings recalls line 15.

Generally there is agreement on the last letter of the line (not counting the traces of three wedges that Lewis sees following b). Otherwise, the reading of the line is extremely disputed. After over four hours of looking at the line with Bruce

Zuckerman, I can report that none of the current readings can be sustained. The penultimate letter, if read as _t_ (as by *CTA*, CAT, and Gulde) is problematic, since its bottom wedge curving down to the right should be visible on the surface. At this point, the surface is clear and undamaged, but it shows no such wedge. Therefore, it would rule out _t_. Similarly, the reading _ṭ_ (as given by Lewis) is also a problem, in terms of the head of the vertical wedge expected. Physically, ʾ*a*, _t_ or *q* would be possible, but it is impossible to confirm any reading, only to rule out letters.

An observation may be made about Lewis's reading of the beginning of the line. When the same letters of line 15 are superimposed on Lewis's reconstruction of the same for line 29, there is no space for [*š*]*bʿd* at the beginning of line 29. Even allowing for squeezing in letters, two or three letters reconstructed by Lewis at the head of the line would not fit onto the tablet. From the point of space, it may be that Lewis's reconstruction could work without [*š*]*bʿd* (which might be explained as scribal haplography). Even so, the reading is open to dispute. All in all, it is impossible at present to offer a convincing reading for line 29.

This section reiterates the song of the fourth section, in lines 13–15. The fourth section couples the song with the consumable cooked in fire. The song of this last section, in lines 28–29, then arguably complements the offering mentioned in the preceding section. In the discussion of lines 13 and 16 above, I have entertained the possibility that lines 13 and 28 may belong to narrative embedded within ritual along the same lines as line 16. At least line 16 suggests knowledge of narrative associated with the goddess's hunt, and one might speculate that the game taken in the hunt may be one element of the ritual firstfruits of the *šd* of the goddess. This narrative embedded in ritual, at least in line 16 and arguably in lines 13 and 28 as well, constitutes a different angle on the ritual actions compared to the narrative after the ritual acts presented in lines 30–76.

Lines 1–29 represent a series of ritual pieces, which shows considerable variety compared to other ritual texts from Ugarit.[43] The components are not like the administrative format known from many Ugaritic ritual texts. Lines 1–29 contain no time signals and few structural indicators. The references to participants and professionals are uneven. The sections shift from one ritual mode to another with limited directions. The whole is oriented toward recitation or presentation (unlike the administrative presentation in Ugaritic ritual, for example, with its series of offerings). At the same time, within lines 1–29, there are some repetitions suggesting some sort of ritual coherence, or at least relationships. Sections 1 (lines 1–7) and 8 (lines 23–27) correspond closely, as do sections 4 (lines 13–15) and 9 (lines 28–29). The most explicit repetitions include

---

43. For this discussion, I wish to acknowledge the help that Daniel Fleming provided me.

the first and last sections, as well as two of the sections in between. I suggested above that section 5 (lines 16–18), with its presentation of the hunting goddess, may also be related thematically to sections 4 (lines 13–15) and 9 (lines 28–29), with their references to the field of Athirat wa-Rahmay. Section 3 (line 12) bears a sevenfold instructional rubric that resembles the sevenfold instruction of section 4 (lines 13–15). In view of these lines of connection, it would seem that some type of ritual coherence runs through most of lines 1–29; the only parts where this is not clear are section 2 (lines 8–11), section 6 (lines 19–20), and section 7 (lines 21–22). Given the ritual relations of the sections that are evident in the greater bulk of lines 1–29, it follows that where such relations are less in evidence, it would seem that though these simply lie beyond the perception of modern readers, these would have been apparent to their ancient participants.

It may be suggested that the dominant theme of lines 1–29 appears in the repetitions of lines 1–7//23–27, followed by the resumption of line 13 in line 28. Together these parts envelop the entire series of ritual pieces in lines 1–29. The parallel of lines 1–7//23–27 are of further note, because these include the only first-person material in the ritual section. As a major departure from Ugaritic ritual texts (as noted at the outset of this chapter), this first-person material offers a window into the ritual world of lines 1–29, which is rarely, if ever, seen in the Ugaritic ritual corpus. That the first-person invocation is of such immense importance may be gathered further from the fact that it is precisely this material within lines 1–29 that shares the same basic theme as the mythic narrative of lines 30–76.

In placing such weight on the lines 1–7//23–27, it is not my intention to flatten out the variety of material within lines 1–29. On the contrary, it is arguable that different mythical understandings accompany these ritual materials. The theme of the goddess in the hunt (line 16) is one such mythology, which would seem to differ from the theme of Death's destruction in section 2 (lines 8–11). We may think that both take place in the field or countryside (*šd*), and so the two myths are attached to the larger ritual context offering two narratives and therefore two perspectives on the reality of life evoked in the ritual. The narrative of the hunting goddess perhaps signals the availability of the sort of provisions that can be gained through hunting, while the presentation of Death (whether narrative or ritual) relates his demise. In short, these two mythologies offer two perspectives on the related, perhaps even the same, reality, namely, that provisions for living are available and correspondingly Death's power over nature is weakened. I have also suggested that a third mythology of the *'ilm n'mm* is embedded within the invocations of lines 1 and 23–24, namely, that the goddess (perhaps Athirat, I would argue) has given birth to and provides life to the *'ilm n'mm*. At a minimum, this third mythology, as I have called it, suggests that the destructive deities are fed thanks to the goddess. (At this point, we do not know if the mention of the *'ilm n'mm* evokes the narrative of their terrible appetite as known from lines 52–76 or not.) In any case, the goddess is central to life, as with the hunt in line 16 and the field in lines 13 and 28.

The various mythic associations ultimately work together with lines 1–7//23–27 in contributing to the major mythic theme of the Feast of the Goodly Gods. To the narrative presentation of this theme in lines 30–76, we now turn in the following chapter.

3

Lines 30–76: Divine Narrative

Section I, El and His Wives: Lines 30–49

Subsection A, Lines 30–39: El and the *mštʿltm*

Lines 30–35a: First set of *mštʿltm*

30	[ ]l[ ]y[ ]ʾi gp ym	... to the seashore
	wyṣǵd gp thm	And he marches to the shore of the Deep.
31	[ ]x[ ] ʾil mštʿltm	El [...] the two servers (?),
	mštʿltm lrʾiš ʾagn	Servers (?) from the top of the pot.
32	hlh tšpl hlh trm	See her, she's low; see her, she's high.
	hlh tṣḥ ʾad ʾad	See her, she cries: "Daddy, Daddy!"
33	whlh tṣḥ ʾum ʾum	And see her, she cries: "Mommy, Mommy!"
	tʾirkm yd ʾil kym	El's penis lengthens like the sea,
34	wyd ʾil kmdb	Indeed, El's penis, like the flood.
	ʾark yd ʾil kym	El's penis lengthens like the sea,
35	wyd ʾil kmdb	Indeed, El's penis, like the flood.

Line 30

In view of the evident reference to El in the following bicolon, as well as the parallel with line 35, Lewis's reconstruction [ʾi]l and his translation "El [takes(?)]," are quite plausible (*UNP* 210). As in line 35, it might be supposed that the verbal form *yqḥ* is to be reconstructed in line 30. However, it may be that these lines are parallel yet also preliminary to the actions in lines 35–36. Perhaps at this point, El sees the two females involved in their activity; he does not yet take them.

It is often assumed that El is old in this text, an understandable view given other texts that portray El as elderly (such as the Baal Cycle). For example,

Gordon (1949:58) refers to his "old age." Cross (1973:24) calls El "a vigorous and prodigiously lusty, old man." Kapelrud (1952:73), Pope (1955:40, 41; 1979), Margalit (1981:138 n. 4), Porter (1981:4), Segert (1986:218) also operate under this assumption. Lewis (*UNP* 206) more circumspectly characterizes the god as a "so-called old timer." However, as noted by Gibson (*CML*² 30 n. 1) as well as Cutler and Macdonald (1982:34), El in this text is a younger god, since his divine procreation seems to belong to distant antiquity relative to the events presented in the Baal Cycle where he is an older figure. Van Selms (1970:252) similarly comments that in this text "El plays a more active role than in the Baal Cycle" and that 1.23 "reflects a somewhat older mythography." In view of his role as father, El here seems to be in the prime of his physical life; he is not yet an old patriarch with grown-up divine children. This text depicts him as he is having his children, and this differs from the Baal Cycle, where this stage of his divine life seems to have long passed. (As noted above in the discussion of line 16, a similar issue regarding the goddess may be raised.)

The choice of verb in the second line, *wyṣġd*, may be contextually driven: it perhaps denotes procession of the god from his abode, as it does with Baal in 1.10 III 7.¹ According to Walls (1992:147), the choice of locale by the water "may be a widespread ancient Near Eastern literary motif." Walls compares Baal's copulation on the banks of a lake in CAT 1.10, as well as Enlil's sexual relations with Ninlil in a boat (Jacobsen 1987:174), and Enki's seduction of his daughters in a marshland setting (*ANET* 39). Komoróczy (1971:76–77) had already compared the theogony of some Sumerian narratives to 1.23. At the same time, the setting suits El, who arrives perhaps from his abode in the midst of the confluence of the cosmic waters (as known from CAT 1.3 V 6–7; 1.4 IV 21–22; and 1.100.3; M. S. Smith 1994b:225–34).

Line 31

The noun *mšt'ltm* has inspired a wide variety of interpretations. A rather mundane view based on etymology and the type-scene identified is proposed below, following a short review of the proposals:

1. *Firebrands or torches* (with or without astral significance). Nielsen (1936:82–83), followed by Pope (1955:80–81), interpreted *mšt'ltm* as "brands, torches" (cf. Arabic *ša'ala*, "kindle, burn, blaze"). Pope suggested that they "may represent the passionate goddesses whom he subsequently impregnates." Pope saw some sort of ritual of sexual relations lying behind this term. Pope would also relate

---

1. Commentators often compare BH *ṣ'd (e.g., in Ps 68:8) despite the problem that the biblical root is thought to be cognate with Arabic ṣa'ida, "to climb up" (see *KB* [1999, ed. M. E. J. Richardson] 1040; also Tsumura 1973:59 and *DUL* 780). It is plausible to disassociate the Ugaritic and Hebrew words from the putative Arabic cognate with the Hebrew word.

the double-torches to pairs of torches in Indo-European religious symbolism.[2] In accordance with this view, Pope takes *ʾagn* as "fire," an Indo-European loanword (cf. Sanskrit *agni*, Latin *ignis*), but most scholars take the word as "pot" or the like, supported by 6.70.1, which refers to *ʾagn z pʿl* PN, "basin which PN made" (see *DUL* 26; see the discussion in line 15). This detail is, however, not crucial to Pope's case.

Lewis's understanding of the word's etymology is similar to that of Pope, as he translates "a pair of brands." This etymology fits the immediate context with the basin (note the coals in line 39). In Lewis's view, this "pair of firebrands" is the pair of females who appear throughout lines 39–61 (*UNP* 209).

2. *Cultic personnel.* Some scholars see in this word "elevated, consecrated women," possibly a cultic title (see *DUL* 595). As support, they cite Akkadian *mušēlû* (*AHw* 682; *CAD M/2*:265). The view is possible, but it assumes a projection of the human level onto the divine plane. Indeed, the narrative of lines 30–76 seems to involve deities and not humans.

3. *Offerings*, etc. *TO* (1.357, 373 n. z) analyzes the form as a dual feminine substantive of the Ct of **ʿly*. *TO*, following Gaster (*Thespis* 235–26) and Driver (*CML*[1] 23), proposes to see a water-pouring ritual here: "les deux femmes *qui font monter (l'eau).*" Lipiński (1986:208–10) renders *mštʿltm lrʾiš ʾagn* "those raising themselves as high as the top of the basin," based on the Akkadian expression *šutēlû ana*, "to reach as high as" (*CAD E*:135). According to Lipiński, the women are filling the basin for a water-pouring ritual. Porter (1981:4) argues that such a ritual "would have little relevance in the context of the poem." Segert (1986:219) is critical of the view, given the lack of evidence.

Operating with the same morphological understanding, de Moor (1972:2.21 n. 89) proposed "scales." This proposal would appear problematic, in view of the fact that the word for scales in Ugaritic poetry is *mznm* (1.24.35). With the same morphological analysis, de Moor (1987:123) later rendered "two girl-acrobats." There is little in the context to support either of these translations.

Dietrich and Loretz (1977) propose to see two "Schälchen": "*mštʿltm* könnte somit eine Bezeichnung für 'Schwimmer, Schälchen' sein, die für die Durchführung der mantischen Handlung wichtig waren." Again, little in the context favors this proposal.

Pardee (1997b: 280 n. 44; Bordreuil and Pardee 2004:2.35) agrees with other scholars that the word refers to the females and sees the form as the Ct of **ʿly*, hence those who make an offering to El (see also Hettema 1989–90:83 n. 26). For contextual reasons given below, I provisionally accept this view.

---

2. See Pope 1979:702–4 and his comparison with the Dioscuri, echoing Gaster 1946:70.

Wyatt (2002:330 n. 31) likewise uses the same morphological analysis for his rendering "the two inflamed ones," but he takes *ʿly with the putative sense "to be aroused."

4. *Handfuls, ladlesful.* Citing BH *šōʿal*, Albright (1934:134) translates: "two handfuls" (see also Gaster 1946:53; *CML*[1] 123; Dahood 1969:32). Cross (1973:22) renders: "ʾEl takes two ladlesful, Two ladlesful filling a flagon." According to Cross, this sentence describes "ʾĒl preparing a meal at his abode near the sea." The etymology is possible, but I doubt that El ever prepared a meal in his life.

5. *Two coals* (Ginsberg 1935:67). This translation derives evidently from a sense of context, but it enjoys no etymological support.

6. *Two effigies* (*UT* 19.2458; Gordon 1966:95; Tsumura 1973:60–63). The idea, evidently inspired by El's creation of Shataqatu in 1.16 V, is that El as creator animates two female effigies. Trujillo (1973:151) comments: "This explanation calls for some unparalleled action on the part of El and seems the least likely of all."

7. *Two concubines* (Trujillo 1973:151–52, 154). This proposal would be generally suitable to the context. It is based on an etymology with Arabic *ʿallat*, "a woman's fellow wife, her husband's wife." The suggestion fits the overall context admirably, but Trujillo himself identifies several problems with the proposal. The first meaning of this word given in Lane is "a (single) second draught." The participial form in the Št-stem also does not suit this explanation. Trujillo also notes that this translation does not work in the immediate context, with the prepositional phrase in lines 31//36.

Despite the significant disparity of views, the solution may be a relatively simple one. The morphological analysis offered by *TO*, Pardee, and others is impeccable. The sense may be suggested first by relating this word to its immediate context. With the phrase that follows, *lrʾiš ʾagn*, the line looks as if it means "to cause to *ʿly to/from/at the top of the pot," although a different syntactical understanding is possible ("to cause to *ʿly the pot to/from/at top"). As noted above, Lipiński suggested water "brought up" for a water-pouring ritual, but the substance in question may be some sort of foodstuff. As an analogy, one might compare *ʿly used in 1 Sam 2:14 for bringing food up out of a cooking pot.[3] The sort of meat broths cooked in a pot is well known in Mesopotamian cuisines (Bottéro 1995:8–11; 2004:26–29).

In 1.23, the meaning of *ʿly may be general, with the sense "to serve" (cf. Akkadian *šēlû*, *CAD* E:130).[4] The infix -t in *mštʿltm* could imply a reflexive-recip-

---

3. The C-stem of BH *yṣʾ appears in a comparable usage in Ezek 24:6 (was this root selected in this context, in part because of the G-stem of the same root in the preceding poetic line?). Cf. also BH *yṣq, "to pour," for serving food from a pot in 2 Kgs 4:40, 41.

rocal meaning that the females "bring up/serve (foodstuff)." In Ugaritic, verbal -*t* forms refer commonly to action performed with the body or parts of the body.[5] Many of these forms are active verbs (some transitive), and several lack explicit reflexivity. So the form would not need to be rendered with an explicit reflexive-reciprocal sense. I would follow Pardee, then, in taking the form with the specific sense that the females make an offering, but with the more specific nuance of serving cooked food.

If this reasoning holds, then the next question is identifying the type of scene involved. This situation here may be analogous to the picture of Athirat in 1.4 II 3–10. In this scene, she is at work with domestic chores at the edge of the sea. These include setting a pot on the fire. We may have a comparable scene here in 1.23.30. If so, it would suggest a rather mundane picture of two females engaged in the domestic activity of lifting some foodstuff from a pot. I would therefore choose a simpler understanding of them as "servers." According to Cross (1973:22), it is El who is preparing a meal; I think it is the other way around. The difference between the two scenes is that Athirat in 1.4 II is understood already as El's wife, while in 1.23.30–31, the females in question are not yet his wives. In sum, El has taken two females who had attracted him (perhaps inadvertently) as they prepare food. There is a further indication that this scene involves such a domestic matter: the cry of the two females to their parents is described in the next two lines.

Lines 32–33

The verb may refer throughout to both females (Pope 1955:37), or they may be referring to the two females in turn ("one bends low, another arcs high, now one cries..., now cries the other..."), as construed by Lewis (*UNP* 210). The grammar favors the second approach. At this point in the narrative, the two females are foregrounded with the presentative particle *hl-*, with *-h* (*DUL* 337), the third feminine singular suffix, which repeatedly focuses attention on them. The fourfold repetition of *hlh* in these lines (observed by W. G. E. Watson 1982:267) has parallels: *ḥš* in 1.4 V 51–54; *ṯm* in 1.22 I 4–9 (noted by Tuttle cited in Pope 1977:68 = 1994:196); and *k-* in 1.169.3–4. The presentative particle *hl-* has been discussed by Brown (1987:202–7) and Tropper (*UG* 750), who compare Amarna Akkadian *allû* and some instances of BH *hălōʾ* (cf. *CAD* A/1:358; see also Sivan 1997:185). My translation, "See...," is designed to bring out the presentative force of the particle.

---

4. Aloysius Fitzgerald has drawn my attention to the Akkadian phrase, *1 ša mê šēlî siparri*, "one dipper (lit. to draw water) of copper" in EA 22 iv 18 (*CAD E*:135).

5. See the listing of twenty or so Gt-forms in the discussion of line 51 below (p. 97). See also Greenfield 1979.

The question is what the females are doing in lines 32–33. Cross (1973:23 n. 55) explains the females' behavior: "The two wives ... bob up and down in embarrassment and excitement."[6] Trujillo (1973:155) surmises: "This seems to be a cry for help uttered by the girls while they are being chased and cornered by El." Pardee (1997b:280 n. 47) comments in a similar vein:

> I remain dubious that 'Ilu is here being addressed directly and wittingly as a mother.... we may surmise that the women were engaging in the activity with the express purpose of catching a male, indeed a divine one.... If such be the case, the cries in lines 32–33 are addressed to their own parents, as in Daddy, mommy, what do we do now?

Cross, Trujillo, and Pardee have put their finger on the problem, although there is no indication that the females are trying to catch El. In context, El might be trying to "take" them, as he is attracted to them and engages in flirtatious behavior with them, and so they appeal to their parents (for permission or for guidance?). If correct, we might compare several biblical scenes involving females communicating with one or another of their parents after meeting a potential suitor (or his representative) at the well: Rebekah runs to her mother's household after encountering Abraham's servant at the well (Gen 24:28); Rachel hurries to her father after encountering Jacob at the well (Gen 29:12); and Zipporah and her sisters tell their father about meeting Moses at the well (Exod 2:19).[7] In the last of the three cases, the females are ordered by their father to offer food and drink to the man. In terms of the verbal formulation in 1.23.32–33, one may note Isa 8:4, which refers to the lower age of when a youth "knows to call 'daddy' [literally, 'my father'] and 'mommy' [literally, 'my mother']." In contrast, the two females whom El approaches are at the upper end of their life-stage under parental authority.

In contrast to this line of interpretation, Wyatt (2004, 2005a, 2005b) has argued that the females are referring not to their parents off-stage but to El himself as father and mother, in his capacity as their androgenous progenitor. The context militates against this view, as no creation of the females is described. Indeed, El is seen relating to them as females in a stage of life well after their births. Moreover, the West Semitic texts that are putatively parallel offer no clear evidence of El as an androgenous figure, much less one who procreates without an accompanying goddess. Indeed, El's consort, Athirat, is known as "the pro-

---

6. I would qualify Cross's characterization of the women as his wives at this point in the narrative, as they do not show this status until lines 46–49.

7. I wish to thank Susan Ackerman for suggesting these comparisons.

genitress of the gods" (*qnyt ʾilm*) in 1.4 I 22; 1.4 III 26, 30, 35; 1.4 IV 32; and 1.8 II 2. This title in itself strongly militates against Wyatt's hypothesis.

A more mundane interpretation is that lines 32–33 characterize the females doing their cooking that is referred to in the previous line 31.[8] El is looking on as they work at the pot. They call to their parents, perhaps as an invitation to eat (for *ṣwḥ in this usage, see 1.4 VI 44, 45; 1.15 IV 6). In this context, El is attracted to the females, as indicated by lines 33–35. Lichtenstein (1968, 1977) has noted the order of food preparation followed by invitation; so the order in this context in lines 31–33, if it is to be understood in this manner, follows suit. If this approach is correct, the description of the females as high and low would seem unusual, even if it refers to their stirring and drawing up meat broth from the pot.

Lines 33–35a

For Ugaritic *ḫṭ*, "staff," for "penis," see 1.169.1–2. Ugaritic *yd*, "hand," is an euphemism for penis as well as a word for "love, passion."[9] This is evident also in 1.4 IV 38–39, which uses both *yd* and *ʾahbt* in a sexual manner. After Athirat's journey to El, he offers her food and drink and then more:

> Or, does the love (*yd*) of El the King excite you,
> The affection (*ʾahbt*) of the Bull arouse you?

Ugaritic *yd* is literally "hand," but as these passages indicate, the word is also a term for "love," with the connotation of "penis." Two roots seem to underlie Ugaritic *yd*, namely, the primitive biconsonantal *yd, "hand," and *wdd, "love." In Ugaritic these two roots have coalesced and their meanings seem to have affected one another. It would appear that the semantic connotation of "love" of *wdd came to exert a connotation on the literal meaning of *yd, "hand." Accordingly, Ugaritic *yd* has the nuance of penis. De Moor and van der Lugt (1974:14) have suggested that the two uses of *yd* retain a slight semantic distinction, that *yd* in 1.23.33–35 indeed refers to the penis, but in 1.4 IV 38 it means affection. The semantic distinction is suggested, to them, by the difference in grammatical gender: the former governs a feminine verbal form (*tʾirkm*),[10] while the latter

---

8. This alternative was suggested by my student Stephen Russell.

9. See, for example, Gordon 1966:95 n. 44; Delcor 1967; Fitzgerald 1967; Cross 1973:23 n. 56; Trujillo 1973:155; *TO* 1.205 n. i; Pope 1979:706; Seow 1989:110 n. 88. For a survey and discussion, see Dietrich and Loretz 2003:160–62. For further evidence in Egyptian and Akkadian, see Paul 2005:247–48 n. 32, 302–3.

10. However counterintuitive it may seem, the word for penis is grammatically feminine; it is to be remembered in this context that breasts in Biblical Hebrew are masculine in gender.

takes a masculine verbal form (*yḫssk*). It is possible that some nuance might be maintained, but the two meanings are closely associated.

Pope (1979:706) argues for wordplay in 1.23.33–35. According to this reconstruction, El achieves penile extension as a result of the foreplay in lines 32–33; whether and how the action in line 31 contributes to his achievement is unclear. Another picture may be entertained. There may be no foreplay here. Instead, as El gazes at the two females engaged in their domestic activity, he experiences an erection expressed by *yd*, which is repeated for emphasis. The image of the flood elsewhere is used in a comparison in describing Baal's enthronement (1.101.1–2): "Baal sits (enthroned) like the sitting of a mountain (*b'l yṯb kṯbt ǵr*), Haddu ... like the (cosmic) ocean (*hd r*[ ] *kmdb*)." In both comparisons, superhuman size is evoked.

Lines 33–35 present El's penis as measuring up, or lengthening (*t'arkm// 'ark*). The root **'rk* appears first in the G-prefix indicative followed by the infinitive absolute. This sequence of forms within a close context (and in this case parallel clauses) indicates the subject of the infinitive absolute in Ugaritic narrative.[11]

LINES 35B–39: SECOND SET OF *MŠT'LTM*

35	yqḥ 'il mšt'ltm	El takes the two servers (?),
36	mšt'ltm lr'iš 'agn	Servers (?) from the top of the pot.
	yqḥ yš<t> bbth	He takes, se<t>s (them) in his house.
37	'il ḫth nḫt	As for El, his staff descends (?),
	'il ymnn mṭ ydh	As for El, his love-shaft droops (?).
37–38	yš'u/yr šmmh	He lifts (his hand), he shoots skyward,
38	yr bšmm 'ṣr	He shoots in the sky a bird,
38–39	yḫrt yšt/lpḥm	He plucks, sets (it) on the coals;
	'il 'aṯtm kypt	El indeed entices the two females.

Line 35

At this point, it is evident that El takes the two females for himself. As explained in line 36, he installs them in his house, evidently with the intention of their becoming his wives. Akkadian *leqû* is a standard verb for "taking" a wife. Attestations include an example from Ras Shamra (RS 17.159.6; *CAD* L:137): "Ammishtamru took (*il-te-qè*) the daughter of Benteshina as his wife." The BH

---

11. For further discussion, see Gai 1982. Note also the infinitive absolutes evidently in line 68.

formula "to take someone to oneself as a wife" (*lqḥ PN l- l'šh) signals marriage,[12] which is likewise the larger context of lines 39–49. The end of the section, in lines 48–49, indicates that the two women become wives of El. More broadly, the BH verb *lqḥ is used as prelude to sexual relations in Gen 20:2–3, where Abimelech "takes" Sarah (verse 4: "Abimelech had not approached her"). In Gen 34:2, Shechem takes Dinah and lies with her (cf. Deut 22:28–29); then he asks his father to acquire her as his wife (verse 4). The allegory of Jerusalem personified as God's wife in Ezek 16:32 uses the root for sexual relations outside of marriage (cf. Gen 30:15; *DCH* 4:573).

Line 37

The syntax of the bicolon, especially with its double *casus pendens*, suggests that the line provides descriptive information rather than a continuation of the narrative line. Since the usual way to continue narrative line is the prefix form of the verb in initial position, the suffix form of the verb in final position also suggests that line 37 does not continue the narration of events as such.

The staff functions in a number of capacities in Ugaritic myth. In 1.23.8–9, the staff symbolizes the power of the deity. In 1.3 II 15–16, the goddess uses a staff (*mṭm*) and a bow-string (*bksl qšth*) as weapons. The former can refer to a common staff (1.19 III 49; 1.23.47), but it is also a weapon (Cross 1973:23). In Hab 3:9 and 14, the noun stands in parallelism with *qšt*, "bow," which in this context may mean "shaft." If it were modified by *yd*, the word would be patently El's sexual organ (Pope 1955:38); accordingly, the bow would symbolize virility (Pope 1987:226, citing Job 29:19–20).

It has been argued that *ydh* goes with the following verb (Verreet 1986:369; Voigt 1990:408). If so, it issues in two features that suit Ugaritic poetry. First, the second line of the bicolon of line 37 is not longer than the first. It is quite normal in Ugaritic poetry for the second line to be about the same length as or shorter than the first line. The interpretation of *ydh* with the following verb would issue in a notable poetic balance in line 37. Second, construing *ydh* with *yš'u* provides the verb with its direct object. Otherwise, the object remains implicit, which is possible. These are hardly definitive arguments, and indeed a very strong contextual factor favors taking *yd* with the preceding noun *mṭ*: the expression *mṭ ydh* occurs three times in relative proximity, in lines 40, 44, and 47. Voigt's further claim that *ydh yš'u* belongs to the category of "Spalsätze" (cleft sentences) has not met with acceptance.

---

12. For example, Gen 4:19; 6:2; 11:29; 12:19; Judg 14:2, 3, 8; cf. CD MS A 5:7. See BDB 543; *DCH* 4:573.

The word order, whether it is to be regarded as *casus pendens* (as rendered here) or not, does not simply continue the narrative. Moreover, this bicolon fronts the name of the god; as noted above, the usual syntax for continuation of narrative sequence is a fronted prefix indicative verb. Based on these features of the clause, the condition described in line 37 takes place in the same time frame as the actions described in lines 35–36.

Lines 37b–39

Some of the terms in the cooking scene in 1.23.38–39, 41, 44–45 appear also in 1.4 II 8–9: *yšt lpḥmm* and *l'išt//lpḥmm*. The bicolon in 1.4 II 8–9 describes Athirat cooking on *'išt*, "fire," parallel to *pḥm*. This noun is cognate with Akkadian *pēmtu*, BH *peḥām*, and Arabic *faḥm, faham*, "(char)coal." The noun also consti-tutes a commodity (CAT 2.73.9; 3.1.22–39; 4.132.1, 4, 5; 4.203.3, 5, 6). It also occurs in protases of lunar observations (1.172.2; see line 6), thought to be part of a Ugaritic translation of a Sin-tablet belonging to the series Enuma Anu Enlil or a related series (van Soldt 1990:342): *hm yrh b'lyh wpḥm*, "If the moon is at its rising and it is *pḥm*."[13] Van Soldt concludes from his study of the word in Ugaritic: "the word *pḥm* literally means 'glowing charcoal'. It was also used to indicate a type of wool, probably red in color."

There is more to the comparison between 1.23.37–39 and 1.4 II 8–9, noted above in the discussion of line 31. The scene in 1.4 II 8–9 takes place at the shore of the sea, with El's female, Athirat. This scene describes her in a series of actions that appear domestic. She wields a spindle in lines 3–4, she conveys her garment into the sea in lines 5–7, she sets a pot on the fire in lines 8–9, and then she is said to make eyes at El (or exalt him?) in lines 10–11. It is to be noted that in both this section of the Baal Cycle and in the Feast of the Goodly Gods, the scene takes place at the seashore. There are differences between the two scenes as well. In 1.4 II 3–11 Athirat cleans up, has put something on the fire perhaps to attract El, and possibly makes flirtatious eyes in his direction, but in 1.23.37–39 El evidently initiates the action to charm or attract (**pty*) the females (*CML*[1] 30 n. 1). As noted by Pardee (1997b:281 n. 52), biblical pas-sages use **pty* for both lawful and unlawful sexual enticement. Male initiation of sexual interaction is discussed in illicit terms in Exod 22:15 [22:16 English] (*wĕkî-yĕpatteh 'îš bĕtûlâ*), but in Hos 2:16 the root expresses Yahweh's licit court-ship of Israel (*lākēn hinnēh 'ānōkî mĕpattêhâ*.[14] The behavior in these two biblical verses is suggestive of some sort of sexual activity in lines 37–38.

---

13. Van Soldt's translation instead renders the two clauses as a single unit.

14. 11QT[a] 66:8, though largely based on Deut 22:28, uses *ypth* from Exod 22:19. In contrast, Deut 22:28 uses **mṣ'*, which perhaps should be noted in relation to El's movement in line 30 above.

Tsumura (1973:66) evidently accepts that a third-weak root is involved, but he translates: "El indeed tests the two women" (Tsumura 1973:120). The basis for this particular semantic sense from *pty* is unclear, as is his reason for rejecting the picture of El's charming or attracting his females: "Such a sense is not justified here, because the two women referred to are already El's, either as daughters or as wives." However, this stage of matters is not reached until lines 48–49. As an alternative, Dahood (1969:24) proposed to take *'il* not as the subject but as a *casus pendens* with *'attm* as the subject of *kypt:* "El, his two wives are truly beautiful." The rendering makes sense of *ypt* in context, but the logic behind the lack of concord between the subject and the verb is notable. Dahood offers an explanation: "Of course, *k* parses as the emphatic particle, and since it is predicative, not attributive, plural *ypt* instead of dual *yptm*, is permissible." This putative solution has not been accepted.

EXCURSUS 2: THE VIRILITY OF EL

The verbs *nḫt//ymnn* in line 37 stand at the center of a controversy over El's sexual capacities, which is a major component of the narrative (Xella 1973:122–37). Appearing first here in line 37 and then in lines 40, 43–44, and 46–47, the two verbs are difficult (see *DUL* 628, 968). Translating both "lower," Albright (1934:135 n. 184) derived *nḫt* from *nḫt*, "to descend," and he took *ymnn* from *mnn* to "lower," based on Arabic *manna*, "to be weary." Albright (1934:135 n. 186) supposed:

> It is not impossible that the whole description refers to the *hieros gamos*, and the strange imagery is erotic. In ancient and modern oriental imagery, both staff and bird may mean penis; the sinking of the staff may refer to the subsidence of the penis after sexual intercourse, while the roasting of the bird may refer to male sexual excitement.[15]

Early commentators were divided over Albright's interpretation. Several scholars accepted his view.[16] Gaster (1946:67 n. 89) does not address the etymol-

---

Like the man who entices the women in Exod 22:19, in the same case in Deut 22:28, he first meets (*mṣ'*) her. Note also 1 Kgs 22:20, 21, where NJPS translates the root *pth* by "entice."

15. Albright then cites "*AfO* 5, 119b." This is a reference to Albright's earlier article on "The Second Campaign at Tell Beit Mirsim." Albright (1928–29:119) describes one figurine: "One figurine represents the naked goddess holding a dove with outstretched wings to her bosom (evidently symbolic of male procreative power; *ráfraf ṭêr el-ḥamâm* is used in modern Arabic of the male in coitus)."

16. Ginsberg 1935:56: "fallen down"//"weakened"; *CML*[1] 123: "is lowered"//"laid aside (?)"; Tsumura 1973:14: "goes down"//"is lowered"; Xella 1973:37: "abbassa"//"lascia cadere."

ogy of the crucial verbs that he saw as relating El's setting aside his staff, and his translation is ambiguous: "Having let his baton drop, having with his rod dispensed (?)" (*Thespis* 429). The virtue of Gaster's rendering is his recognition of the difficulty of line 37.

Pope (1955:40, and in M. S. Smith 1998b:663–64) marked a new direction, although he followed Albright's etymology: "There is, however, no indication that intercourse occurs before l. 49b. Therefore, the drooping of El's rod, we suggest, represents his inability to achieve and maintain an erection rather than post-coital detumescence." This showed El as a *deus otiosus* for Pope as well as some other commentators.[17] In contrast, Cross (1973:22–24) understood the verbs in the opposite manner: they denote El's erection that he maintains throughout the scene, a picture defended also by Trujillo (1973:161). Cross (1973:23 n. 58) viewed *ymnn* and the related form *mmnnm* (lines 40, 44, 47) as denominative from the noun *ymn*, "right hand," with the alleged meaning "to draw with the right hand."[18] Broadly speaking, Trujillo (1973:164) follows Cross, though with his own view of the roots, **nḥt//mnh:* "aim"//"directs" (cognate with BH *mnh*, "to divide in parts").[19]

Cross's view was strongly criticized by Pope (1979:706; 1987:225–26) and later Renfroe (1992:129), because of the lack of evidence for the putative denominative verb. Pope (1987:226) also suspected that a putative D-stem prefix indicative of **ymn* would yield forms such as **ywmn*, just as the D-stem form of **ysr* is attested as *ywsrnn* (energic indicative plus suffix). Good (1986:155–56) defended Cross's etymology by suggesting that the second *n* in the related masculine singular form *mmnnm* may be an energic suffix to a participle.[20] Good also criticized Pope's citation of **mnn*, in suggesting that the Arabic evidence includes *munnatun*, "strength."

Along the lines suggested by Good, Cross changed his mind about his etymology. As reported in Olyan (1988:42 n. 13), Cross later derived the verb from **mnn* "to make taut," a verb in Arabic that can mean "to weary" and "to be strong":

> Cross will argue in a future article that the original meaning of *mnn* is "to strain," "make taut." The secondary meaning would be "to become weak,"

---

17. For a listing and discussion, see Xella 1973:124–37.

18. So also *DUL* 968; de Moor 1972:2.92; Pardee 1997b:280–81 n. 51.

19. Apart from the semantic development, one may wonder about the required morphology for the second root. No instance of the D-stem of a third-weak verb, with reduplication of the middle radical, is listed by Tropper (*UG* 669–70). One might try to salvage the proposed etymology by arguing that Ugaritic **mnn* or **mwn* is a biform of BH **mnh*. In view of the semantics required, this seems inadvisable.

20. This is possible, but if so, the form has not one but two sufformative elements, which is unpersuasive.

"weary" (as a result of straining). He will cite Akkadian *manānu*, "sinews,"
nerves," and Syriac *minnîn/minnē*, "sinew, hair," in defense of this position.

Olyan circumspectly comments in turn:

> The cruces of this text remain unresolved. It is certainly clear that El is not
> impotent; there is intercourse between El and the two goddesses, producing
> offspring. However, Cross's arguments are not altogether convincing either.
> The Arabic cognate root *MNN* is simply too ambiguous, and we can assume
> nothing about its range of meaning in Ugaritic.

A more recent survey of the issue favors the meaning "to be weakened" for
mnn. Renfroe (1992:128–30) stresses the meaning "weakness" not only in Arabic
but also in Ethiopic. At the same time, Renfroe argues that this meaning for
Ugaritic forms is "arguable though unprovable." On the translation of the verbs,
more recent translations are divided. Wyatt (1998:331) follows Albright's view:
"lowered"//"drooping." Paul (2005:248 n. 32) does as well: "is down" //"droops."
Lewis (*UNP* 210) evidently follows Cross's overall interpretation in translating the
verbs *nḫt//ymnn* as "lowers"//"is generous." More neutrally, Pardee (1997b:281)
translates: "prepare your staff"//"grasp your rod."

As a cautionary analogy, the image of the "taut cords" could imply either
an erection or tumescence. In Mesopotamian potency incantations, the image
of "taut cords" is used sometimes for the erect penis (Biggs 1967:35, no. 15, line
15; Leick 1994:200), but in other contexts, "taut cords" (*qé-e šad-du-ti*) represents
also an image for the slack penis (Biggs 1967:17, no. 2, line 9; 20–21, no. 4, lines
12, 16), in other words, "taut cords (when they are loosed)." El is indeed potent as
lines 33–34 amply illustrate. At the same time, it is unclear that El maintains his
erect condition throughout, as in Cross's view. This question hinges ultimately
on the language of *mšt'ltm//lr'iš 'agn* in lines 31//35–36 and the shooting of the
bird put on the fire in lines 37–39. Is it metaphorical for sexual passion (in heat)
in lines 31//35–36, or does it refer to some sort of further action within the narrative? Similarly, is the shooting of the bird itself metaphorical wordplay?

Commentators are quite divided. On one side are those who see actual sexual
relations being expressed, or at least double-entendre for such copulation. De
Moor takes the stick as a real one (1972:2.21 n. 91), but with a double-entendre (1972:21 n. 93): "the stick (penis) will enter the innocent bird (girl, almost
universal imagery, *e.g.* Hebr. *yōnā*) which will be roasted." For Hettema (1989–
90:87–88), shooting the bird and putting it on the fire in lines 37–39 stand for
sexual penetration. W. G. E. Watson (1977:281), followed by de Moor (1987:124
n. 43), views the image of plucking as double-entendre and as support cites
Babylonian Love-Lyrics: "with the plucking of a bird will I pluck you" (*ba-qa-an
iṣ-ṣu-[r]u-um-ma lu-ub-qu-un-ki*; Lambert 1975:110, line 35); see Paul 2005:248 n.

32, 302). For Albright, as for de Moor, Hettema, Pardee, and others, the language was metaphorical double-entendre.

For other scholars, lines 37–39 depict preparations for an aphrodisiac. For Pope, in lines 37–39 there is "a ritual designed to produce this coveted state" (see also Gray 1965:100; Gaster, *Thespis* 413). As a third option, might the language be metaphorical but also evoke the imagery known for such preparations? De Moor (1972:2.21 n. 93; cf. 1987:123 n. 35, 124 n. 43) seems to hold such a view of matters, since he maintains a metaphorical view of the language, yet cites the use of birds in Babylonian potency rituals (see further below). So is the image of the bird shot, plucked, and cooked on the fire in this section simply a metaphor for El's sexual heat, as Albright suggested? Or, does it refer to some sort of ritual, as Pope proposed?

In the corpus of the Ugaritic texts, sexual passion is otherwise never described in this manner. This is not to say that such double-entendre was unknown in the ancient Near East. A good instance of sexual double-entendre appears in a short Sumerian tale that references sexual arousal or passion with reference to a bird as well as other images. In "The Fowler and his Wife," a fowler drinks and ignores his wife, who then says to him (Leick 1994:37–38):

> "The net was cast upon an *esig*-bird,
> the net was drawn up upon a raven.
> The water has dried up in the little swamp
> So that your boat touches the ground.
> A whirlwind blew.
> Fowler, let not your net be drawn up, let not your net...,
> Let the raven rise!"

This speech is suggestive of the metaphorical use to which birds could be put in a sexual context. Every line is an allusion to sex or bodily parts, as Leick (1994:38) explains:

> the little swamp drying up is an obvious reference to her neglected vulva. The whirlwind is often invoked in potency incantations, and the "rising" of the raven, a most useless bird to be caught, points to the desired effect of the fowler's phallus and, at the same time, the proper professional course of action to take.

The image of the bird in this passage is driven, at least in part, by the man's profession. The treatment of the bird in this context therefore differs from what we see in 1.23.37–39. Its movement symbolizes erection; in contrast, in 1.23.37–39, this bird is shot, plucked, and cooked. Accordingly, the image of the raven rising in this sexual context seems to be quite removed from the cooked bird in

1.23.37–39. Still, poetry is pliable, and different ways to use the image of the bird sexually can hardly be discounted.[21]

Rituals pertaining to male sexual performance also reference birds. In the incantations for male potency, Biggs (1967:4) observes: "a number of items prescribed in the rituals are derived from animals and birds." For example, *KUB* 4.48 I 1–7 (Biggs 1967:4, 54, 56):

> If a man becomes impotent (literally "if a man's potency ends") in the month of Nisannu, you catch a male partridge (?),[22] pluck its wings, strangle it, flatten (?) (it), scatter salt (on it); you dry (it), crush (it) together with seeds of the mountain-*dadānu* plant; you give (it) to him to drink in beer; that man will regain potency.

Other potency rituals, using various forms of this bird for a drink, follow in this text (lines 8–11 and lines 12–16; see also no. 35, line 6′ in Biggs 1967:50; see Leick 1994:207). One detail in the quoted incantation echoes what appears in 1.23.37–39, and that is the plucking of the bird as part of the process. If some sort of potency ritual lies behind lines 37–39 as a way of conveying El's need for a little help at this juncture, it peeks through only in an abbreviated form that an audience would have presumably understood. As Pope recognized (as stated in M. S. Smith 1998b:664), birds are frequently used in the rituals cited by Biggs (1967), but there are no examples of roasting. In the end, the parallels do not really determine the correct interpretation of 1.23.37–39, nor are the proposed etymologies definitive. Instead, both criteria can be conformed to the picture of either a virile El or an El who could use some love charm or aphrodisiac (see Pardee 1997b:281 n. 51).

To my mind, there is reason to hew to Albright's view of metaphorical double-entendre. As noted above in the discussion of line 30, Cross and Pope, like several commentators before and after them, assumed that El in this text is an old figure.[23] However, this presumption is certainly not verified by the text. Gibson (*CML*[2] 30 n. 1) noted that El is young relative to the presentation of this figure in the Baal Cycle. Cutler and Macdonald (1982:34) comment in a similar way:

---

21. A similar question perhaps applies to the story of Aqhat. Given the sexual associations with bird imagery noted in this context, is it possible that Anat's attack on Aqhat via Ytpn among the hovering birds in 1.18 IV resonated, for the text's ancient audience, with her propositioning of him for his bow, earlier in 1.17 VI? I thank Susan Ackerman for suggesting this possibility.

22. For the *iṣṣur ḫurri*, "partridge (?)," see *CAD* I/J:207–8, no. 2; Landsberger 1966:262–64.

23. See Gordon 1949:58; Kapelrud 1952:73; Pope 1955:40, 41; 1979; Cross 1973:24; Porter 1981:4; Segert 1986:218. Cf. Lewis, *UNP* 206: a "so-called old timer." See above, pp. 73–74.

It is striking that this ritual and mythological text makes no mention of Baal or Anat, and this fact raises the question whether our text is older (at least in origin) than the other extant mythological texts. At the same time El is represented as rigorously fertile. Here is a different picture of El than that painted in the other mythological texts. He is not here the old, ineffectual El to whom we are accustomed from later (?) mythological texts.

Even if we do not accept the idea of earlier and later texts as posed by Cutler and Macdonald, it appears that the the events represented in 1.23 belong to an earlier time relative to events narrated in the Baal Cycle. In 1.23, El and Athirat are in the spring of their divine lives, producing their divine children. Accordingly, El is a relatively young man and not an old figure.

The question about El's drooping penis in lines 37, 40, 43–44, and 47 seems to work against this picture. However, this may misconstrue the picture of virility being presented. El first experiences an erection in lines 33–35. El then takes the females to his house (lines 35–36), and in the transition, his penis "lowers" (line 37); that is, his initial erection subsides. Then he "shoots skyward," perhaps an allusion to a new erection. He shoots a bird, perhaps an allusion to the females whom "he plucks," as seen above as an image of sexual play. At this point, there seems to be no problem with El: he is the one who is charming or seducing the women with the acts described in this line (see *CML*[2] 30 n. 1). So with the females in heat ("bird roasting on the coals") (lines 41//44–45//47–48), he is ready to impregnate them (lines 49–50), and he does so twice. Reading double-entendre through lines 30–49, El is quite potent, achieving erection at at least three and arguably four different points: first with the explicit reference to his penis at lines 33–34; then a second time expressed in the double-entendre of shooting, plucking, and roasting the bird (a k a the women) in lines 37–39; a third time for the initial impregnation in lines 49–51, with the double-entendre of the hot women (cooking bird) in lines 47–48; and a fourth time for the impregnation in lines 55–56, this time with neither a double-entendre nor any explicit reference to the condition of El's penis. Accordingly, it may be that the language depicts a young god who heats up several times. In conclusion, Albright seems to have been closest to the mark.

SUBSECTION B, LINES 39B–49: EL SECURES HIS WIVES

LINES 39B–42: FIRST CONDITION EXPRESSED

39	hm ʾaṯtm tṣḥn	If the two females cry:
40	ymt mt	"O man, man!
	nḥtm ḫṭk	Your staff droops,

mmnnm mṭ ydk	Your love-staff sinks!

41	h[l] ʿṣr	Lo[ok] a bird
	tḫrr lʾišt	You're roasting on the fire,
	ṣḥrrt lpḥmm	Browning on the coals."

| 42 | ʾa[t]tm ʾatt ʾil | (Then) the two fe[mal]es will be wives of El, |
| | ʾatt ʾil wʿlmh | Wives of El, and his forever. |

EXCURSUS 3: THE IDENTITY OF THE FEMALES

The identity of the two females has long been a matter of debate. The primary basis for identification has relied on the comparison of lines 58–59//61 with 23–24, which names Athirat explicitly, but this view assumes that the goddesses who give birth (or at least one of them) is then suckled by Athirat in lines 58–59//61. Olyan (1988:57) notes, however, that there is no clear connection: "There is no evidence that the two scenes and the goddesses are connected in any way." While it is true that there is no such evidence, it is not unreasonable to suppose that the female(s) nursing the newborns may be their mother(s) (see the discussion of lines 58–59 and 61 below).

There is another potential objection to Athirat as a candidate here, when one compares her in other texts. It might be thought that Athirat is considered too old for the job, since she is the elderly matriarch of the divine family in the Baal Cycle. However, the ages of El and Athirat arguably differ here. In 1.23, El is at the age when he is producing divine children, while in the Baal Cycle, this time seems to have long passed. It would follow that Athirat in 1.23 is younger than she is in the Baal Cycle. Accordingly, Athirat appears to be a viable candidate as at least one of the two females.

The identity of the other female is in doubt. Because of the epithet *rḥmy* in line 16, there have been proposals (e.g., *CML*[2] 123 n. 10) to identify Anat as the second female in this binomial name. This approach has been driven by the fact that Anat has the similar title *rḥm* in 1.6 II 27 (cf. 1.6 II 5). In 1.15 II 26–27, Raḥmay appears as the name or title of a goddess, but which one is unclear. In addition, the pairing of Athirat and Anat appears in a manner that evokes lines 23–24//58–59//61. Kirta's son, YṢB, is said to be one who "sucks the milk of A[thi]rat, draws the breast of Adolescent [Anat], the wet nurses [of the gods]" (1.15 II 26–27). In view of this information, Anat has long been regarded as the leading candidate (Xella 1973:53, 120–21). As with the goddess in line 16, Anat is a huntress (1.22 I 10).

There are some problems with this proposed identification. One difficulty involves the observation made above that the time frame differs in the

Baal Cycle from that in 1.23. Anat is perhaps not yet born in 1.23, or at best she would be a young child. In any case, Anat seems tied to the mythology of Baal, as known for example in the Baal Cycle; there really is no hint of Baal and Anat in 1.23. However, what we could have in 1.23 is an alternative mythology for El and his family compared to the Baal Cycle, and this alternative mythology could have included a different understanding of Anat. Interestingly, these different mythologies seem to have been maintained by the same cultic or ritual circles. The other issue concerns the form of the title *rḥmy*. As Wyatt (1996:229) correctly points out, Anat's title is not *rḥmy*, but *rḥm*; there is a small difference, perhaps even inconsequential, but it is to be taken into consideration.

Astarte could be another candidate as Rahmay here. Like Anat, Astarte hunts (1.114.23–24), a predication of the Rahmay in 1.23.16. With Athirat and Rahmay in line 13, along with the hunting theme of line 16, it would seem natural to posit a younger hunting goddess, like Astarte (or Anat). This view would seem to be supported by *PE* 1.10.22–23 (Attridge and Oden 1981:51), where Astarte is said to be one of El's wives, as noted by Olyan (1988:44 n. 22). What this different tradition suggests is a number of versions about El's wives varying in period and location. Within the context of 1.23, Astarte like Anat may belong to the wrong generation, however.

There is another approach that would see Rahmay not as a separate goddess as Athirat, but essentially as her title. Indeed, the word *rḥmy* may be applied to a variety of young females depending on context. In 1.23, it would seem that Athirat is the young female with a compound name.[24] This approach would seem to generate a new difficulty, which is the dual number in the description of the females. There is a parallel for this usage: Kothar wa-Hasis, another binomial name for a single deity, is treated as dual in 1.17 V 20 and 30.[25]

There is also a literary parallel for this usage. Each of the two weapons used by Baal against Yamm in 1.2 IV 11 and 18 is separately presented in the plural:

kṯr ṣmdm ynḥt	Kothar fashions the weapons,
wyp'r šmthm	And he proclaims their names.

In the narrative context, it is clear however that the weapon is singular in each instance (see *UBC* 1.338; Cross 1998:143 n. 24). The text presents two weapons in a sequence, both in the plural, a situation that perhaps underlies the presentation of the females in 1.23. There may be only one goddess at each stage of 1.23.30–76, although she is presented as dual. In this case, Athirat wa-Rahmay could be a binomial that actually represents a single female, despite her being

---

24. See Mullen 1980:18 n. 22 and Oden 1977:84–85, discussed in Olyan 1988:57 n. 82.

25. Accordingly, Parker in *UNP* 58–59 translates "them" for the craftsman-god in this context.

presented literarily in the dual. Above the suckling of Kirta's son by both Athirat and Anat is compared by scholars to 1.23.23–24//58–59//61, but it is to be noted that in this text Rahmay is not a party to suckling to the newborn gods. It may be that more than one female involved in suckling the newborn gods.

To understand the relations between the females in these two major sections of 1.23, I would entertain the possibility that lines 30–76 narrate two sets of double figures. Lines 30–76 generate two sets of "doubles" (or "twinning"), relative to comparable figures attested in lines 1–29. By this I mean that lines 30–76 show double-figures (except for El) where other lines show one. The first instance of such doubles or twinning is to present the single figure of Athirat wa-Rahmay in lines 13 and 28 (also probably line 16) as two females in lines 30–76. The second example of twinning may be the *'ilm n'mm* (which might include *mt*, "Death"). While it is possible that a second figure (such as Yamm) is involved, it is also plausible to entertain the possibility that the *'ilm n'mm* represent a twinning of the individual figure *mt w-šr*, known from line 8. However, this suggestion remains hypothetical at best. In short, it is possible that Athirat wa-Rahmay is presented as two females. The other possibility is that the text presents an alternative mythology of El with two wives, only one of whom is Athirat.

It is important to mention one last alternative proposal for the females, namely, that they are not divine but human (see Xella 1973:93; see also Wyatt 1998:324–25 n. 1; Tsumura 1973:203, 1999:235). Tsumura in particular offers a reason for his view: the noun *'aṭt* is not used for goddesses, only humans. Tsumura's claim does not quite hold. 1.2 III 22 refers to *'aṭt* in a purely divine context, and in 1.3 IV 40 Baal's female is designated by this noun. In neither case is a human evidently involved. As further support in this direction, *TO* (1.375) compares the biblical episode of Lot and his two daughters in Gen 19:30–38 (see also Porter 1981), but this is a literary observation, and in any case it does not seem to aid in identifying the females.

The very need for this discussion highlights a general issue about the females in this text: Why aren't they named? It might be supposed that the answer was known by the ancient audience; it would have understood the identity of El's wife (or wives). Therefore, it may have been unnecessary to name the females. One might speculate that there is some additional aspect of the goddesses' anonymity that is significant for the telling of the story. It might be that it represents a means of emphasizing other features or figures in the text. For example, the stress in the text, it could be argued, falls on El and his sexual relations with the females. Or, it might be speculated that their anonymity is related to weightier matters about the nature of the cosmos, specifically that the females' dual number as well as their anonymity is not only a literary matter but also an ontological statement about reality. Where El signifies the ultimate, single point of cosmic origins, the two females signal the duality in the cosmos.

A comparable point may apply to the double sets of the two births. Chapter 5 (under "The Royal Construction of Cosmic Duality and Unity in 1.23.30–76") follows up this question. As the discussion at this point would suggest, it is impossible to determine firmly the identity of the females.

Line 41

I have translated the line as a tricolon instead of the common rendering as a bicolon. This translation better highlights the sonant parallelism of the second and third lines, in particular the verbs. It also focuses on the presentative force of the particle *hl*.[26] As noted for lines 32–33, the translation, "See…," is designed to bring out the particle's presentative force.

The bird is not the subject of the two verbs that follow (cf. *UNP* 211), as it is a masculine noun (31 times in the masculine plural, as listed by *CPU* 1590–91);[27] in contrast, the following verbs have a *t*-prefix. Since the verbs cannot be third feminine singular, they are second masculine singular, in this case referring back to El. It is possible that an asyndetic relative clause is involved: "see the bird (that)// you're roasting on the fire,//browning on the coals." However, if the verbs are intransitive, then El himself would be their subject, and the picture of El's own passion, symbolized by the "bird," would be the apparent topic.

This barbecued "bird" goes back to lines 38–39, as suggested by the mention of the bird on the coal in lines 38–39 and in line 41 (and also in lines 44–45 and 47–48). In addition, the verb in line 38, *yḫrṭ*, has sonant association with the sonant parallel verbs, *thrr* and *ṣhrrt*, in line 41. The word *ṣhrrt* may refer to either the yellow-brown color as in Arabic, Hebrew, and Syriac cognates (see *SPUMB* 114), or perhaps burning, as in a number of Modern South Arabian dialects (see Rendsburg 1987:625). Both meanings have been attributed to the root in 1.23.41 and 45.[28]

Line 42

The syntax of *w-* here and in lines 46 and 49 serves to highlight rather than simply coordinate, as in a number of other passages:[29]

št ʾalp qdmh	He set an ox before him,

---

26. See Brown 1987; *UG* 750; and the discussion above at lines 32–33.

27. I am grateful to my student KellyAnn Falkenberg-Wolfe for directing my attention to this point of grammar.

28. For the first instance, see *CML*[2] 125, and for the second, see Pardee 1997a:254; cf. Grabbe 1976:58–59, esp. 59 n. 4.

29. For a poetic example with asyndesis (lacking –w), note 1.3 V 32-33 = 1.4 IV 43-44:

mlkn ʾalʾiyn bʿl	Our king is Mightiest Baal,
tpṭn ʾin dʿlnh	Our ruler, with none above him.

| mr’a wtk pnh | A fatling right before him. |
| | (1.4 V 45–46) |

| ‘bdk ’an wd‘lmk | "Your servant I am, indeed forever yours" |
| | (1.5 II 12, 19–20; Tsumura 1973:68–69).[30] |

| w‘lmh | "… and to eternity" (1.19 IV 5–6) |
| | (+ w- + ‘lm + locative -h)[31] |

In these passages,[32] the *w-* serves a syntactical-semantic function of marking (or perhaps better, demarcating) the noun (or nominal referent) or phrase that follows.

The case from 1.3 V 32–33 = 1.4 IV 43–44 also contains two of the components of *d‘lmh* in 1.23.42//45–46//49, namely, the syntax of relative *d-* plus the third masculine singular pronominal suffix, *-h*. The example from 1.15 II 12 is further pertinent to 1.23.42 and its parallels in lines 45–46 and 49, as it contains the syntax of *w-* + the noun *‘lm* + pronominal suffix. A partially corresponding use of *‘l* + pronominal suffix occurs in Ps 16:2: "I said to Yahweh: 'You are my lord, with none above You (*bal-‘ālêkā*).' "[33] In sum, line 42 and its parallels in lines 45–46 and 49, with their seemingly unusual syntactical patterns, fall within the range of syntax found in Ugaritic texts.

LINES 42–46A: SECOND CONDITION EXPRESSED

| 42–43 | whm/’aṯtm tṣḥn | But if the two females cry: |

43	y ’ad ’ad	"O Daddy, Daddy!
	nḥtm ḥṭk	Your staff droops,
44	mmnnm mṭ ydk	Your love-staff sinks!

| | hl ‘ṣr | Look a bird |
| | ṯhrr l’išt | You're roasting on the fire, |

---

30. For this formula, cf. EA 287:64–70, 289:101 (van der Toorn 2000:101).

31. Cf. *p‘lmh* in 1.19 III 48//55; see *UG* 324.

32. According to Sivan 1997:179, *w‘lm* in 1.164.10 is to be rendered "… and above all" (= *w-* + *‘l* + adverbial *-m*). However, other commentartors understand the phrase differently. Pardee (2002:75) translates: "And on the next day." Tropper (*UG* 332) renders similarly: "am folgenden/nächsten (Tag)."

33. The parallel was noted by Dahood 1966:87. Pope took *‘ālêkā* as a corruption of Baal's title, ‘Aliy (though without versional evidence); see *RSP III* 457.

45   wṣḥrrt lpḥmm   Browning on the coals."

          btm bt ʾil   (Then) the two females will be daughters of El,
45–46   bt ʾil wʿlmh   Daughters of El, and his forever.

Line 43

The vocative particle is set off as a separate word. In light of the observation of Horwitz (1974:80), the presence of a word-divider following this particle in lines 43, 46, and 64 would suggest that the scribe apparently thought it was a word.

There are two differences between this portion and the preceding parallel part. The condition states that if the two females identify El as "father," then they will be his daughters (cf. Baal as the father of Pidray in 1.24.23–27, but she is one of his brides or fiancées in 1.3 IV 50–53//1.3 V 41–44//1.4 I 14–18). The result stated here sounds like the formula of Esth 2:7 MT: *lĕqâḥâh mordŏkay lô lĕbat*, "Mordecai took her [Esther] to himself as a daughter." This instance is regarded as an adoption formula (so NJPS: "adopted her"), but the LXX reads instead *epaideusen autēn seautō eis gynaika*, "he brought her up for himself as a wife." The discrepancy between the MT and LXX Esth 2:7 corresponds to the two options represented in 1.23. To explain the difference, Levenson (1997:58) comments that adoption is known in anticipation of matrimony (to this effect he cites Ezek 16:1–14).

Apart from this difference, the stated conditions in this section of 1.23 are virtually the same. What distinguishes the two is how the females react to El, and specifically to his staff. The two conditions differ in whether the females identify him as a man (or husband) or as father. Pardee (1997b:281 n. 53) states: "The function of this test seems to be to determine whether the women are mature enough to discern the sexual function of the roasting birds or whether they will simply see in ʾIlu a father figure providing them with food." The outcome described in the following part shows that they react to him as man (or husband). They evidently see El and his staff, probably at this point pointed in their direction. At this point, it is clear that the women favorably react to El in his aroused state.

Second, the text uses *ʾaṯtm* in two different ways. For line 42, where it is parallel to *btm* in 45–46, *ʾaṯtm* means "wives" as opposed to "daughters." However, at the head of each of these parts of text, in line 39//line 43, it is evident that the word means "females" or "women."

The double-conditional sentences for a narrative may seem odd, if the point is simply to narrate El's sexual relations. However, the style of twin conditional sentences followed by the realization of one or the other is attested in 1.6 III, with El's dream vision concerning Baal's return to life. Similarly, the pairing of conditional sentences of this sort is known from various rituals, including potency rituals (e.g., Biggs 1967:p. 46 no. 27, line 10). It has been observed that the scene here reflects the praxis of dream-divination. Trujillo (1973:162–63) notes an Assyrian ritual (BM 121 206 X:53–57) that describes two alternative recitations in conditional sentences to indicate which is to be accepted. As a result, Trujillo sees a ritual recitation lying behind this section.

LINES 46B–49A: FIRST CONDITION REALIZED

46	whn ʾaṯtm tṣḥn	And see, the two females cry:
	y mt mt	"O man, man!
47	nḥtm ḫṭk	Your staff droops,
	mmnnm mṭ ydk	Your love-staff sinks!
	hl ʿṣr	Look a bird,
48	tḥrr lʾišt	You're roasting on the fire,
	wṣḥr<r>t lpḥmm	Brow<n>ing on the coals."
	ʾaṯtm ʾaṯ[t ʾil]	(So) the two females are wiv[es of El],
49	ʾaṯt ʾil wʿlmh	Wives of El, and his forever.

Apart from the opening particle *whn* in line 46 (cf. *hm* in lines 39 and 42) and textual lacuna and mistake, lines 46–49 are verbally identical to lines 39b–42. The condition expressed in lines 39b–42 is realized in lines 46–49.

The translation of line 46 is designed to bring out the presentative force of *hn* (see also lines 50a and 55b). The preceding *w-* suggests continuity or at least connection with the preceding unit.[34] The structural parallelism of the particles *hm* (line 39)//*hm* (line 42)//*whn* (line 46) suggests the unity of lines 46–49 with the preceding sections of lines 39–42 and 42–46.

SECTION II, BIRTHS OF THE PAIRS: LINES 49B–64

SUBSECTION A, LINES 49B–59: DAWN AND DUSK

LINES 49B–52A: SEXUAL RELATIONS AND BIRTH

| 49 | yhbr špthm yšq | He bends down, kisses their lips, |
| 50 | hn špthm mtqtm | See how sweet their lips are, |

---

34. See the general considerations of BH *w-* offered in Steiner 2000.

	mtqtm klrmn[m]	Sweet as pomegranate[s].
51	bm nšq whr	As he kisses, there's conception,
	bḥbq ḥmḥmt	As he embraces, there's passion.
51–52	tqt[nṣn w]/tldn	The two cr[ouch and] give birth
	šḥr wšlm	to Dawn and Dusk.

Line 50

The translation of line 50a (see also line 55b; cf. line 46) is designed to bring out the force of the presentative particle *hn*. The line may be rendered more literally, "behold, their lips are sweet."

The word *lrmn[m]* was recognized as pomegranates by Virolleaud (1933:147), based on Akkadian cognates, *lurmû*, *lurînu*, and *nurmû*.[35] From the context here, it is "sweet." This characterization fits with its attestation as a summer fruit in 4.751.9–11, where it appears with figs (*dblt*) and raisins (*ṣmqm*) (see Heltzer 1980:414 n. 11). The Akkadian and Ugaritic terms are evidently related to BH *rimmôn*; the variation in spellings suggests the possibility of a loan-process or *Kulturwort*.

Line 51a

The same formulas largely occur in 1.17 I 39–40 (Aitken 1989:19, 29), though with *whr* perhaps falling in a lacuna (*MLC* 370; Wright 2001:70). The syntax is explained by Pope (1955:40–41 n. 74; followed by Trujillo 1973:179): *hr* and *ḥmḥmt* are nouns serving as the apodoses of temporal sentences (see also Wright 2001:70, 79, in particular for the second noun). As another example, Pope cites *nhmmt* in 1.14 I 32 (cf. 1.14 III 50–51). The notion that *w-* is "an existential particle" (Tsumura 1973:71, 145 n. 335, citing *UT* 12.9, 13.103) has no basis in the grammar. The nouns *hr* and *ḥmḥmt* may be more semantically parallel than the translation indicates. The root **ḥmm* refers to mating in Gen 30:38, 39.[36]

The parallel in 1.17 I 39–40 suggests that it is El who is subject of the infinitives, although one could translate more neutrally, as in *UNP* 212: "In kissing, conception,//In embracing, pregnant heat." The verb **ḥbq* is used in 1.23.51, 56 for physical embrace. The pair **nš'//*šyt* contextually functions here in the same manner as **ḥbq//*šyt* in 1.4 IV 13–14. In both contexts, it would seem, then, that **ḥbq* means to hold someone by wrapping one's arms around the person. El evidently hugs or embraces his females.

---

35. *DUL* 504, citing *CAD* L:255–56; N/2:345–46; *AHw* 564. See also Tsumura 1973:70.

36. I am grateful to my student Sara Milstein for directing my attention to this reference.

Line 51b

The verb **qnṣ* has an infix -*t*, perhaps for physical action of the body. In context, the verb refers to action prior or preparatory for giving birth. The infix –*t* suggests reflexive or repeated action using the body or some part of it, as observed by Greenfield (1979). The following is a representative sampling of the form:

1. ytmr bʿl bnth	"Baal sees his daughters" (1.3 I 22)
2–3. tmtḫṣ//tḫtṣb	"she fights"//"she battles" (1.3 II 5–7; see the *t*-forms of these verbs in lines 19–20, 23, 24, 29–30)
4. tštql	"She betakes herself" (1.3 II 18; cf. 1.6 VI 42; 1.17 II 25; 1.19 IV 18–19; 1.100.68, 72; 1.114.17)
5. ttpp	"She beautifies herself" (1.3 III 1)
6. tštḥwy	"You shall bow down" (1.3 III 10)
7. lʾištbm tnn	"I surely bound (**šbm*)/captured (**šby*) Tunnanu" (1.3 III 40)
8. ʿmy twtḥ ʾišdk	"To me let your legs race" (1.3 III 19–20//IV 12)
9. bʿl ytlk wyṣd	"Baal goes about hunting" (1.12 I 34)
10. ytʿn	"They eye each other" (1.6 VI 16)
11. ʾitbd/yʾitbd	"It perished" (1.14 I 8, 24)
12. yʾitsp	"He gathered" (1.14 I 18)
13. ttpl	"It was felled" (or: "it fell") (1.14 I 21)
14. trtḥṣ/yrtḥṣ	"Wash yourself" (1.14 II 9), "he washes himself" (1.14 III 52; cf. 1.19 IV 41)
15. ʾiḫtrš	"I will work" (1.16 V 26)
16. ʾištmʿ	"Listen up" (1.16 VI 29//42)
17. ytšʾu	"He lifts himself up" (1.17 V 6; cf 1.19 I 21)

Most, if not all, of these forms are arguably active verbs; many are also reflexive, and some are transitive. All involve bodily functions. Following suit, the verb *tqtnṣn* in 1.23.51//58 involves physical action with the body.

It is evident that *tqtnṣn* does not mean "to go into labor," which is designated in the Ugaritic corpus by **ḥwl*, as in 1.12 I 25.[37] In this text, El sends off divine female servants to give birth into the wilderness, and about their offspring he says to the females in line 25–29 (see Parker, *UNP* 189):

____

37. For *ḥl* in this passage as well as parallels, see Stol 2000:121, 122–23.

ḫl ld ʾaklm	"Labor, give birth to the Eaters
tbrkk	—May they (the gods) bless you!
wld ʿqqm	Give birth to the Tearers
ʾilm ypʿr šmthm	—May El pronounce their names!"

For *tqtnṣn* in 1.23.51//58, many treatments, including Stol (2000:124) and *DUL* (706), suggest "squat, crouch." Despite the phonological irregularity of the consonants, the most likely cognate is Akkadian *kamāṣu* (cited by *DUL* and others).[38] It is used for crouching before birthing (*walādu*) in the Middle Assyrian version of the Cow of Sin from Nimrud (labeled text b, line 26, in Veldhuis 1991:10). The basic Akkadian root is unclear; *CAD K*:117–20 lists *kamāṣu* with *kamāsu* and *kamāšu*.[39] In any case, the meaning "squat, crouch" seems to be a reasonable supposition even if it cannot be further verified.

Lines 52b–54: The birth announcement

52	rgm lʾil ybl	Word to El was brought:
52–53	ʾat̠[ty]/ʾil ylt	"El's [two wi]ves have given birth."
	mh ylt	"What have they born?"
	yldy šḥr w šl[m]	"A newborn pair, Dawn and Dus[k]."
54	šʾu ʿdb lšpš rbt	"Make an offering to Lady Sun,
	wlkbkbm knm	And to the stationary stars."

Line 52

The introduction to the speech begins with the standard formula for announcing a message by using the G-passive stem plus the noun *rgm* (Sivan 1997:126). The root *rgm* for an announcement is used similarly in the divine announcement in 1.4 V 12: "Let it be told (*yrgm*) to Mightiest Baal." In 1.10 III 32–36, the birth announcement is made also with a passive verb (*UNP* 186). The passive is common to the type-scene of the birth announcement in Ugaritic and biblical literatures. It is to be noted that 1.23.12 also uses *rgm* in the passive voice to give directions for ritual recitation.

---

38. Leslau 435 commenting on Ethiopic *qanaṣa, qannaṣa, qanṣa*, "leap, spring away," remarks: "the connection with Ug. *qnṣ* 'go into labor, travail' suggested by [M.] Fisher [1969:]178 is unlikely."

39. If so, it would seem that the other Akkadian forms have influenced a shift of the initial consonant from *q > *k (see Tsumura 1973:72) and/or of the middle consonant from *n > *m.

Lines 52–53

The dialogue over the announcement seems to take place between an unnamed messenger and El.[40] The unnamed announcer brings the announcement of birth to El, and it would seem that, though unnamed at this point, he is the respondent to the question *mh ylt* (= **yalattā*, third feminine dual of **yld*; *UG* 636; see Parker 1989:65). The answer to El's question about the children presupposes the verb *ylt* from the question, according to C. L. Miller (1999:369). Miller further supposes that *yldy* should be rendered "my (two) sons," given the pronominal suffix. In contrast, Tropper (*UG* 468) regards *yldy* as a third masculine dual G-stem passive **qatala* form plus an "EP (enklitische Partikel)." Tropper (1994:475) ventures an explanation: "Die Funktion der EP -*y* besteht offensichtlich darin, den Anfang einer wörtlichen Rede zu markieren." While a noun (so Miller) makes eminent sense, the final -*y* suffix (so Tropper) does not appear in context to be pronominal.

It does not seem in context that the speaker of the announcement would be either parent. According to Tsumura (1973:75), it is the human husband of the two women who makes the announcement. It might be thought that the birth announcement would be delivered by a female rather than a male. Anat exercizes this role in 1.10 III, and she serves as the announcer in 1.4 V 20–35 (note also *hambaśśĕrôt* in Ps 68:12). This would be particularly suitable for a woman messenger to give the announcement of a birth in particular. The unidentified announcer informs El of the birth, and after El asks (Tsumura 1973:77) what the two women have borne, the pair of Dawn and Dusk is given as the answer.

Line 54

El replies by giving instructions for an offering, perhaps made for the occasion of the birth of children or in lieu of the children (cf. Num 18:13–15). Tsevat suggests (1978:26*) that ʿ*db* in line 54 refers to food offered (**nšʾ*): *šʾu ʿdb lšpš rbt wlkbkbm*, "arrange preparations (an offering) for Shapshu and the stars." He applies the same view to line 65: *šʾu ʿdb tk mdbr qdš*, "arrange preparations for the holy outback/steppe of QDSH." Elsewhere **ʿdb* is generally taken to mean, "to prepare, arrange," as illustrated by the verbal usages in 1.4 IV 7, 12 and V 46. The verb applies to food preparation (1.14 II 27, IV 9, V 19; 1.17 V 16, 22; Tsevat 1978:26* n. 22; Pardee 1997a:261 n. 176). In 1.4 VIII 14b–20a Baal's messengers are warned to be careful lest Mot "makes (prepares) you" (*yʿdbkm*) like a lamb in his mouth (cf. 1.23.63–64); this is exactly the "preparation" that in 1.6 II 22–23 Mot says he made of Baal. The verb **ʿdb* used in the context of El's feasting in 1.114.6–8 has been understood in this way as well (Lewis, *UNP* 194). Levine and

---

40. For the type-scene in Ugaritic and biblical literature, see Parker 1989:63–70.

de Tarragon (1993:81, 95) as well as del Olmo Lete (1995:42) note this verb in a ritual text (1.41.10; cf. 1.100.71), to denote the preparation (*ʿdb) of the animals for the sacrificial feast.[41] As a grammatical alternative provisionally accepted here, Dietrich and Loretz (2002:92) suggest that ʿdb in this context and in line 64 is not a verb but a noun ("eine Gabe"). To anticipate the description of the ʾilm nʿmm in lines 61–64, the word ʿdb serves to highlight a contrast, between what they ravenously devour in line 64 and what is given in a proper offering as expressed here in line 54.

The recipients of the offering are Shapshu the sun-goddess and the stars, perhaps because of their astral affiliation with Dawn and Dusk. Here Shapshu bears the epithet rbt, sometimes with nyr, "light, lamp," sometimes without.[42] The title is indicative of her status relative to other celestial bodies in the Ugaritic pantheon. In Ugaritic literary texts, the title rbt is applied also to Athirat. The goddess Athirat is addressed in the full form of her title, rbt, literally "great one" and often translated "Lady."[43] The term denotes the goddess's status. Following Gordon (1988) and others, Wiggins (1993:65–67) considers the use of rbt for Athirat to be modeled on the application of the title rabîtu to the mother of the king or dowager queen, who was a major force behind the throne (for this view, see also Binger 1997:81). This view makes sense of her role in the selection of Athtar for kingship in 1.6 I (although it is to be noted that her candidate falls short in his bid for kingship). In their discussions, Greenfield (1987:36 n. 6) and Gordon (1988:127) compare Athirat's role in this passage. Gordon comments: "The pinnacle of status for a woman in the royal harem was to be designated the rbt/rabîtu with the legal contractual right to bear her royal husband's successor."[44] Gordon notes the Akkadian evidence at Ugarit, in the term rabîtu used as a title of the wife of Benteshina, king of Amurru (RS 17.318+.19, 26, 29; 17.348 rev. 4; 17.372A+.11).[45] EA 29:8, 63, 67 likewise uses ra-bi-tum to designate Teye as the principal wife of Nimmureya (Amenophis III), who was apparently involved in the successful royal succession of her son Amenophis IV. Evidence for this royal female rank from Ebla and Mari is associated with the term AMA.GAL, according to Owen (1995:574 n. 4). The distribution of the Akkadian evidence for rabîtu in this particular usage suggests a peripheral western Akkadian usage, perhaps even as a loan from early West Semitic rbt.

---

41. See also Renfroe 1992:21; Dietrich and Loretz 1993:129; 2002:94.

42. CAT 1.16 I 36, 38; 1.23.54; 1.161.19; see Wiggins 1996.

43. In literary texts, 1.3 IV 40–41; 1.4 I 13–14, 21, II 28–29, 31, III 27–28, 34, IV 31, 40, 53, V 2–3; 1.6 I 44, 45, 47, 53; 1.8 II 1–2; and, in an incantation, 1.169.16.

44. For a critique of the "Orientalist" use of the term "harem" for ancient Near Eastern societies, see Van De Mieroop 1999:146–54.

45. See Kühne 1973; van Soldt 1991:15; CAD R:26a; Márquez Rowe 2000.

Gordon and others have further identified the *rbt* with BH *gĕbîrâ*, sometimes with specific associations with the figure of Asherah (see also Ackerman
1993). The biblical evidence has recently been the subject of a critical reading
that would question the freight of the term *gĕbîrâ* (Bowen 2001), specifically
whether a specifically "legal contractual right to bear her royal husband's
successor" (as Gordon commented) obtained in the case of the *rbt/rabîtu*. At
a minimum, the terms seem to refer to the most important royal female at a
given time. Here we may note (and contrast) its use to denote the eldest female
child in a household: the one who lodges a complaint, according to one of the
many Neo-Assyrian sale documents, "shall burn either his first born son or his
eldest daughter" (DUMU.MI-*šu ra-bi-tu*; Mattila 2002:68, lines 7–8). What its
application to both Athirat and Shapshu seems to denote is their rank within
their class or category: Athirat is the chief female within the household of El,
while Shapshu is evidently the chief ranking figure among the stars mentioned
here in this context.

These stars are characterized as *knm*, evidently established, fixed, or set in
the firmament (Gaster 1946:57). Psalm 8:4 refers to the works of Yahweh's hands
as "the moon and the stars which you established" (*kônānĕtâh*). Wyatt (1996:242,
247) argues that procreation may underlie the use of **kwn* in both line 54 and
Ps 8:4,[46] but the meaning "to procreate" is expressed in the D-stem (or L-stem)
and not by the G-stem. It would appear preferable to compare the word with
Akkadian *kânu* in the sense "to be stationary," predicated of planets (*CAD* K:160).
Jupiter, for example, is said to have "reached its culmination point and remained
stationary in its 'seat'" (*ašar niṣirtri ikšudamma ina šubtišu ikun*; *CAD* K:160). Psalm
8:4 provides a general analogue for 1.23.54, insofar as it displays the relationship of the astral bodies to the creator-deity. In this psalm, the deity established
or fixed them in the sky; these are "the works of your hands." This expression
of the god's creation may represent a thematic variant to Job 38:7, where the
morning stars are not the creation but the children of the creator-god called
Elohim, arguably the same figure as the protagonist of this part of 1.23 (see
Wyatt 1996:245). Analogous to Job 38:7, the stars also seem to be El's children, if
the parallelism in 1.10 I 3–5 is correctly understood:[47]

... which the sons of El do not know (?) ...	[ ]h dlyd' bn 'il
... the assembly of the stars ...	[ ]pḫr kkbm
... the circle of those of heaven ...	[ ]dr dt šmm

---

46. The proposal that the "sucklings" in Ps 8:3 are these cosmic forces goes back at least to
Shedl 1964; see Loretz 1971:104–12, with earlier literature; Ringgren 1979:721. See also M. S. Smith
1997.

47. For the readings, see CAT and Parker, *UNP* 182.

On the face of it, the three expressions seem to be parallel.[48] The first identifies the group involved as El's family, while the other two phrases clearly use astral language for it. In short, the picture of Shapshu and the stars appears to be a reference to gods generally (see *TO* 1.363; Wyatt 1998:333) and specifically to El's astral family.

Shapshu is called *nrt 'il/'ilm*, "the lamp of El."[49] Elsewhere she serves as El's special envoy (1.6 IV, VI). Shapshu and the stars constitute a way to refer to El's heavenly or astral family, which includes major figures of the pantheon (M. S. Smith 2001:61–65).[50] El's family may also constitute the following group designations: *mpḫrt bn 'il*, "the council of the sons of El" (which lacks –*m* on the final word, which marks it a singular noun and therefore probably the god's name; 1.65.3; cf. 1.40.25, 42; cf. 34); *bn 'il*, "the sons of El" (1.40.33, 41, and its reconstruction in parallel lines in the same text, lines 7, 16, 24; 1.62.7; 1.65.1; 1.123.15); *dr 'il*, "the circle of El" (1.15 III 19); *dr 'il wpḫr b'l*, "the circle of El and the assembly of Baal" (1.39.7; 1.62.16; 1.87.18); and *dr bn 'il*, "the circle of the sons of El" (1.40.25, 33–34). The understanding of El's own family as astral is important in view of the offspring sired by El here in 1.23, namely, Dawn and Dusk. This part of the narrative serves as a prelude to the ultimate interest in this narrative, namely, "the Goodly Gods," but this prelude shows the theogony of El's astral family as the backdrop.

I would like to anticipate a point to be raised below, that this astral family in this form has nothing to do with the storm-god, Baal. The mythology of this text has no stage scene of conflict for supremacy; in this respect, it is of an utterly different character from the Baal Cycle and other narratives pertaining to the storm-god. We may note another major difference between 1.23 and the mythologies of Baal attested in other texts. 1.23 arguably represents a mythology of summer precipitation that would contrast with what we see in Aqhat and the Baal Cycle (see Healy, *DDD* 249–50). In Aqhat, rain and dew are elements attributed to Baal in 1.19 I 38–46 (see also 1.3 II 39–40). The Ugaritic word-pair *ṭl*//*rbb* is attested here of precipitation as generated by Baal (1.19 I 44–46): *bl ṭl bl rbb/bl šr' thmtm/bl ṭbn ql b'l*, "No dew, no downpour, No swirling of the deeps, No welcome voice of Baal" (Parker, *UNP* 69). In the Baal Cycle, the association is

---

48. So also Parker, *UNP* 182.

49. The form without –*m* is clear in RS 92.2016.38 published by Caquot and Dalix, in Yon and Arnaud 2001: 394, 402–3, with a photograph on p. 405; for the form with –*m*, see 1.6 IV 8, 17. In view of the attestation in RS 92.2016.38, the often-proposed emendation of *'il* to *'ilm* in 1.6 III 24 (e.g., M. S. Smith, *UNP* 158) would appear to be unnecessary.

50. For a Mesopotamian analogue, note "the stars, the seven gods, the great gods" in MUL. APIN, in Hunger and Pingree 1989:30, tablet I I i 44. For another example, see the discussion in Reiner 1995:18.

mythologized in the name of one of Baal's females, "Dewy" (*tly*) (1.3 I 24, III 7, IV 51, etc.). However, dew could also be thought of as a product of the stars and not associated with rains as such. The notion that the stars provide precipitation (*TO* 1.161 n. e) is known from an Akkadian text from Ugarit, if correctly interpreted (*Ugaritica VI*, pp. 393–408), col. III, line 41', which reads *ki-ma na-áš-š[i šá* MUL.MEŠ], "like the dew [of the stars]" (see W. G. E. Watson 1977:274). Weinfeld (1983:133 n. 56) compares Isa 26:19: "For your dew is like the dew of light." Given the overall agricultural setting of 1.23, the astral family of El, in providing dew for the summer fruit, provides a point of intersection between the cosmic and terrestrial planes of reality.

Many scholars relate this portion of the theogony to the order of creation in Gen 1. Gibson (*CML*[2] 30 n. 2), for example, comments: "Dawn and Dusk may have been born first because they represent the division of day and night, which in Israel too (Gen. I 3–4) was considered the first act of creation." With the sun-goddess and the stars present in the text, it would appear that Shahar and Shalim are not the first but last in the series of divine births. The procreation of the other deities, signaled by the sun and the stars, is skipped over, as it is not the interest of the text. The final act of procreation preceding the generation of the *'ilm n'mm* is sufficient to set the stage. This observation dovetails with the comparison of Pardee (2000b:56), between the positions of Shalim in CAT 1.39 and here in 1.23. He suggests that Shalim in both contexts represents an organization of a form of the Ugaritic pantheon that places him at the end of the children of El and Athirat. One might object, as Wyatt (2001:703) has, that CAT 1.23 goes on to narrate another set of children. However, this objection misses the important point that the birth of Shahar and Shalim signals the standard story of theogony associated with El and Athirat, while the next pair of children moves to the specific interest of the story.

SUBSECTION B, LINES 55–64: THE GOODLY GODS

LINES 55–59A: SEXUAL RELATIONS AND BIRTH

55	yhbr špthm yšq	He bends down, kisses their lips,
	hn špthm mtqt[m]	See how swee[t] their lips are,
	<mtqtm klrmnm>	<Sweet as pomegranates.>
56	bm nšq whr	As he kisses, there's conception,
	bḥbq ḥ[m]ḥmt	As he embraces, there's pa[s]sion.
56–57	yt̲bn/yspr lḥmš	He sits, counts to five,
57	lṣ[...]šr pḫr	For the ... [...] the assembly sings (?).

57–58	kl'at/tqtnṣn wtldn	The two crouch and give birth,
58	tld ['i]lm n'mm	Give birth to the Goodly [G]ods,
58–59	'agzr ym/bn ym	Day-old devourers, one-day-old boys,
59	ynqm b'ap dd	Who suck the nipple of the breast.

Line 55

The end of the line is reconstructed based on its parallel in line 50. Lewis (*UNP* 212) uses square brackets, which would suggest that a lacuna would have contained these words. This is not the case.

Lines 56–57

Most early commentators assume for the first line a ritual instruction for repetition (Trujillo 1973:174–75; Xella 1973:71), as expressed in the translation proposed by Lewis (*UNP* 212): "They recite again five more times//[...] the assembly [si]ngs (?)." In other instances of such an instruction within a narrative, the scribe usually deploys scribal lines to demarcate it. Given that the scribe ably uses such scribal lines in lines 1–29, the lack of such lines here suggests that a scribal instruction is not involved here. Instead, Tsumura (1973:78–80; 1978a, 1981) reads these lines as narrative, in accordance with the context:

ytb[n]/yspr	He sits (and) counts,
lḥmš lṣb['i]	to five for growth
[l']šr pḫr kl'at	[to t]en for total completion.

This approach has been adopted also by Hettema (1989–90:85) and by Pardee (1997b:282). As noted by Tsumura and commentators, this proposal gains support from 1.17 II 43–45: *ytb dn'il [ls]pr yrḫh*, "Danil sits to count her months" (Parker, *UNP* 57). Tsumura offers another fine parallel in Atra-hasis I, lines 278–279: "And Nintu [sa]t [cou]nting the months" ([*wa-aš-ba*]-*at* ᵈ*nin-tu* [*i-ma*]-*an-nu arḫi*; Lambert and Millard 1969:62–63). In 1.23.56, *ḥmš* stands in the same semantic slot as *yrḫ* in 1.17 II 43. The syntaxes of **spr lḥmš* and *spr yrḫ* differ slightly, but this may be a difference only between using the ordinal, "counting to the fifth," as opposed to a collective noun for the months of pregnancy, "counting her months." For the beginning of the unit, Tsumura's proposal makes good sense.

It is not clear that Tsumura's interpretation applies equally well to the rest of lines 57–58. Lipiński (1986:214 n. 34) criticizes this part of the proposal for requiring unusual meanings for *pḫr* and *kl'at*. Wright (2001:84–85 n. 12) also notes differences in the readings between lines 57–58 and the parallel in 1.17 II 43–45. The first word *pḫr* commonly refers to a group, and that may be the case here (e.g., Lewis, *UNP* 212): "the assembly sings" (*wšr pḫr*). The common usages for the assembly are predicated of divinities: "the assembly of the gods," *pḫr 'ilm* (1.47.29; 1.118.28; 1.148.9); "the assembly of the divine sons," *pḫr bn 'ilm* (1.4 III 14); and "the assembly of the council," *pḫr m'd* (1.2 I 14, 15, 20, 31). It is possible that 1.23.57 contains a picture of the divine assembly, in the form of El's astral family, singing perhaps in anticipation of the birth of the Goodly Gods. As a parallel, the reference to this astral group's singing at creation in Job 38:7 might be compared:

> When the morning stars sang together,
> All the sons of Elohim celebrated?

If this understanding of 1.23.57b is correct, it would suggest that it is the stars (presumably with Shapshu) of line 54 along with Shahar wa-Shalim who sing to celebrate in anticipation of the newborn children. The proposal remains debatable, since the lacuna without any clearly parallel passage prevents any final determination of the correct sense of line 57. However, the virtue of this proposal is that it interprets all the words in ways attested for them elsewhere in Ugaritic.

Lines 58–59

Merlo (1996) discusses the issue of whether *št* is to be reconstructed in the lacuna that follows *dd*, based on the evident parallel in line 61.[51] Merlo finds the emendation in line 59 unnecessary, and following *TO* (1.377), he would construe *št* in line 61 not as a title of the goddess but as the verb (**šyt*) governing *špt l'arṣ// špt lšmm* in lines 61–62. Despite this acceptable rearrangement, it seems likely from context that they are the same females who give birth to the children and nurse them. In view of the similar formulation in line 24, it would still appear to involve Athirat despite no precise verification of this view in the immediate context of lines 58–59 and 61.

Excursus 4: The Identity of the *'ilm n'mm* (Part 2)

The identity of *'ilm n'mm* is a matter of great debate. Sometimes they are identified with Dawn and Dusk,[52] sometimes not.[53] Del Olmo Lete, Dijkstra, and

---

51. So Virolleaud 1933:132, 149; Lewis, *UNP* 213, etc. See the critical discussion in Wright 2001:212–13.

52. For example, Gaster 1946:67–68, 69; Foley 1980:186; *MLC* 438; Pardee 1997b:274; Dijkstra 1998:270; Wyatt 1976:417; 1977:381; 1996:223, 227; 1998:324–25.

53. *CML*[1] 23; Komoróczy 1971:79–80; Xella 1973:90–93; *TO* 1.358–59; Tsevat 1978:26*–27*; Porter 1981:5; Hettema 1989–90:90–91; Gulde 1998:320–22, 333.

Wyatt identify both sets of births with Athtar (as the Venus star), a speculation strongly criticized by Pardee (1997b:281 n. 58; see the introduction above). Wyatt (1986:386) further equates Shahar and Shalim with Mot. Tsumura (1973:192–99) sees a "septad" of children, based on his understanding of line 64. Tsumura assumes the reading of the noun *šbny*, "septad," but commentators now accept Ginsberg's reading of a verbal form here, *tšbʿn*.[54] Even if Tsumura's interpretation of this feature is not shared by other scholars, his observations about the number seven in this text are otherwise worthwhile.

The issue of whether the gods of the two sets of birth are to be equated hinges on understanding the similarities as well as the differences between the narrative presentation of the two sets of birth. Lewis succinctly presents the state of the question (*UNP* 207):

> Some scholars take great pains to show that these are separate groups of gods while others collapse the two into one because they feel that the repetitious nature of the poetry is simply a device that was not meant to be understood sequentially.

Many commentators, including Hettema and Pardee, note the literary parallels between the two sets of births. In view of this approach used to support the identification, it is important to observe the differences as well as the similarities. These extend to the manner of their gestation and the actions following their births, especially the appetite of the latter and their consignment to the *mdbr*. In short, these features differ considerably, in turn suggesting different identities for the sets of divine figures (Xella 1973:91).

Perhaps some sort of literary analogy from Ugaritic literature can provide some insight into this question. The analogy that seems to fit this issue best is Kothar's commission of the weapons for Baal's conflict with Yamm in 1.2 IV. In this conflict, Kothar makes two different weapons (each with its own name), which are, however, presented partially as grammatically dual (or plural). If any insight from this replication of weapons in 1.2 IV can be applied to 1.23.30–76, it is that Dawn and Dusk and *ʾilm nʿmm* are not the same figures.

Sometimes the argument for the identification is made as a matter of default, that if the two sets of births are to be identified, then the text lacks any purpose for Shahar and Shalim (e.g., Foley 1980:186–87). This objection is interesting, but it is also answerable. There are various purposes to the presentation of Shahar and Shalim. Their births may not only parallel but also anticipate the births of the *ʾilm nʿmm*. In this text, the births of Shahar wa-Shalim may demar-

---

54. For the reading of the verb, see Ginsberg cited in Albright 1938:37; for criticism of the "septad" view, see Trujillo 1973:187.

cate the births of the astral children of El. Following their births, the behavior of Shahar wa-Shalim conforms to the norms of divine society and therefore provide a foil to the ravenous, destructive *'ilm n'mm*. This contrast is signaled in the varying use of the word *'db* in lines 54 and 64. As noted above, the word *'db* in line 64 serves in a description of what they ravenously devour, not what is given to Shapshu in a proper offering as expressed in line 54. Following suit, the description of Dawn and Dusk provides a marker of the nature of El's astral family, again in contrast to the *'ilm n'mm*. Later I will also suggest that it is this astral family of El from which the *'ilm n'mm* are expelled in lines 64–68 and to which they implicitly gain access, in terms of shared space in the sown (*mdr'*) as a sort of momentary reconciliation or integration.

On the assumption that the *'ilm n'mm* are not Shahar and Shalim, the next question involves their identity (see the survey in Gulde 1998:318–20). Nearly all commentators have noted the correspondence between the description of lines 62–63 and Mot's cosmic appetite in 1.5 II 2–3, with lips to earth and heavens (the opposite order). In this connection, Hab 2:5 in its comparison to Sheol// Mot may be noted, as it is said to have a massive "appetite" (*napšô*), one that "is not satisfied" (*wělō' yiśbā'*). The picture of the appetite that "is not satisfied" is exactly what is stated in line 64 (*wl[.]tšb'n*). To judge from 1.5 II 2–3 and Hab 2:5, the picture of Mot's insatiable appetite was a standard West Semitic motif. Not surprisingly, many commentators concluded that the same motif as expressed about the *'ilm n'mm* suggests Mot as at least one of these figures. Ginsberg (1935:59) acknowledged these points, yet added a cautionary note:

> The first guess of 99 per cent of scholars will be that it is Môt, the arch-enemy of Ba'l and the notorious cannibal ... who swallows this mouthful. But, of course, certainty will only be possible if the context of these lines is suffi- ciently well preserved.

There is a central feature of the mythologies of Mot in the Baal Cycle and of *'ilm n'mm* that meets Ginsberg's contextual criterion. The gods are consigned to the *mdbr*, a feature that, as Komoróczy (1971:79–80) argued, fits Mot (see Gulde 1998:319). Death's home lies at the edge of the *dbr*, where he finds Baal and devours him in 1.6 II 19–20. Indeed, in Mesopotamian texts, the wilderness is analogous to the netherworld (Talmon 1976:946; Anderson 1991:74). Further- more, following Komoróczy (1971:78–79), Hettema (1989–90:92) compares the use of *n'm* for Mot's abode in 1.5 III 9–10, 25–26 (even though Hettema does not identify Mot as *'ilm n'mm*). The larger context of 1.23 might be seen as militat- ing in favor of this identification. Given the attestation of *mt w-šr* in line 8, who is reasonably understood to be Mot, it also stands to reason that Mot could be at least one of the *'ilm n'mm*, except that these two sets of figures are evidently distinguished in lines 1–7 and 8–11.

Critics of this view have sought to explain the parallel between 1.5 II 2–3 and 1.23.64. After noting the parallel, Wyatt (1977:381) summarizes his view:

> this relationship is to be explained on the grounds that both the twins of *CTA* 23 (and of *CTA* 12) and Mot are to be regarded as hypostases of ʿAttar, whose birth, in geminated form, is the subject of the present text. On this understanding of the text, it would be illogical to have Mot appearing before the hierogamy of which, in twin form, he is later to become the offspring.

Wyatt's view depends on his identifications of both sets of births in 1.23 and of the further identification of both of these sets with Athtar as the Venus star. With Mot as yet another hypostasis of these others (Wyatt 1986:386), Wyatt's approach requires four sets of identifications for which there is no explicit evidence.

Other alternatives have been proposed. Tsevat (1978:26*–27*) saw these gods as "minor gods who populate nature." Tsevat (1978:26*) acknowledges the significance of *mdbr* versus *mdrʿ* in this text, but it plays no real role in his analysis of the deities in question. Equally telling, he does not take into account or even mention the parallel description of Mot's mouth, which had long been cited (see the comment of Ginsberg above). Not so different is the view of Hettema (1989–90:90–91), who states: "the birth of the other astral gods is told ... by reiterating the birth story of Shahar and Shalim." Operating with this presupposition, Hettema equates these astral gods with the seventy sons of Athirat in 1.4 VI 46. Clemens (2001:86 n. 296) offers yet a further alternative, based on a number of general similarities between 1.23 and 1.161 (RS 34.126): "it can be hypothesized that the *ʾilm nʿmm* in fact correspond to the *rpʾum* of RS 34.126." The views of Tsevat, Hettema, and Clemens may have a certain appeal; indeed, the number of the gods in question is simply given as plural. However, the single greatest difficulty with these approaches is that the deities identified as the *ʾilm nʿmm* do not have ravenous appetites, nor do they belong to the *mdbr*.

As yet another alternative, Porter (1981:6) sugests that *ʾilm nʿmm* are "earth beings." This view cannot be ruled out absolutely by the fact that they are called *ʾilm*. However, the consistent use of this term does not inspire confidence in the view. It also assumes that the females are human, a view that is dubious (see excursus 3). In short, these alternatives do not address the specifics about these figures in 1.23. It would appear that the consensus view enjoys the most support from the context.

There is a further question whether there is a second figure under the designation of *ʾilm nʿmm*. It would seem so, since Dawn and Dusk are apparently two figures linked in nature. Above it is shown that the binomial name of Mot represents a single figure, not two figures, and perhaps then the same applies here. In this case, the single figure of *mt w-šr* as known in lines 8–11 is represented in a "twinned form." Or, we may have an alternative mythology with a second monstrous newborn paired with Mot, as argued by Komoroćzy (1971:79–80).[55] In building a case for Yamm as this twin, Komoroćzy took the word *ym* in lines 58–59//61 as the name of Yamm (and not "day"). He is hardly alone in the view that the gods are called "sons of sea" (see line 23). Even if this proposal is not accepted, one might still nominate Yamm, since only Yamm and Mot receive the titles, *ydd 'il* and *mdd 'il*, "beloved of El." It may be noted further that these titles suggest their shared identity and association with El, a major figure here. In the case of 1.23, this relationship would be one of affiliation. On this assumption, one might think that the narrative's references to the *'ilm n'mm* could be a reference to both Mot and Yamm. There is no way to confirm this speculation, but in view of the pairing of Dawn and Dusk, as well as the dual or plural form of *'ilm n'mm*, it might be thought that Mot may not be operating by himself.

1.23.30–76 shows a number of pairings in terms of both agents and descriptions, and perhaps this is the case here, unless this phrase were understood as a title for *mt w-šr*. The notion of *mt w-šr* in a "twinned" form parallels the proposal made about Athirat wa-Rahmay, mentioned from lines 13 and 28, possibly in a "twinned" form as the wives of El in lines 30–76. In chapter 5 (under "The Royal Construction of Cosmic Duality and Unity in 1.23.30–76"), I suggest a reason for these "twinnings." Despite such considerations, in the end it seems better not to import Mot or Yamm into the identity of *'ilm n'mm* without a further indicator of either figure. Indeed, with the Goodly Gods mentioned in lines 1–7 and *mt w-šr* in lines 8–11, it seems unlikely that these two sets of divine figures are to be identified. It is important to be clear that the overall interpretation of lines 30–76 offered in this study does not depend on this specific reading of the gods, only that they are destructive divinities. It may be simpler to conclude that these unnamed gods share Mot's destructive character and function as seen in the Baal Cycle; a direct identification is arguably unnecessary and perhaps incorrect. So if these gods do not include Mot per se in any form, it may be said instead that they share his character as destructive forces. One may remain inclined to see the *'ilm n'mm* as a duality rather than a plurality in view of all the other pairings in this text, but this, too, would be no more than an operating assumption.

LINES 59B–61A: THE BIRTH ANNOUNCEMENT

| 59 | rgm l'il ybl | Word to El was brought: |
| 60 | 'aṯty 'il ylt | "El's two wives have given birth." |

---

55. Gulde 1998:318–19 discusses the idea of two infernal deities here.

	mh ylt	"What have they borne?"
	ʾilmy nʿmm	"Twin (?) Goodly Gods,
61	ʾagzr ym bn ym	Day-old devourers, one-day-old boys,
	ynqm bʾap ḏd	Who suck the nipple of the breast."

Line 60

According to Rainey (1995:705–6), *ʾatty* is a construct nominative dual form with –*y* being an uncontracted –*ay* suffix or contracted –*ê* with *y* as vowel indicator (see also Blau and Loewenstamm 1970:29–30). *CTA* (p. 100) and Sivan (1997:84) see a scribal error here; the scribe has accidentally treated the form as an oblique construct dual with –*y* vowel indicator instead of a nominative construct dual. Tropper (*UG* 306–7, 833) views the final –*y* as an enclitic particle. The views of Sivan and Tropper fit the attestation of *ʾatt ʾil* in lines 42 and 49. At this point, there is no means available to confirm any of these theories.

Line 61

Most commentators take *št* with *bʾap ḏd*. For the argument for taking *št* as a verb governing *špt* in the next bicolon, see below.

Lines 61b–64a: Aftermath of birth, the appetite of the goodly gods

61–62	št špt/lʾarṣ	They set a lip to earth,
62	špt lšmm	A lip to heaven.
	wyʿrb bphm	Then enter their mouths
	ʿṣr šmm	Fowl of the sky,
63	wdg bym	And fish from the sea.
	wndd gzr l<g>zr	As they move, bite upon <bi>te,
63–64	yʿdb ʾuymn/ʾušmʾal	They stuff—on both their right and left—
	bphm wl tšbʿn	Into their mouths, but they are unsated.

Lines 61–62

The initial four words (with their own parallelism) would appear to constitute an example of a *qtl suffix verbal clause providing backdrop to the resumption of narrative marked by *w-* + *yqtl verb (cf. Blake 1951:80 n. 1). Alternatively, the clause could be what Blau (1977) calls an extrapositional clause dependent on the following clause separated by *w-*. There is yet a third possibility. As noted in the discussion of lines 58–59, Merlo (1996) construes *št* in line 61 not as a title of the goddess but as the verb (*šyt) governing *špt l'arṣ*//*špt lšmm* in lines 61–62. Unfortunately, the parallel in 1.5 II 2 (discussed in the next paragraph) has a significant lacuna where a verbal form such as *št* might have been slotted. Merlo's view holds no particular verification from the content as compared to the standard view, which takes *št* as the "lady," a title for a goddess. Although line 24 stands at a considerable distance from line 61, their similar formulations have been viewed as evidence in favor of *št* as a term for the goddess. The standard view may well be correct here, but I think an extrapositional clause of a full bicolon is unlikely. Moreover, a biform of *šyt*, namely, *štt*,[56] underlies the verbal form in the one biblical passage that has been compared to this line,[57] Ps 73:9: *šattû baššāmayim pîhem*, "they set their mouths against heaven" (NJPS). Merlo mentions neither of these points, but they militate in favor of his proposal. Although I would tentatively adopt Merlo's proposal, the similarity of content between lines 58–59, 61 and line 24 would nonetheless suggest that they refer to the breasts of the goddess. Merlo himself is critical of this view. Olyan (1988:57), too, questions the connection: "There is no evidence that the two scenes and the goddesses are connected in any way." At the same time, neither scholar offers a better way to understand the similarity of content between these lines. Just as the ritual and narrative sections refer to the *'ilm n'mm*, so they may refer to the goddess as well.

As many commentators have noted, lines 61–62 approximate 1.5 II 2, a description of Mot's magnificent appetite, which adds in line 3: [*l*]*šn lkbkbm*. The two passages differ in the order of cosmic components, earth and heaven in lines 61–62, but heaven and earth in 1.5 II 2–3.[58] Mot's mouth is massive, as in 1.4 VIII 14–20 presenting Baal's warning against its power, which ironically becomes Baal's own fate, as described in 1.6 II 21–23. To these evocations of Mot's mouth, commentators often add the picture of the rapacious appetite against heaven and earth in Ps 73:9 (noted in the preceding paragraph). The parallel afforded by Ps 73:9 involves the content of the motif of the maw of the destructive cosmic forces, in all these instances arrayed against the order of the cosmos. Also cited as a parallel is the mouth of Sheol described in connection to famine in Isa 5:13–14 (Cutler and Macdonald 1982:43).

Albright added Jonah to the list of biblical parallels. After crediting Ginsberg's oral communication explaining the parallel in 1.5 II 2, Albright comments: "note the curious parallel to the Jonah motive!" (1934:137). By this remark, Albright seems to have meant that Jonah being swallowed by the fish of the sea

---

56. *BDB* 1060; *KB* (1999, ed. M. E. J. Richardson) 1672.

57. See *SPUMB* 178; Pope 1978:150 n. 7; and Ringgren 1979:720–21, with citations.

58. Cf. the difference of order of heaven and earth in Gen 1:1 versus earth and heaven in Gen 2:4, discussed by Albright 1934:137 n. 194.

Pozo Moro monument. Photo Archive National Archeology Museum, Madrid. Used by permission.

Below. Detail of the relief.

echoes the motif found here (see the further discussion below in lines 63–64). More precisely, the prose writer of Jonah perhaps found in the combination of the poetic images of Sheol's belly (2:3) and the heart of the seas (2:4) the inspiration for the prose presentation of Jonah swallowed by the great fish in the sea (also the reference to prayer in 2:8; cf. 2:2).

A further parallel to the gigantic maw of the gods in 1.23 may be suggested. The site of Pozo Moro, located about 125 kilometers southwest of Valencia, yielded what has been interpreted as a funerary monument dating to the sixth century B.C.E. based on the associated Attic ware (for a picture of the monument as reconstructed, see page opposite; also Vicente 2003:57). One block of this monument depicts a monstrous figure with a human body and two heads with tongues receiving an offering of a child (Almagro-Gorbea 1983; Kennedy 1981; Rundin 2004; for bibliography and further description, see Vicente 2003:56–57). The figure has been thought to go back to Levantine prototypes, in view of its style as well as its depiction of child sacrifice. The enthroned recipient of the offering, in particular the presentation of its double-heads, fits typologically with the monstrous figures of the Goodly Gods, especially with the emphasis on their massive appetites. Given the distance between this iconography and CAT 1.23, the possible putative parallel appears thematic at best.

Line 62

The singular verb precedes the double subject. The second subject is clearly singular, and it is arguable from the parallel that the first subject is as well. Accordingly, we may see here a double-collective subject preceded by a verb in the singular. It may be noted that the parallel between lines 61–62a and 1.5 II 2–3 extends to line 62–63 and 1.5 II 3–6, with its description of Baal entering Mot's innards compared to "a dried (?) olive, the produce of the earth and fruit of the trees." The verb of entering (*ʿrb) followed by reference to the natural phenomena that are consumable is common to both lines 62–63 and 1.15 II 3–6. One important difference between these two passages casts additional light on lines 62–63. The produce that enters Mot's mouth in 1.5 II 2–3 includes the produce of the earth, while the natural products devoured by the ʾilm nʿmm are limited to the other natural realms, namely, the sky and sea. This presentation leaves open, and perhaps anticipates, the earthly plenty to be enjoyed in lines 70–76.

Lines 63–64

The opening verb is formed from the N-stem of *dwd and is cognate with Akkadian izuzzu, as Pope (1947) and Rosenthal (1940:293 n. 1) noted independently.[59] Elsewhere in Ugaritic, the verb evidently means to rise: "he stood

---

59. Endorsed by Huehnergard 2002; see also Pardee 1997b:282 n. 62.

(*ndd*), served, and offered him drink" (1.3 I 8). In its position in the tricolon of lines 8–11, *ndd* is parallel to *qm* relative to its position in the cola in lines 4–8 and line 18–19. Hettema (1989–90:85 n. 30) takes the verb as a G-stem participle from **ndd* in the sense "to hurry." Lewis (*UNP* 213) also takes the verb in this direction ("rushing"). Hettema believes that the suffix form is less probable because of the following prefix form, but this may be a matter of sequence of tenses sequentially coordinated, in this case two **qtl*-forms, *ndd* and *gzr*, followed by a **yqtl*-form, *y'db*. The type of sequence, **qtl*-form followed by **yqtl*-form, was noted by Blake (1951:80 n. 1). Despite the flaw in his reasoning about the semantics of *ndd*, Hettema could be correct, as **ndd* shows the meaning of movement (1.20 II 2; 1.21 II 4; 1.22 I 10; and 1.22 II 21). Accordingly, **ndd* may denote movement to stand up or to move about ("to hasten, hurry"). The meaning of *ndd* here may presuppose that as newborns the gods are faced with providing for themselves, and they therefore stand up and search for food to their left and right; or, they simply move about to their left and right to find provisions. A good biblical parallel, Job 15:23, was noted by Driver (*CML*[1] 123 n. 14), followed by Xella (1973:73, with other biblical references): "He wanders about for bread—where is it?" (NJPS).[60]

Many scholars take *gzr l<g>zr* in line 63 as a phrase, "bite upon bite" or the like (*TO* 1.377). Gibson (*CML*[2] 126) offers an alternative: "And they did stand, 'cleaver' by 'cleaver.' " Tropper and Verreet (1988:346), taking this phrase with *ndd*, render "Es standen Zerteiler bei Zerteiler." Pardee (1997b:282) renders: "When they stand, delimitation to <deli>mitation" (see also Bordreuil and Pardee 2004:31, 36). In this view, *gzr* refers to the "extremity of the horizon," a suggestion that would work with the theme of the pair's monstrous appetite taking in the whole of the cosmos. This division makes better sense of the parallelism, but the sense is questionable. From the point of view of the line's semantics, the words *gzr l<g>zr* would seem to go syntactically with the verb that follows.[61] It is also possible, though less likely, that *gzr l<g>zr* is to be understood as an infinitive absolute plus asseverative *l-* plus **qatala* verb: "truly they ravenously devour."

Even if the syntax remains somewhat elusive, the overall sense is not. The key to this section, and in particular to *gzr*, is the contextual parallel with Isa 9:19, as noted by Albright (1938:37), followed by Trujillo (1973:187) and Xella (1973:59):

---

60. In view of *'ay* in 1.23.6–7, Trujillo (1973:69–70) suggests that the same particle may be attested in Job 15:23: "He wanders (looking) (*nōdēd*) for any (*'ayyēh*) food." This understanding would account for the lack of pronominal suffix presupposed by the NJPS translation.

61. Hypothetically, one might instead take *gzr l<g>zr* as infinitive absolute plus asseverative *l-* plus finite verb, but usually the finite verb in question is a prefix indicative form and not a suffix form.

> It slaughters (*gzr) on the right, but remains hungry (*rʿb),
> And eats (*ʾkl) on the left without being sated (*śbʿ).
> Each one eats the flesh of his kin.

This biblical verse provides a good parallel with 1.23.63–64 on a number of scores. In Isa 9:19 the root *gzr appears in a manner similar to its use in 1.23.63–64. The root means to "tear, divide."[62] In Isa 9:19 it seems to refer to tearing meat off of animals for consumption.[63] The biblical passage offers an image of a ravenous people whose appetite is violent in its tenor. A similar effect applies to the picture of the gods in 1.23.63–64. The motif of the ravenous party eating on both the right and the left (as a way of saying, in every direction) appears in both lines 63–64 and Isa 9:19. Finally, the motif of unsatiated ravenous eating appears in both passages. Similar motifs occur in Hab 2:5 in its comparison to Sheol//Mot, said to have a massive appetite (napšô), one that is not satisfied (wĕlōʾ yiśbāʿ); compare the belly of Sheol in Jonah 2:3. With the word gzr, the ʾilm nʿmm evidently display what their epithet ʾagzr in lines 58//61 (and presumably line 23, where the term is reconstructed based on these parallels) suggests about them.

As Ginsberg (1935:60) observed, the double use of the particle ʾu in 1.23.63–64 seems to express inclusion ("both … and …") rather than alternatives ("either … or …"), as in 1.4 VII 43: ʾumlk ʾubl mlk, literally "either king or nonking." The double use ʾu may express inclusion or alternatives, which extends the particle's meaning "or" (cognate with BH ʾô, "or"; see further the apparent multiple attestations of ʾu in the form of ʾulp in 1.40). The binary pair of "left" and "right" expresses "completezza," as noted by Xella (1973:73), following Rinaldi (1968). Xella's characterization is particularly useful: this left-right pair provides a horizontal opposition that matches the vertical opposition of earth-heaven in lines 61–62. The two pairs cover four points on a plane (down and up, left and right), and therefore everything in between (merismus), in other words, everything completely.

The final verbal clause in lines 63–64, with w tšbʿn,[64] is paralleled closely in 1.3 II 19–20, where Anat is said to be unsated (wlšbʿt) with "her fighting in the

---

62. For the root, especially Arabic jazara, "cut, slaughter," see Leslau 211.

63. BH haggĕzārîm for halves of animals in Gen 15:7 is compared in TO 1.377 n. o.

64. As noted above, Tsumura (1973:85–89, 192–99; 1999:232) instead reads a noun šbʿny, "a heptad," as a designation of the gods born to the women. This interpretation leaves unexplained the reading of the preceding t. Most read a word-divider after n (e.g., CAT), favored by the spacing available between n and y. It would seem that the word-divider is filled by deposit (a feature of a number of letters in this area, e.g., the ʿayin in yʿdb above in line 63). If correct, it would militate against Tsumura's view. Commentators otherwise accept Ginsberg's reading of a verbal form

valley//With battling between the two towns." Anat then sates herself with the captives taken to her house, where she consumes "until she is sated (ʿd tšbʿ) with fighting in the house, with battling between the tables" (1.3 II 29–30). In the case of lines 19–20, which mention that Anat is not sated, they mark a minor break in the narrative, which next moves to a further description of her being sated in lines 29–30. Similarly, in 1.23.64, the mention of the ʾilm nʿmm not being sated anticipates the next episode's resolution of this problem.

SECTION III, THE GOODLY GODS IN THE OUTBACK AND THE SOWN:
LINES 64B–76

SUBSECTION A, LINES 64B–68: THEIR CONSIGNMENT TO THE OUTBACK

64	y ʾaṯt ʾitrḫ	"O wives I have espoused,
65	y bn ʾašld	O sons I have begotten:
	šʾu ʿdb tk mdbr qdš	Make an offering amid the holy outback,
66	ṯm tgrgr lʾabnm wlʿṣm	There sojourn mid rocks and brush."
66–67	šbʿ šnt/tmt	For seven years complete,
67	ṯmn nqpt ʿd	Eight cycles duration,
	ʾilm nʿmm ttlkn šd	The Goodly Gods roam the steppe,
68	tṣdn pʾat mdbr	They hunt to the edge of the outback.

Lines 64–65

From the context, it is evident that El is the speaker, as the direct discourse opens with an address to "my wives." W. G. E. Watson (1990:417–18) counts the bicolon of lines 64–65 as one of several examples of unintroduced direct speech (what he calls "abrupt speech"). The parallel dual vocatives are in construct to the parallel asyndetic verbal clauses that follow (for discussion of the line, especially the verb, see Dietrich and Loretz 1999:156). As pointed out in *DUL* (878), the verb is denominative from the *t-* preformative noun, *trḫ*.[65] As noted in the lexica (*UT* 19.2603; *WUS* 328; and *DUL* 878), it is related to Akkadian *terḫatu*, "bride-price" (*AHw* 1348), thought by some scholars to derive from *reḫû* (see Dahood 1969:34).

---

here, *tšbʿn*. See Ginsberg cited in Albright 1938:37; for criticism of the "septad" view, see Trujillo 1973:187.

65. Note Ugaritic *trḫ*, "newlywed," in 1.14 II 47, IV 26, and *trḫtt*, "dowry," in 1.111.20.

Lines 65-66

The first command here echoes the command for an offering in line 54. Both use the phrase *š'u 'db* (see the discussion of line 54 above). Line 65 also differs from line 54 in not naming the recipient of the offering and instead focusing on the location where the activity is to take place, namely, in the *mdbr qdš*. The word *mdbr* signals the outback, which marks the boundary of human activities such as grazing and hunting (for the latter, see 1.12.34–35; 1.92.3) and here begins the area of dangerous forces. Accordingly, in the cosmic geography of the Baal Cycle, *dbr*, "outback," is part of the designation for the locale where Baal meets Mot, the god of "Death" (CAT 1.6 II 20; cf. 1.5 VI 6, 29); this place would appear to be the edge of the underworld (CAT 1.6 I 8–14). The *mdbr* is also the site where Baal's foes are to be given birth and to confront him in 1.12 I 19–22.[66] This usage reflects the correlation of beneficial deities in the center, called the "sown" (*mdr'*), and of destructive deities dwelling beyond the periphery, labeled the "outback" (*mdbr*).[67]

The significance of *qdš* in this context is less clear. Early on in Ugaritic studies, the phrase was compared with *mdbr qdš* in Ps 29:8 by Ginsberg (see *KU* 86) and followed by others (e.g., Cross 1973:154; Tsumura 1973:92; Pardee 2005:169). While a good deal of attention centered on the question of the biblical parallel in Ps 29:8, less energy was devoted to its significance. De Moor (1987:127 n. 66; see also 118 n. 9) suggested that this is an oasis site. Pardee (2005:167) suggests that the phrase in both cases refers to a specific area, "a sparsely populated area in the vicinity of Qadesh on the Orontes that was widely known as 'the steppeland of Qadesh.'" While a specific location is plausible, it seems that more may be involved here. The appearance of Qadesh as a place-name elsewhere (e.g., biblical Kadesh-barnea) would point to a general type of holy site. Moreover, it could be that the outback itself is designated as holy in both texts. The parallelism in lines 65–66 does not suggest the steppeland near a sanctuary site called Qadesh; instead, it sounds like the outback itself is being called "holy." In context, it appears to be a set phrase for a sanctuary space either near or in the outback as opposed to the sacred center of shrines or temples (in cities or towns).

Many commentators have suggested that the verb **grgr* is a reduplicated form of **gwr*, "to sojourn" (cf. BH **gwr*, noun *gēr*).[68] As an alternative, com-

---

66. Parker's recent translation of these pertinent lines renders *mdbr 'il š'iy* as "the god-awful wilderness." See *UNP* 189.

67. For the correlation of cosmic topography and deities, see Smith 2001:29–30. See also Xella 1973:96–106; Wyatt 1987a:esp. 380–85. For further references and discussion, see below in lines 67–69 on p. 120.

68. See Barton 1934:66; *TO* 1.378 n. r, with listing of scholars; Tsumura 1973:93; Pope 1978; Dietrich and Loretz 2002:92 n. 97.

parison has been made with Ethiopic *grgr*, "to wallow, revolve, roll, roll oneself, make one roll about, spin, drive around (tr., intr.), flop around, wiggle (one possessed by a demon)," issuing in the translation, "to bustle about, make haste."[69] This proposal assumes a semantic gap between the Ugaritic word and the cognates cited. In context, the gods move around or go about the landscape in search of food (see lines 66–67), which would work well with the first proposal. The periphery or "outback" is characterized as a terrain of "rocks and brush" (*l'abnm wl'ṣm*, in 1.23.66). This may be a further specification of the outback. Pope (1978 = 1994:45–50) compares this line and Exod 7:19: "the phrase 'wood and stones,' or the reverse, aptly characterizes the arid and barren desert area beyond the sown where both food and water are scarce, though not entirely lacking."

Lines 66–67

The indication of time is fronted before the mention of the gods themselves in lines 68–69. In view of the seven-year theme, a fitting parallel might be the seven years of lean and of plenty in Gen 41. In this biblical story as well as CAT 1.12 II 45 and 1.23.66–67, Gordon (1949:56) saw the seven-year sabbatical cycle of famine and abundance. He also saw this theme operative in the seven-year period between Baal's smiting of Athirat's sons in 1.6 V (especially lines 8–10) and the renewal of the Baal-Mot struggle in 1.6 VI. Gordon's ideas are developed by Tsumura (1973:222–23, cited in 1999:236 n. 73):

> The main theme and purpose of the cult depicted in UT 52 is the fertility of the land through the birth of the Good Gods of fertility which assures food and drink for the community of Ugarit. Hence, its goal is the inauguration of a new seven year cycle of plenty in the land by means of banishing the destructive power by sympathetic magic, giving assurance of enough bread and wine to the new-born Gods of fertility, a "Heptad", in the act of drama and introducing into the ritual the heptad-theme in terms of the "traditional" sevenfold performances of liturgy and the motif of "good-"ness in keeping with the atmosphere of [the] entire rite. This cult was probably reenacted at the end or toward the end of the seven year cycle of famine.

Gordon's view was reviewed and criticized by de Moor (*SPUMB* 25–27, 32–34). Also rejecting Gordon's theory, Dijkstra (1998:275) relates the seven-year period instead to astronomical reckoning. The astronomical approach of Dikjstra (like Wyatt's) relies explicitly on the identification of Dawn and Dusk with the morn-

---

69. Driver (*CML*[1] 146), Xella (1973:74), and de Moor (1987:127 n. 63). For these and some further alternatives, see Dietrich and Loretz 2002:92 n. 97.

ing and evening star (Venus star), but most commentators would relate the Venus star in its evening and morning manifestation to the deities Athtar and Athtart. Dijkstra's astral approach relies too heavily on a problematic series of undemonstrated assumptions. Still for the larger backdrop of the text, perhaps as it relates to the moon and the vernal equinox, Dijkstra shows a well-placed sensitivity to the possible astral dimensions of this text.

While de Moor criticized the weaknesses in Gordon's "sabbatical theory," the point remains that seven-year periods serve some sort of literary purpose that hardly enhances de Moor's seasonal theory. Wyatt (1998:335 n. 57) sees "a ritual period" in the seven-year period in 1.23, and seven years in fact constitutes "a ritual period" in the expansion of the *zukru*-ritual in Emar 373 (Fleming 2000:54, 56, 63–68). It might well be that seven-year ritual cycles have informed the use of seven-year periods in literary contexts, including the Baal Cycle and 1.23. Seven-year periods arguably serve a general literary purpose (cf. the seven-year periods of service performed by Jacob in Gen 29),[70] perhaps as "an undetermined period of time" (Trujillo 1973:190), "an indefinite period" (Porter 1981:7), or "a considerable interval of time" (Segert 1986:220). If a seven-year period intervening between Mot's humiliation at the hands of Anat and his later engagement with Baal (1.6 V 8–10) was interpreted agriculturally, it might suggest seven years of plenty with Baal dominant over Mot (thanks to Anat). Seven years is also a lengthy period, after which Athirat remembers the vow that Kirta made to her (1.15 III 22).

Some of the examples of seven-year periods from the Ugaritic texts denote a long period marking seminal junctures in the lives of families, human and divine. After seven years, Danilu finishes mourning and the narrative moves on (1.19 IV 15–18). The same parallelism of seven years and eight cycles is attested in 1.12 II 45, after which family tensions between Baal and his half-siblings (?) require resolution (Xella 1973:75). The conflict between Baal and Mot might also be read in terms of family conflict. If this context were to be related to 1.23.66–67, it might suggest the seven-year gap as a period of "family feuds," unresolved relations within the context of the divine family.

With these literary usages in mind, let us reconsider the view of Gordon and Tsumura. As Tsumura (1973:222–23, cited in 1999:236 n. 73) rightly stresses, sevenfold components mark the ritual of 1.23 in particular (lines 12, 20, 29). If seven symbolically marks completion or fullness, then such sevenfold actions perhaps generate ritual completion or fullness. The mention of the seven-year period in the narrative, in line 66, may connect to this notion rather than an actual

---

70. As my daughter Rachel Smith reminds me.

seven-year ritual period. The narrative here may echo the ritual without being the same as the ritual or corresponding precisely to it.

Lines 67–68

The image is stereotypical for destructive forces operating in the steppe, for example locusts in 1.14 II 50–III 1//IV 29–30. In this passage, the picture of locusts may not suggest simply the edge of the outback, but everywhere in between the edges of the steppeland. In contrast, the parallel language used of Baal out hunting in the steppeland in 1.12 I 34–35 suggests roaming around the edge of that zone (see van Zijl 1972:258). Unlike Baal and perhaps more like locusts, the ʾilm nʿmm seem to wander all around the steppeland for a substantial period of time. The use of the same two verbal roots, in line 16 and here in lines 67–68, would suggest that the activity of the ʾilm nʿmm resembles the movement of Rahmay in line 16. Her hunt moves her from the sown to the outback (as in other divine hunting scenes; see the discussion of line 16). In contrast, the ʾilm nʿmm hunt in the outback, and presumably unsuccessful there, they move to the sown in search of food. The two hunts may be read as inverse movements: the goddess moves outward from the sown to the outback for food, while the gods move inward from the outback to the sown in search of sustenance. To the action of the Goodly Gods, Cutler and Macdonald (1982:46) compare Amos 8:11–12, which suggest wandering everywhere.

SUBSECTION B, LINES 68B–76: THEIR ADMISSION INTO THE SOWN

68–69	wngš hm nǵr/mdrʿ	The two approach the Guard of the sown,
69	wṣḥ hm ʿm nǵr mdrʿ	And the two cry to the Guard of the sown:
69–70	y nǵr/nǵr ptḥ	"O Guard, Guard, open!"
70	wptḥ hw prṣ bʿdhm	And he himself opens a breach for them,
71	wʿrb hm	And the two enter:
	hm [ʾiṯ ṯmt (?) l]ḥm	"If [there is there (?) f]ood,
71–72	wtn/wnlḥm	Give that we may eat!
72	hm ʾiṯ [ṯmt (?) yn],	If there is [there (?) wine],
	[w]tn wnšt	Give that we may drink!"
73	wʿn hm nǵr mdrʿ	And the Guard of the sown answers them:
	[ʾiṯ lḥm d...]xt[...]	"[There is food for the one who ... (?)] ...,

74   ʾiṯ yn dʿrb bṯk[...]   There is wine for whoever enters ...[...].”

75   mǵ hw   ... he himself approaches,
          lhn lg ynh[...]   He serves a measure of his wine ...
76   wḥbrh mlʾa yn[...]   And his companion fills (it [?]) with wine ...

Lines 68–69

These lines feature the "sown" (*mdrʿ*) versus "outback, steppe" (*mdbr*) in the preceding lines.[71] The sown denotes in agrarian terms the center versus the periphery of the outback. This use of "sown" appears also in administrative lists, twice for royal workers (4.141 III 16 and 4.618.6) and once for a record of wine (4.149.16; Trujillo 1973:193). As noted in the introductory chapter, this last reference (4.149.14–16) is of further interest, as it shows cultic devotion in the "sown" (unless this is the name of a town):

          ḥmš yn   five (jars of) wine
          bdbḥ mlkt bmdrʿ   for the sacrifice of the queen in the sown

Here the sown is a special zone. Cutler and Macdonald (1982:35) speak of "temple-land." If this understanding may be pursued along the model proposed by Schloen (1993), it would seem that in gaining access to the sown, the *ʾilm nʿmm* gain access to the land of plenty (the fertility emphasized in *TO* 1.363–65), produced by the bounty of El and his family, who are considered the "normal" deities. In contrast, the *ʾilm nʿmm*, though born of El, do not belong to this astral family. Their entry into the sown constitutes a spatial expression of being allowed in the sown or center. In terms of the paradigm of the divine family, they are "allowed home," if only for a ritual moment. Though they come from the same parents, they are opposite in nature from the astral family (M. S. Smith 2001:61–65), and in this narrative, then, we may see the reconciliation of cosmic opposites that derived from a common origin.

In ritual terms, in lines 1–7 and 23–27 the royal parents and their various ministers are joined by the gods at home in the sown. Like the gatekeeper in line 70, they allow the most threatening forces into their midst. In the ritual (lines 1–7, 23–27), they do not merely admit, they even invite, the Goodly Gods into the sown. We may note here a difference of detail that may be indicative of a slight difference in sensibility between lines 1–7 and 23–27, on the one hand, and, on the other hand, lines 68–76: the former invites the Goodly Gods, while the latter

____

71. See Xella 1973:96–106; Wyatt 1987:esp. 380–85; M. S. Smith 2001:29–30. See also the important survey of the biblical material in Talmon 1997:87–118. More recently, Xella (2003:237–39) has touched on this topic.

issues no invitation but admits the gods to the sown. Instead of someone calling to them as in lines 1–7 and 23–27, in this section they call for admission to the sown. In this slight difference, we may detect an ambivalent attitude toward the Goodly Gods.

In both the ritual and mythic parts, we see the formulation of a theology of destruction: it comes into the human and cosmic orders not always as a terrible threat but sometimes in relative weakness when life is at its most fertile; and under these circumstances, destruction too can share in the plenitude without crippling effects. Whereas lines 8–11 offer a theology of death, that the death of death allows life, here we glimpse a very different viewpoint, that destruction can enter in the midst of life and for a ritual moment be unthreatening as the larger celebration of life overshadows the threat of destruction.

The identity of the Guardian is unknown. Gibson (*CML*[2] 127 n. 3) compares the guardian cherubim of Gen 3:24 and the gatekeeper in the Descent of Inanna (lines 12–13; *ANET* 107). Dijkstra (1994:119) notes, at least for form, the phrase *nǵr krm*, "the watchman of the vineyard," in 1.92.23 (see also 4.609.12). Dijkstra (1998:278–79, 287) also suggests a further possibility that the watchman is to be identified as an astral constellation that served as "gatekeeper" for the divine astral twins. It is possible that through an astronomical speculation, the cosmic reality experienced on earth was read also in the stars.

There are more precise Ugaritic parallels for 1.23.68–69. Particularly germane is CAT 4.141 III 16–17, as noted by Trujillo (1973:23, 192). Before the phrase *nǵr krm*, "guard of the vineyard," in 4.141 III 17, there is in 4.141 III 16 the same phrase as in 1.23.68–69 and 73, *nǵr mdrʿ*, "guard of the sown"; it also occurs in 4.618.6. For this usage, we may also compare more generally Akkadian *naṣāru*, which in some texts from Mari refers to guards of fields (*CAD* N/2:35, 37). Similarly, the image of the watchman (*nōṣēr) over the vineyard is applied to the deity and Israel in Isa 27:2–3.[72] The watchman (*nōṣēr*) in Job 27:18 makes a booth, likewise suggesting the fall interchange setting as found in 1.23. The Ugaritic parallels, especially 4.141, remain the most helpful to the immediate context of 1.23. The *nǵr mdrʿ* in 4.141 III 16 and *nǵr krm* in 4.141 III 17 belong to *bnš ml[k]*, according to the heading in line 4.141 I 1. In view of the fact that these roles are ascribed to royal workers, one may see this as the broad backdrop for the same figure in 1.23.30–76, as this narrative is situated within the royal sacrificial liturgy of 1.23. Ritually speaking, the gatekeeper parallels those who make the offering in lines 26–27, following the invitation to the *ʾilm nʿmm* in lines 23–24.

---

72. This passage itself seems to represent a literary echoing of the "song of the vineyard" in Isa 5:1–7.

Line 70

For the question of this meaning for *bʿd*, see Young (1977:302) and Margalit (1995:297). The parallels cited by them are not particularly strong, but the sense suits the context here.

Lines 71–72

With the verb **ʿrb*, the text marks a thematic reversal, compared to line 62, where the same verb occurs. There the produce of the world enters the mouths of the Goodly Gods, while here in line 71 the Goodly Gods enter the sown to enjoy its produce.

The reconstructions for the parallel clauses in the lacunas (*hm* ['*iṯ ṯmt* (?) *l*]*ḥm*//*hm* '*iṯ* [*ṯmt yn*]) in these lines essentially follow from the invitation of the guardian in line 74. As the drawing of the lines by Bordreuil and Pardee (2004:2.124) nicely illustrates, there is more than sufficient space in the lacunas for the reconstructions entertained here.

The two instances of *w-* preceding the imperative *tn* involve the *w-* of the apodosis following the protasis beginning with the particle *hm*. Therefore, *w-* in these cases requires no translation, as the *w-* links the two clauses (see Steiner 2000). The apodoses are syndetic clauses (with *w-*), unlike several asyndetic clauses otherwise showing the same sort of syntax of imperative followed by volitive (see Verreet 1984:313; Tropper 1991:348–49). The overall reference to the plenty might be compared with the invitation in Isa 55:1–2 (see Clifford 1983).

Line 74

The end of the line remains unexplained.

Lines 75–76

The one debated term is *lhn*, sometimes related to Arabic *lahhana*, "to proffer (a morsel) before a meal" (so *CML*[1] 158 n. 15), or to BH *hîn*, a liquid measure (like *lg* following it), which would be preceded by the preposition *l-*(Gordon 1966:98 n. 50; Trujillo 1973:196; Xella 1973:77; de Moor 1987:128 n. 69). The mention of two measures in a row in this manner seems less likely. In either case, service of wine is narrated. It may be assumed that this is *yn ṭb*, "good wine," as opposed to *yn d l ṭb*, "wine that is not good" or even *yn ḫlq*, "spoiled (?) wine" (CAT 4.213; Heltzer 1990:128).

The identity of the companion to the *nǵr mdrʿ* is unknown. We might speculate that the companion is the *nǵr krm*, just as *nǵr mdrʿ* and *nǵr krm* are mentioned in 4.141 III 16–17. At the same time, the gap at the end of lines 75 and 76 possibly points to a lack of parallelism of figures.

PART 3

GENERAL INTERPRETATION

4

THE QUESTION OF "SACRED MARRIAGE" AND
THE TEXTUAL RELATIONS BETWEEN LINES 1–29 AND 30–76

This chapter examines the textual relations between the ritual material of lines 1–29 and the mythic narrative of lines 30–76, in order to address a long-standing claim made about this text. It has been often argued that the text attests to a "sacred marriage" (*hieros gamos*), that is, sexual relations between humans as ritual imitation of the sexual relations on the divine plane designed to promote fertility, or at least a symbolic representation or evocation of such sexual relations. A major cornerstone of this theory has involved the way the relations between lines 1–29 and 30–76 have been construed: the first has ritual, and the second has sexual relations, and therefore the text as a whole witnesses to sexual relations in the cult. To unpack this assumption and the evidence for it, the first two sections examine the case for sexual relations in lines 1–29 and their role in lines 30–76, while the last two sections focus on the nature of the textual relations between lines 1–29 and 30–76. To anticipate the findings of this chapter, it is evident that the material shared between these two major sections does not include the theme of sexual relations, as sacred marriage is entirely lacking in the rituals of the text. Sexual relations do appear in the longer narrative section, but there it plays a relatively subordinate role to the larger theme of the feast for the Goodly Gods. Sexual relations in this text represent background information only in the narrative for the main theme named in both the rituals and the narrative. In short, "sacred marriage" is not the concern or context for this text.

1. IS THERE A "SACRED MARRIAGE" IN 1.23?

At this point in Ugaritic studies, recent evaluations are quite split over the question about whether a sacred marriage or *hieros gamos* is expressed in, or underlies, this text. A number of scholars would see "sacred marriage" (*hieros gamos*) as a fundamental feature in both the ritual and narrative of this text. De Moor (1972:2.18; 1987:117–18) would identify in this "sacred marriage" the

-127-

king as El, Athirat as the queen, and Anat as a high priestess (probably a princess). Anat as a high priestess may be left out of the question, since it is unclear that the text attests to either Anat or a high priestess. Lipiński (1986:211) has also defended the possibility of a sacred marriage ritual within 1.23, on the basis of the narrative in lines 30–76. In his view, sexual relations could have been actually performed. Wyatt (1996:216–68; 1998:324–25; 2002:325) has reaffirmed this view of the text. He stresses "the royal dimension" of this *hieros gamos* in lines 30–76. Referring to the text as a *hieros gamos*, Wyatt comments (1998:325; Wyatt's italics):

> It is here that I think that the *royal* dimension is important. A mythic paradigm is established here which is used to convey basic notions about the concern for the chief deity for the created order, and the implicit identification of his offspring with kings becomes the means whereby royal duties are represented as actualizing the theological programme.

One would hardly dispute the royal significance underlying this text, in view of the mention of royal participants in line 7. At the same time, it may be noted that the recognition of an important royal dimension does not require seeing "sacred marriage" in 1.23.

In contrast, other commentators (Pardee 1997b:275; Gulde 1998:328–30) at most entertain a more restricted notion of "sacred marriage" (less as an actual act of ritual sexual relations and more as an expression of social well-being). Indeed, many scholars are highly critical of seeing "sacred marriage" in this text. Trujillo (1973:146) observes: "there is no evidence to prove that the recitation of CTA 23: 30ff. was enacted in any way." Tsumura (1999:234–36) has also reviewed the question. He notes that the single figure of the queen could not represent the two women in a *hieros gamos*. Tsumura (1999:236) concludes: "The sexual union between El and the two women is mentioned euphemistically, and the result of that 'union', i.e. the 'birth' of the Good Gods (*'ilm n'mm*), is emphasized more than the 'union' itself." Lapinkivi (2004:2) likewise comments: "the extant mythological texts do not provide confirmation for sacred marriage." Other scholars, such as Frevel (1995:598–618) and Marsman (2003:528–31),[1] have also noted difficulties with the theory of sacred marriage in this text.

More recent discussions of myths and rituals in the ancient Near Eastern world indicate that the correspondences that would have seemed obvious a generation or two ago are now highly controverted. Well before Gaster's heyday, it was commonly assumed in many circles of classical and Near Eastern studies that myth was part of ritual, that it was the spoken part of the acted rite (see the

---

1. Marsman does remain open to the idea of 1.23 "as a *divine* marriage which was symbolically re-enacted in the cult" (Marsman's italics).

survey in Versnel 1990:28–41). By the 1960s, this view came in for strong criticism in the fields of classics and anthropology. The difficulty lies not only in the particulars upon which the theory was based, but also in the necessary assumption that myth generally was to be seen as part of some ritual.[2] Near Eastern specialists have strongly criticized the "myth and ritual" approach (see Xella 1973:18–22, 83–85, with citations), and it has largely passed from the field.

Oden (1979:49) noted just how exceptional 1.23 was relative to other myths. It is precisely because 1.23 shows ritual along with myth that one may suspect some relations between the myth and ritual in this text; in contrast, the myths with no ritual should be viewed as having no ritual counterpart. In Oden's words, "one cannot argue from the particular [here 1.23] to the general [myths with no ritual] and therefore conclude that all Ugaritic myths are the libretti of various cultic productions." As a result, Walls (2001:4) could list the "myth and ritual" interpretations among the interpretive approaches now considered outdated. As reflected in the citation of Wyatt's work above, the approach is not totally dead in the ancient Near Eastern field, and there have been occasional efforts to resuscitate some of the crucial elements of the theory (e.g., the discussion of so-called "dying and rising gods" in Mettinger 2001). Yet major components for this idea have been found to be critically lacking.[3] Among classicists, Versnel (1990) has more recently defended the contribution made by the approach. However, his version of the theory radically differs from older versions of the theory, which indicates just how unacceptable the basic tenets of the theory remain. Bell (1997:3–22, esp. 7–8) has seconded several of the critical assessments in her review of Gaster's work.

Crucial to Gaster's approach to 1.23 was the corollary character presumed for the ritual and myth in the text. An important contribution to this question has been made by studies that could determine the relative priority or date of related myths and rituals. In his study of Babylonian myths and rituals pertaining to ritual combat, Livingstone (1986:150–67) was able to demonstrate that there was some correlation between the two. However, Livingstone (1986:166) goes on to comment:

> Myths did not originally belong to the rituals, and the rituals did not originally mean the myths. Since some of the myths are older it could be argued that originally the ritual had mythological meanings different from the myths that require a late date, and the names of the protagonists were changed to suit different theological conditions. Nevertheless, the point remains that in

---

2. See the critical assessments of Fontenrose 1966 and Kirk 1971; see also the critically important but overlooked study of J. Z. Smith 1969, with a summary in J. Z. Smith 1978:208–39.

3. In addition to the critiques of J. Z. Smith 1969, 1978:208–39, 1989, see M. S. Smith 1998a.

the myth and ritual works many of the myths originated later than and independently of the rituals.

These comments, which pertain to a rather specific type of texts known as
explanatory works about myths and rituals, apply more broadly to ancient Near
Eastern myths. There are many myths embedded in texts that are clearly not
a libretto to any ritual as such, yet have some sort of relation to ritual.[4] The
prescription for a hangover in CAT 1.114.29–31 is prefaced by the story of El's
drunkenness ending with Astarte and Anat hunting for the ingredients for a
cure (lines 1–28). Over the broader ancient Near East,[5] we find many examples
of myth and ritual combined in a variety of ways. Some notable examples may
be mentioned. In "Enki and the World Order," the myth shifts to ritual at lines
140–154 and then reverts to myth (Averbeck 2003). The myth of the "Cow of
Sin" serves as an etiology for a ritual to facilitate childbirth (Veldhuis 1991).
An Akkadian incantation for a toothache contains only one of the many variations of the creation account (see Foster 1993:878). The main text of the Telepinu
myth (*KUB* 17.10) includes a ritual (ii 9–32) designed to appease the god's anger
(*ANET* 126–28; *COS* 1.57:151–53; see Kellerman 1986). In the complex case of the
Enuma Elish (*ANET* 60–72, 501–3; *COS* 1.111:390–402), the myth originally did not
serve in the context of the Babylonian New Year Festival (Akitu), but its recitation came to comprise an important component of the festival.[6] In this case,
the myth predated the ritual setting that used it. In all of these texts, it is clear
that the myth is not the narrative libretto to the nonmythic material; instead,
the mythic and non-mythic parts of these texts have been brought into various
sorts of textual alignment. In some cases, myths may involve no such alignment
at all but are perhaps to be regarded as ancient "classics," transmitted by scribes
thanks to the cultural values and sense of identity that the texts expressed. In
short, myths may (or may not) be brought into alignment with rituals, as well as
many other sorts of genres.

There are many instructive points here for the study of CAT 1.23. The first
that is most directly applicable is the need to make no a priori assumptions
about the relations between the myths and the rituals, apart from clear indicators of shared material. Some myths and rituals may be correlated in some
manner, and these may vary tremendously; in other cases, there may be no such

---

4. I wish to thank Dr. Beate Pongratz-Leisten for her critical questions and remarks on this
discussion.

5. For the variety of relations between Greek myths and rituals (including none at all), see Kirk
1974:66–68.

6. Enuma Elish and the first millennium *akitu*-festival lie beyond the scope of this discussion.
See Pongratz-Leisten 1994 (with bibliography); Bidmead 2002; note also Livingstone 1986:156–58.

relationship involved. Here Tsumura (1999:234) judiciously remarks: "it seems that the mythological portion (30–76) had existed originally in a separate form without any liturgical setting." Trujillo (1973:147) remarks in a similar vein: "a distinction between a 'ritual part' and a 'mythological part' of the text is useless." This is not to say that lines 30–76 stand apart from the rest of the text,[7] only that the relations between this narrative and the rest of the text are complex; they cannot be simply presumed but require a full discussion and defense (as provided further below in this chapter and developed further in the next one).

A further lesson for 1.23 concerns the possible disjunctions between the formulations of mythic materials in different parts of the text: various sections may treat the same mythic notions differently. Finally, claims about ritual cannot be based on narrative within the text; there may be no intrinsic connection between the settings of the rituals in lines 1–29 and the narrative material in lines 30–76, apart from the topics shared by lines 1–29 (in particular, lines 1–7//23–27) and lines 30–76. Although it has been claimed that lines 30–76 were at least read for the occasion of the ritual in lines 1–29 (so Trujillo 1973), even this view enjoys no support from the text.

At most, it may be said that for the scribe and the royal establishment that sponsored the transmission of this text, lines 30–76 may offer a narrative showing the worldview that underlies the ritual allusions to the same topics interspersed in lines 1–29 (lines 1–7//23–27). 1.23 is a scribally produced work, in which the scribe of the ritual rubrics added the larger mythic narrative (or, the version of the myth as known in his scribal circles). The text is reducible to neither rituals nor literary myth. Nor does the text merely juxtapose rituals with myths; instead, both rituals and myths interpenetrate one another. The work is thus not simply a scribal production that merely transmits traditional texts. It is a product of an intellectual, scribal culture (see Rochberg 2004:210–36; van der Toorn forthcoming) that could and would combine different modes of discourse, in this case rituals, myths, and mythic images, in representing more fully the realities to which these different materials referred.

Without wading any further into the long discussion about the so-called "myth and ritual" approach, I would suggest that Gaster's way of viewing textual relations tended to flatten out the reading of this text, which was the best test case for his "myth and ritual" theory. Moreover, it was unfortunate that Gaster switched to a springtime ritual setting, evidently driven largely by the misunderstanding of the "kid in its mother's milk" in line 14. Gaster's contri-

---

7. Trujillo also comments (1973:18), "The whole text is rather a ritual which includes prayers, hymns and readings from the mythological literature of the day which were recited during the ceremony, just as in a modern church service the ceremonies include rituals, prayers and readings from the sacred books."

bution remains, nonetheless, if only because there is no denying that 1.23 contains both ritual actions and narrative. In this vein, Cutler and Macdonald (1982) could argue for the text as a ritual and myth text designed to avert famine. Later, Ratner and Zuckerman (1986:34) could characterize the text as an "annotated choreography." There remains some merit to Gaster's ritual observations, especially concerning firstfruits, but it is to be noted that his far-ranging comparisons have been jettisoned in favor of the more local parallels, especially within the Ugaritic literature and then within the West Semitic world.

The critical view taken here is borne out by studies of "sacred marriage" (*hieros gamos*) in the wider ancient world. J. S. Cooper (1993:82) notes that "*hieros gamos*" applied to the marriage of Zeus and Hera, and as observed by B. Pongratz-Leisten (forthcoming), the expression was also used to describe the union between Demeter and the mortal Jason (Homer, *Odyssey* 5.125–128). Classicists generalized the term to refer to marriages between deities or between gods and humans, especially when ritually enacted. In his famous work, *The Golden Bough*, Sir James George Frazer (1890) extended the term to cover a variety of sexual acts in myths and rituals designed to promote fertility. Later this notion was applied by the "myth and ritual" school to a number of ancient Near Eastern texts.

In Assyriology today, "sacred marriage" refers to the ritual enactment of marriage involving a deity, with either a human or divine partner. It is known from the Early Dynastic period down to the first millennium (for surveys, see Renger 1972–75; Frayne 1985; Cooper 1993; Pongratz-Leisten 2000; Lapinkivi 2004; see also Nissinen 2001). The "classical sacred marriage" (Cooper 1993:84–87) involved sexual relations between kings of Ur and Isin and the goddess Inanna represented by an unnamed human (a priestess?). In general, scholars identify two sorts of "sacred marriage," the first between a deity and a human (ritually played out with sexual relations), and the second between deities (ritually played out by sexual relations imagined between deities and paralleled by sexual relations between corresponding humans). In her work on sacred marriage, Pongratz-Leisten (forthcoming) speaks of hierogamy (the union between a goddess and a king) and theogamy (union between a god and a goddess). From the second millennium onwards, the latter predominates; it is unclear that the former is attested in this period (Lapinkivi 2004:2).

Sacred marriage ritual (hierogamy) in Sumerian texts has been long thought to involve sexual relations between the king and a female representing the goddess, customarily Inanna, which helps to engender fertility of the land (Kramer 1969; Jacobsen 1976:23–24).[8] Doubts have been expressed as to whether actual

---

8. For a full treatment of scholarly views, with detailed discussion and bibliography, see Lapinkivi 2004. The texts used as "evidence" in Lapinkivi's study extend well beyond the ancient Near East. Their relationship to the ancient Near Eastern material is controversial.

sexual relations are present in either type (see Pongratz-Leisten 2000; Lapinkivi 2004:69, 243). More recently other theories have been forwarded for Mesopotamian sacred marriage. Hallo (1987) focuses on the royal setting of the ritual and argues that the purpose of the ritual was to secure a royal heir. Cooper (1993:90; Cooper's italics) takes his cue from a hymn (Ishmedagan K) that indicates the reason for the ritual: "so that justice would be done for the numerous people … so that the person with violent intentions [*would not succeed*] … Enlil and Ninlil gave Ishmedagan, the perpetual provider … as a spouse." Responsibility for maintaining the care and feeding of the gods follows. The point is to secure royal legitimacy and divine blessings (including fertility) and to reaffirm human obligations to the deities. According to Cooper, the Mesopotamian texts show no particular emphasis on agricultural fertility.

West Semitic material offers a limited picture of sacred marriage. In his discussion of the ritual of the installation of the *entu*-priestess, Fleming (1992:191) notes the lack of sexual aspects in the Emar sacred marriage ritual (Emar 369), and it is evident that there is no human couple replicating a divine couple in an act of procreative fertility. Moreover, Fleming suggests that the features of marriage appear in the ritual simply "because of the nature of the office." In this context, marriage evidently serves as means to express the relationship established between the god and his priestess (see futher Lapinkivi 2004:9–10).

From this discussion of "sacred marriage," it is evident that Frazer's model has dominated the discussion despite the departures from his model in the attested texts. What is to be made of marriage motifs in various ritual texts? Nissinen (2001:129) rightly asks: "If the concept of 'sacred marriage' is all too burdened with post-Frazerian connotations, as it seems, could we just talk about 'rituals and poetry of divine love'?" Cooper's view of the issue has much to recommend it: sacred marriage is expressive of the hope and desire for societal well-being, which includes agricultural fertility. Operating with this sort of understanding, the field may continue to employ the term "sacred marriage," yet it is equally clear that this notion is far removed from what its older proponents had in mind. Moreover, as more recent commentators observe, the understanding of such "marriage" may well vary in the ancient Near East.

To begin a parsing of the case for sacred marriage in 1.23, it is necessary first to examine the case for ritual marriage in the rituals of lines 1–29. (The next section examines the basis for the argument that the mythological sexual relations in lines 30–76 reflect sacred marriage in this text.) In lines 1–29, there is not a shred of evidence for sacred marriage. There is no priestess in the text, a feature of several sacred marriage texts mentioned above. De Moor seems aware of this difficulty in suggesting that a priestess be assumed in 1.23.

What might evidence for sacred marriage look like in Ugaritic? It might be argued, with Marsman (2003:528–31), that 1.132.1–3 mentions the goddess

Pidray in what may be understood as a sexual context pointing to some sort of "sacred marriage": *btš‘ ‘šrh trbd ‘rš pdry bšt mlk*, "on the nineteenth of the month you are to prepare the bed of Pidray with the king's bed-covers."[9] Following several sections of sacrifices, the final ritual of the last day ends in lines 25–26 with the instructions: "before nightfall, you will remove the bed" (*pn ll tn‘r ‘rš*; Pardee 2002:98–99; for the verb form and meaning, see Dietrich and Mayer 1996:174). Some commentators interpret this text as a reference to "sacred marriage" involving Pidray and the king (Dijkstra 1994:121), although the context affords little insight into the precise nature of this aspect of the ritual (Pardee 2002:96). It could have taken place without any human sexual act.

The evidence from other Syrian sources dating roughly to the same period as 1.132 is equally inconclusive. The ritual of the installation of the *entu*-priestess at Emar (Emar 369.73) mentions "her place of repose" or "bedchamber" (*ur-ši-ša*; Fleming 1992:116; Pentiuc 2001:190–91). In this connection, Fleming observes that the *bit erši*, "bedroom," is a regular feature of Mesopotamian palaces and temples, mostly in the first millennium, but also once at Ugarit (RS 17.28.5 in *PRU* IV, 109). Whatever one is to make of 1.132.1–3, there is no evidence of this sort even suggesting a hint of sacred marriage in the rituals of 1.23.1–29. Even the proponents of this view today offer no specific evidence. In sum, it appears best to conclude that lines 1–29 do not involve a sacred marriage. Yet what of lines 30–76, where sexual relations are mentioned?

2. Is There a Cult Drama of Sexual Relations behind Lines 30–76?

Can or should sacred marriage be seen behind the mythic narrative of 1.23.30–76? Is there a "cult drama" or a "ritual pantomime" presupposed here? Of recent authors, de Moor and Lipiński are perhaps the clearest exponents of this idea. As for lines 30–76, the situation is stated straightforwardly by Segert (1986:219): "No connection with the ritual action is indicated." Tsumura (1973:170–71; 1999:234) gives two reasons for his view that the myth of lines 30–76 was independent of, and antecedent to, the rituals of lines 1–29. First, apart from the *'ilm n‘mm* and the titles of the goddess (lines 23–24, 58–59, 61), the deities of the text appear either in the ritual portion or in the longer mythological portion of lines 30–76, but not both. Second, some key words of the ritual portion (e.g., *'iqr'a/'iqr'an* in lines 1, 23; *šrm* in line 22) do not appear in the mythological portion of lines 30–76. At the same time, scholars recognize that the two major portions of 1.23 share a number of key terms (e.g., *mdbr*, "food" and "wine,"

---

9. Pardee 2002:98. See also Dietrich and Mayer 1996; Moran 1992:199 n. 11. Cf. *EA* 84:13; and texts 54 and 55 in Parpola 1987:50–52.

and the references to "seven"), as well as the main figures of the ʾilm nʿmm and the references to the goddess (in lines 23–24, 58–59, 61). Therefore, it may be argued, following Tsumura (1973), that the rituals of lines 1–29 and the narrative of lines 30–76 have been brought into some sort of alignment (discussed further in section 3 below). At the same time, there are several significant differences between these major parts. Given such thematic disjunctions, the sexual relations in the mythic narrative need not point to implicit sexual relations in the rituals of lines 1–29.

This problem of suspecting ritual action behind the mythic narrative without evidence is a long-standing one in the study of ancient Near Eastern rituals and myths. In his work on Babylonian conflict myths and rituals that clearly show related material, Livingstone (1986:167) asks the very germane question (from which the title of this section derives), is it "cult drama or not?":

> Can the rituals be seen in relation to the myths as what Zimmern called "mimetic", Pallis "religious drama", and Jacobsen "cult drama"? These writers envision a drama in which the victorious gods were represented by people and the defeated gods by animals or objects. This is consistently the principle of the interpretations in the works but whether it is drama which is involved is doubtful.

There are many myths embedded in texts that are clearly not a libretto to any ritual as such. Several were noted in the discussion in section 1 of this chapter (such as 1.114). In these cases, it is clear that the myth is not the narrative libretto to the nonmythic material, only that the mythic and nonmythic have been brought into alignment. And of course, myths may have no such context at all. In many cases, these stand without any sort of context. These would appear to be ancient "classics," transmitted by scribes thanks to the cultural values and identity that they express. In short, myths may (or may not) be brought into alignment with rituals, as well as many other sorts of genres. In the case of 1.23, the calibration relates primarily to the Goodly Gods in the outback.

Livingstone (1986:167) offers some further considerations about a complex group of works known as Mesopotamian explanatory texts:

> Individual actions in, or details of, a ritual are equated with what can only be regarded as a whole myth. To suppose that the ritual enacted myth one would have to imagine that whole myths were repeatedly acted in widely differing minute actions of the ritual. One would also have to imagine that the same myth was enacted in different ways in the same ritual. These considerations show that religious or cult drama in the sense of a conscious enactment of the myth is not involved.

Livingstone's cautionary remarks help to guard against two tendencies in the treatment of 1.23. The first is to see ritual behind lines 30–76. The second is to assume a rather close correspondence between ritual components in lines 1–29 and the mythic narrative in 30–76. There is no doubt the *'ilm n'mm* are central to both sections of the text, and it is also evident that the movement from *mdbr* to the meal in the sown, as it were, is the conceptual goal or end-point of both sections. Some of the same deities are mentioned, certainly Shapshu and arguably Athirat. However, there is no real evidence for "sacred marriage," in the sense of roles acted out by the king and queen (so Tsumura 1999:236).

3. Parallels between 1–29 and 30–76

The relative unimportance of sexual relations in 1.23 can be seen better through an examination of the many correspondences between lines 1–29 and 30–76 that scholars have noted. The mention of the *'ilm n'mm* themselves in both sections initially led scholars in this direction. More recently Xella (1973:79–80) offered a considerable list of textual correspondences between lines 1–29 and 30–76. To Xella's list Tsevat (1978:25*) added a correlation between line 24 and lines 59//61.

The following is largely a compilation of the observations of these scholars, with the added feature of the subdivision of lines 30–76 into lines 29–51 and lines 52–76 (which will be justified below):

PART 1		PART 2
Lines 1–29		Lines 30–76
	A: lines 29–51 Background to the birth of the gods	B: lines 52–76 Birth of the gods and their hunger
Section 1		
Lines 1–7		
Lines 1–2 *'ilm n'mm*		Line 60 *'ilm n'mm*
Line 4 *mdbr*		Lines 65, 67–68 *mdbr*
Lines 6–7 Invitation to the feast		Lines 71–76 Feast
Section 2, lines 8–11		
Lines 8–9 Image of staff of Mot (death)	Line 37 Image of staff of El (life)	

Lines 9–11 Image of the summer produce	Lines 50, 55 (reconstructed) Image of the summer fruit: *lrmn* (see also lines 25–26)

Section 3, line 12

Line 12 Song seven times	

Section 4, lines 13–15

Line 13 (also line 28) "the field…"	Lines 68, 73 "the field"

Line 15 ʾ*agn*	Line 31 ʾ*agn*	

Section 5, line 16

The hunt of the goddess *tlkm rḥmy wtṣd*	Lines 67–69 The hunt of the gods ʾ*ilm nʿmm ttlkn šd* *tṣdn pʾat mdbr*

Section 6, lines 19–20

Section 7, lines 21–22

Section 8, lines 23–27

Lines 23–24	Lines 58–59
…ʾ*ilm nʿmm* [ʾ*agzr ym bn*] *ym* *ynqm bʾap zd* ʾ*atrt*	…[ʾ*i*]*lm nʿmm* ʾ*agzr ym bn ym* *ynqm bʾap dd*
	Lines 60–61 …ʾ*ilm nʿmm* ʾ*agzr ym bn ym* *ynqm bʾap dd*
	Line 63 *gzr*
Line 25 Shapshu	Line 54 offering to Shapshu
Line 26 Summer fruit: *ǵnbm*	Lines 74, 76 wine (produce from *ǵnbm*)

Section 9, lines 28–29

The comparison would suggest that the textual end-point or goal of both lines 1–29 and 30–76 is the food for the ʾilm nʿmm in the *mdbr*, as noted by Hettema (1989–90:92), among others. It is particularly evident that what the two sections share is concentrated in the second section of lines 30–76, specifically lines 52–76. The implications of this observation can be seen better by focusing on the parallels between lines 1–29 and 52–76. Indeed, the parallel columns of correspondences shown above do not distinguish between general thematic and verbal similarities, on the one hand, and, on the other hand, more specific points of thematic contact between the ritual material and the narrative. The latter may be shown in parallel columns:

Lines 1–2 ʾilm nʿmm	Line 60 ʾilm nʿmm
Line 4 mdbr	Lines 65, 67–68 mdbr
Lines 6–7 Invitation to ʾilm nʿmm to the feast	Lines 71–76 Feast of the ʾilm nʿmm
Line 13 (also line 28) "the field…"	Lines 68, 73 "the field"
Line 16 The hunt of the goddess tlkm rḥmy wtṣd	Lines 67–68 The hunt of the gods ʾilm nʿmm ttlkn šd tṣdn pʾat mdbr
Lines 23–24 … ʾilm nʿmm [ʾagzr ym bn] ym ynqm bʾap zd ʾaṯrt	Lines 58–59 …[ʾi]lm nʿmm ʾagzr ym bn ym ynqm bʾap ḏd
	Lines 60–61 … ʾilm nʿmm ʾagzr ym bn ym ynqm bʾap ḏd
	Line 63 gzr

Line 25	Line 54
Shapshu	offering to Shapshu
Line 26	Lines 74–76
Summer fruit: *ǵnbm*	wine (produce from *ǵnbm*)

This set of parallel columns indicates that the ritual material, where it can be correlated with the narrative of lines 30–76, focuses on lines 54–76, in other words, that which pertains to *'ilm n'mm* and their feast. We may note also that the connections are not only between rituals and myths. The segment in line 16 connecting to lines 67–68 is mythic in nature, and not ritual.

The connections between the ritual material in lines 1–29 and the narrative of lines 30–76 are otherwise verbal connections or thematic associations of a relatively secondary order. Viewed in this light, the narrative material in lines 30–54, including the description of sexual relations, appears to serve as background material to the presentation of the *'ilm n'mm* in lines 55–76. This view of lines 30–76 also comports with the subdivision made above between lines 29–51 and lines 52–76. On the whole, lines 1–29 show the feast of the *'ilm n'mm* as its major ritual action (lines 1–7//23–27), and the narrative of lines 30–76 manifests the same thematic trajectory. In this sense, lines 1–7 serve as a prelude to the entire text, invoking a sacrificial offering, whose narrative representation in turn reaches its culmination in lines 70–76. In short, the text begins ritually where it ends mythically. This analysis is relevant to the issue of "sacred marriage" in this text, as it demonstrates that the sexual relations, where they appear at all, play a subordinate role to its main theme. "Sacred marriage," as it appears only in the narrative and not in the rituals, plays a relatively minor role in the overarching theme of the text.

4. Homology of Divine and Human Roles

Instead of seeing ritual roles played out sexually or otherwise, one might think in terms of self-identifications or homologies in royal roles, human and divine. The king and queen preside at the ritual, and they are perhaps as much observers as they are participants (see Tsumura 1999:237). Furthermore, through the roles exercised by El and Athirat in the mythic materials, the human royal couple may convey something of their own roles and powers in the world. One may entertain the following sorts of correspondences between the casts of characters in the material shared in lines 1–29 and 30–76 (cf. de Moor 1987:117–18):

| The Goodly Gods | The Goodly Gods |
| The king and queen | El and Athirat wa-Rahmay (his wife/wives) |

Divine dwellings (*mṯbt ʾilm*)	Shapshu and Dawn and Dusk (El's astral family present at the ritual)
Guards (*ṯnnm*)	Guard of the sown
Guards (*ṯnnm*) and "enterers" (*ʿrbm*) giving the offering	Guard of the sown and his companion, offering food and wine

Given the explicitly shared features between some of the ritual material and the longer narrative, we might see some sort of relationship between the two, but not for the narrative representation of sexual procreation, for which there is no ritual counterpart. There is no reason to suppose that beyond what is mentioned in the ritual there is additional ritual transpiring.

Insofar as the ritual texts point to correspondences of roles, the figures in the mythic world correspond to those undertaken by their human counterparts in the ritual material. Some are indicated as having ritual roles (the presentation of the offering in lines 26–27), while others such as the king and queen are not. The human participants may have imagined that their world connects to this mythic world, but not simply as ritual imitation. Instead, the text offers a representation of an imagined divine reality in which the situation on the ground, as conceived by the royal elite, is reflected. Given the connections between lines 1–29 and 30–76, the ritual material thematically connects to the mythic world that is conjured up. In other words, the narrative of lines 30–76 *evokes* the mythic landscape *invoked* by the ritual material of lines 1–29.

At the same time, the sexual participation of the human in the divine does not appear to be the end-point or trajectory of the mythic world. There are sexual relationships in both sections of 1.23, but not sets of sexual relations ritually related to one another. Instead, as noted above, the trajectory of both major parts of the text is the banquet in the sown. What is celebrated in both the rituals and the mythic narratives is agricultural fertility. Neither the rituals nor the mythic narrative in 1.23 provide evidence for "sacred marriage" as a ritual practice. Indeed, the narrative containing the divine sexual acts belongs to the backdrop of what the text, in both its rituals and narratives, is moving toward, namely, the gods who are hungry and need to be satisfied with the feast. Accordingly, it is evident that the sexual acts in the narrative are not the focus of 1.23, and the absence of any referent to them in the ritual material comports with this conclusion. In other words, the text is not primarily concerned with sexual relations that issue in the birth of the Goodly Gods; the text is about the food for these gods. The absence of any referent to sexual relations or the accoutrements to facilitate it from the ritual material in lines 1–29 supports this view.

A look at the ritual for clues about its setting may benefit from the anthropology of sacrificial ritual. Ritual studies have turned to the larger social context in which ritual is embedded in order to ascertain the significance of its symbols.[10] We may address some features of the rituals and myths in 1.23 to ascertain its symbolic meanings in the context of ancient Ugaritic society, in particular for the royal circles that patronized this text. In 1.23, we do not see ritual marriage. Instead, we see the feast at the center of both the rituals and myths. With the feast lying at the heart of both the rituals and the long mythic narrative, eating functions as both the locus for and expression of the system of prosperity offered by the royal scheme of reality. In his study of food in Thai village rites, Arnold (2000:18) offers comments on eating applicable to 1.23: "Not only is eating a physical act of replenishing the human body, but a mode of meaningfully orienting oneself within a total worldview.... food came into being 'to sustain life and religion'." Or, in the words of Macdonald (2000:28), "Food and the consumption of food speak, on the symbolic level, of the negotiation of social and cosmic relationships."

With the meal at the center of both the rituals and myths, the participants alluded to in the rituals of lines 1–29 are constructed as parties analogous and ritually connected to the divinities mentioned in both these rituals and the myth of lines 64–76. The human participants understand their world as ritually signaled in lines 1–29 to be also the world narrated in lines 30–76 (or at least the two are closely related). The divine forces that operate in the rituals and the narrative are much the same. Allman (2000), in his ritual analysis of the Christian Eucharist, stresses the process of identification of the ritual participants and the figures of the divine story. Applied to 1.23, this notion would suggest that, to some degree, the ritual participants in their functions and identities do connect with their divine counterparts, in this case the royal family with their divine patrons, El and his astral family. The power and nature of the human royalty are effectual insofar as they ritually share or participate in the power and nature of the divine beneficial powers that are evoked in the narrative.

The presentation of food in 1.23 is figured within the context of both stasis and movement of the ritual and mythic figures. Ritual stasis suggested by the enthronement of Mot (line 8) and the divine dwellings (line 19) contrasts with the ritual movement evidenced by the procession (*hlkm*, in line 26); we may also note the movement involved in the hunting of the goddess (line 16). The mythic narrative of lines 30–76 also suggests stasis, in the meeting of El and his females, as well as movement, in the form of the wives and the *'ilm n'mm* moving out beyond the sown and back. In his ritual analysis, Prattis (2001:41–42) emphasizes

---

10. This development has taken place in part as a reaction to Fritz Staal's view of ritual as lacking symbolic meaning apart from its own performance (1978, 1989). For a discussion of Staal with a critique, see Harris 1997; note also Bell 1992:121–22, 1997:71.

the role of movement and stasis in molding ritual participants in the image and likeness of the symbols expressed in ritual:

> The importance of metaphor, the process of connotation and analogy, is that it enables a symbolic concept to register with the mind and senses. As metaphorical meaning is imparted to symbol by our minds in the first place, there is then an engagement of the mind's products with the mind's sensibilities. As I intend to demonstrate, when this engagement occurs within well defined, and orchestrated, ritual sequences that are socially supported, an inordinate impetus for behavioral transformation is engineered.

In the case of 1.23, we do not have access to live performance, and the specifics of the ritual that Prattis studies lie well beyond the textual record of 1.23. How the rituals and myths informed its human patrons can only be inferred. We might suppose that its ritual and mythic behaviors direct the royal participants' attention and action toward the deities named or alluded to in the rituals. As suggested above, we may guess what this ritual process effects upon its human participants, in particular to act analogously to deities and be similar to them. Between the invocations (lines 1, 23), recitation and antiphonal response (line 12), and song (lines 14, 29), oral dimensions of ritual are evident; these provide for the recitation of divine activity in the hearing of the human participants. The mythic narrative, too, involves speech of deities of various sorts, and this narrative would at least express what was being understood for those parts of the ritual that thematically connects with the longer narrative of lines 30–76.

There is a great deal about the sacrificial ritual of 1.23 that goes unmentioned. We do get some reference to color in lines 21–22, apparently with respect to the singers; these seem to signal the royal character of the ritual proceedings. We also get a sense of taste from the alimentary elements of the ritual in lines 6 and 14 and as implied by the hunt of line 16. Otherwise, our ability to decode the text remains at a rather general level. Yet even in this absence of evidence, there may lay a clue about the effect of the rituals and myths. Perhaps the text expresses a general experience of the meal in order to make a broad point about the production of food in the larger environment. We might ask whether the identification of both king and queen also serves a function to generalize the meaning of the ritual across gender lines. In the end, even as the rituals and the myths together generate and express a symbolic worldview in which the human patrons participate, a good deal of the larger setting would seem to lie beyond our recovery at this point.

At this point, we stand at a great distance from the approach taken by the "myth and ritual" school. The "myth and ritual" approach (with the linkage implied by the conjunction "and") provided an interpretational means undeterred by a lack of evidence as well as a lack of coherence in specific examples.

In the case of 1.23, there is no evidence for ritual sexual relations or even for the sort of royal ideology imagined by Wyatt and others. At the same time, Wyatt has rightly emphasized the royal dimension of this text, as well as the symbolic universe generated by this text, questions probed further in the following chapter. In order to appreciate the complexity of the myths and rituals of 1.23, a closer examination of the intersections between the myths and the rituals is required. In the next and final chapter, more details about the construction of 1.23 are offered, with the goal of offering further observations about the text's larger meanings.

5

Intersecting Genres and Cultural Codes

As we observed in the brief history of scholarship in chapter 1, commentators have noted the rare combination of myth and ritual in this text. At the same time, it has been shown in chapters 2 and 3 that the text involves not simply myth and ritual but more precisely myths and rituals as well as myth and mythic images within the ritual sections. Chapter 4 discusses the textual relations between the ritual materials in lines 1–29 and the mythic narrative in lines 30–76. It was observed that there are connections—with differences—further between the mythic material embedded in lines 1–29 and the mythic narrative in lines 30–76. This chapter further probes the nature of the relations between the multiple myths narrated or alluded to in connection with the various rituals (with what might perhaps be called "mythic abbreviations"). Following up this examination, an effort is made in this chapter to examine the settings of these myths and rituals and their larger construction of reality, which are presented in a series of cultural-religious oppositions. As in chapter 4, this discussion draws from the fields of ancient Near Eastern studies and anthropology, especially ritual studies.

1. The Rituals and Myths

As noted in the introduction in chapter 1, the text does not consist simply of two parts, ritual actions (lines 1–29) and mythic narrative (lines 30–76). Within lines 1–29, there are arguably references to three mythic narratives or mythic images.

"Myths"

The first is a picture of Mot as a destructive force sheared of his power (lines 8–11). In terms of scribal lines, it is a self-standing subunit within the ritual actions of lines 1–29. It is noted above that this could be a ritual rubric that prescribes Mot's pruning and binding, but in broad terms it still relates in narrative order a plot about the god.

The second piece of mythic information, appearing in line 16, concerns the goddess Rahmay (evidently called Athirat wa-Rahmay in lines 13 and 28). The goddess in 1.23.16 hunts for game, which would figure as the food on the divine plane corresponding to the food prepared in the ritual on the human plane. For this understanding, one could appeal to 1.114.23–28, where goddesses go hunting and return, possibly with some of the materials that figure in the cure for a hangover. In this case, we have an instance of the mythic description of the hunt by the goddesses corresponding to the material used on the human plane. In short, 1.23 contains two mythic presentations about the *mdbr* as it pertains to food: one where food provision is achieved through hunting (line 16) and a second about food lacking (lines 67–69). As noted in chapter 3, this connection between sections lies not between rituals and myths, but between two myths. The mythic segments in line 16 and in lines 67–68 apply two verbs of the hunt to divinities. The complexity in interpreting 1.23 therefore does not remain as the level of noting similarities and differences between myths and rituals. There is a further level of complexity involving the relationships between the pieces of myth and mythic images in the text. The mythic image of line 16 seems to relate inversely to the larger mythic narrative of lines 30–76: the beneficial goddess goes out to the outback from the sown and returns presumably with game, while the Goodly Gods lacking food in the outback move to the sown to receive food. Despite this interesting parallel, the rest of the unit of lines 16–18 provides little clear information, so that no firm conclusion can be reached on the further significance of this mythic evocation.

A third mythic piece appears in the description of the Goodly Gods, as embedded in their titles (lines 1, 23–24). Assuming the correctness of their reconstruction based on lines 58–59 and 61, lines 23–24 acknowledge the goddess who suckles these gods at their birth. The story of their birth is known from the longer narrative of lines 30–76, so it may be thought that the invocation of the gods in lines 23–24 is designed to evoke this mythic world of lines 30–76. If this reasoning is correct, the result in lines 1–29 is a series of ritual actions joined to the evocation of three myths and mythic images that in turn have a connection to the larger narrative of lines 30–76.

LINKAGES BETWEEN "MYTHS" AND "RITUALS"

The linkage between the three mythic evocations and the ritual actions vary within lines 1–29. As the scribal lines indicate, the first myth, recited about Mot, is self-standing (lines 8–11). The second myth, about Athirat, appears at least once (line 16) and arguably three times, each time followed by ritual actions (lines 13–15, 16–18, 28–29). The third, concerning the Goodly Gods suckled by the goddess Athirat, is embedded within the ritual invocation (lines

23–27). The second and third of these three are related to the rituals to which they are textually tied. In the case of the first, regarding Mot, it may be thought that, from its place within the larger group of ritual actions, it is to be conceptualized within the ritual whole of the text. It would seem from the repetition of the invocation of lines 1–7 repeated in lines 23–27 and from the repetition of line 13 in line 28, that lines 1–29 should be read as some sort of ritual whole, with the various pieces mentioned in between fitting in different ways into the overarching theme of the feast of the Goodly Gods. Accordingly, it may be speculated that the evocations of the three myths somehow belong together.

The combination of various ritual actions and mythic images indicates that rituals are highly complex in their performance, or at least in their composition as we presently have it. In addition, it was noted in chapter 2 that the rituals are further complex, insofar as they do not always consist only of actions as such. As seen above, it is true that there are actions taken; these include invocation (or better, invitation), lines 1–2, 23–24; instructions for offerings (lines 3–4); invitation to divinities to consume offerings (line 6); greetings to ritual participants (lines 7, 26–27); instruction for performance of song (line 12 and probably line 29); instruction for sacrifice prepared (lines 14–15) and presented (line 27). At the same time, it is true that the ritual section embeds narrative (line 16). It also shows a different sort of ritual action, namely, observation on the part of the participants. In lines 25–26, there is no ritual action in the usual sense, but the ritual acknowledgment of Shapshu's aid to the ʾilm nʿmm, perhaps in its effects on the summer fruit (ǵnbm). Accordingly, ritual actions are hardly simply actions taken but include recitation of narrative as well as stated observations. It is arguable that lines 8–11 could be understood in a similar manner, if they are ritual and not simply a recited narrative as entertained above. Lines 8–9 do not sound like an instruction for a ritual action, but a ritual recitation concerning Mot's power; it is followed by what could be either a ritual action, namely, the expression of a wish for the god to be pruned, bound, and felled, or a further narrative about Mot. In either case, the tricolon of lines 8–9, if it is a part of ritual, would be a recited description about Mot, perhaps similar to the ritual mention of Shapshu in lines 25–26.

To offer some sort of picture of how the embedded narratives and ritual acknowledgments hang together with the ritual actions, a quick review of the sections may be helpful. The initial ritual section (lines 1–7) suggests a setting of an offering of food and wine made to the ʾilm nʿ[mm]. The second section (lines 8–11) evokes a picture of the transition from the power of Mot to a time of Mot shorn of his power. It is speculated in chapter 2 that this would be the fall interchange period between the dry and rainy seasons (the term is borrowed from Fitzgerald 2002). In addition, lines 9–11 use the language of viticulture to express this destruction of Death; such language would be particularly suitable to the late summer. When viewed *in tandem*, these first two ritual sections are thematic opposites: the first (lines 1–7) invites the destructive gods into the feast, while the second (lines 8–11) sheers and fells the deadly god. The two sections offer a thematic opposition: the destructive gods invited to celebrate life versus death shorn of life.

The third section (line 12) and the fourth (lines 13–15) offer a little information about their setting. The third section (line 12) indicates ritual song to be performed seven times. The fourth section (lines 13–15) provides what looks like the rubric of a song (line 13) as well as a (partial) recipe made seven times. The reference to the field of the gods suggests a counterbalancing of the beneficial gods in the sown in position to the destructive gods of the outback. The fifth section (lines 16–18) is too unclear to offer much help in determining the larger ritual setting. We seem to have a recitation about the goddess hunting, but it is difficult to add more to the picture from this section. The sixth section (lines 19–20) is arguably more helpful. It seems that the "dwellings of the gods" (line 19) points to the presence of the gods in general terms. This would appear to follow up the reference to the beneficial deities of the fourth section (lines 13–15). Following their invitation to the *ʾilm n*[*mm*] in lines 1–2, the human parties conduct ritual song and offerings in sections 3 (line 12) and 4 (lines 13–15). Then the human participants acknowledge the provisions of the goddess's hunt in the fifth section (lines 16–18), and in the sixth section (lines 19–20) they implicitly acknowledge deities, in addition to the *ʾilm nʿmm*.

To my mind, these would be the beneficial gods who belong to the ritual setting of the "sown." As in lines 52–76, these gods are not named or figure explicitly in the text, although many scholars would identify the general referent as Shapshu and the stars, in other words El's astral family (M. S. Smith 2001:61–65). The focus falls in both the rituals and the long narrative myth on the *ʾilm nʿmm* entering into the sown. However, based on the family model worked out by Schloen (1993), the holders of the dwellings in line 19 would be the gods at home in the sown, the home of human activity, and that would be El's astral family, in particular the sun-goddess, the stars, and the affiliated figures, Shahar and Shalim. Moreover, if the connection of the *mṯbt* in line 19 with the *mṯbt* of 1.41.51 is correct (see chapter 2 for discussion), it suggests the time of the summer fruit harvest as the setting for the text. This proposal for an early fall setting fits also what is suggested about the second section (lines 8–11).

The seventh section (lines 21–22) provides little aid in determining the larger setting. It may be supposed (but little more) that this section describes the decoration for the gods' statues set in the dwellings mentioned in the preceding section 6 (lines 19–20) or decoration for the dwellings themselves. Even if neither of these proposals can be confirmed, at least they would work with the ritual context.

The eighth section (lines 23–27) shows strong connections with the first section (lines 1–7) in the invocation of the *'ilm n'mm* and of the human personnel. Between the two sections, the ritual has moved from acknowledgment of these human personnel to a recognition of their role in sacrificial offering, presumably that which is mentioned in the fourth section (in lines 14–15) and to which the fifth section (in line 16) perhaps gives mythological expression in the form of the allusion to the goddess's hunt. This point is to be underscored, for it would help to understand the relationship between the two rather different mythic pieces of line 16 as opposed to the longer presentation of the *'ilm n'mm*: though not tied to one another, the mythic allusion of line 16 perhaps offers a mythological "score" about the sacrifice to be cooked or served with the substances described in line 14 and to be offered in lines 26–27. With the eighth section, then, the ritual seems to have moved to the presentation of the offering to the *'ilm n'mm* made in the presence of both the human parties of the sown (lines 7 and 26–27) and the gods of the sown (lines 19–20). In addition, this eighth section adds a mention of the sun-goddess in connection to *ǵnbm*, which would tie well into the setting of the fall interchange period, as suggested for sections 2 and 6. The ninth section (lines 28–29) provides no help for the setting. All in all, sections 2, 6 and 8 suggest a setting in the fall interchange period.[1]

Like the rituals, the mythic evocations in lines 1–29 may be related, at least loosely, to the fall interchange period. The setting for Mot in the second section (lines 8–11) seems clear. This is a viticultural evocation of the waning of the god's power, which would suit the period of the fall interchange. The myth of the Goodly Gods evoked only references to them in lines 1 and 26–27 and is perhaps better explained by recourse to the narrative of lines 30–76, which also suggest a feast including the wine of the late summer harvest. The myth of line 16 is more difficult to situate. This is a myth (or mythic abbreviation) about the goddess going off to hunt for game; this could correspond to the food for the offering. This situation is hardly clear.

To unpack the relation of the myths and the rituals, I would like to return to some of the comments made by Livingstone (1986:166):

---

1. The meteorological specification of this time of year as "the fall interchange period" by Fitzgerald (2002) avoids the difficulty of the characterization of the New Year as the rubric for this time, as proposed by de Moor (1972). De Moor's characterization nonetheless deserves credit for locating this text within the early fall seasonal orbit. (In contrast, Barton 1934 and Gaster 1946 had located the festival in the spring.) If some sort of term from the study of Syro-Palestinian cultures needs to be applied to this time frame, it would be Sukkot (*SPUMB* 204) and not the New Year. Further discussion of this question involves a larger area of Israelite religion, which lies beyond the scope of this study.

> Myths did not originally belong to the rituals, and the rituals did not origi
> nally mean the myths. Since some of the myths are older it could be argued
> that originally the ritual had mythological meanings different from the myths
> that require a late date, and the names of the protagonists were changed to
> suit different theological conditions. Nevertheless, the point remains that in
> the myth and ritual works many of the myths originated later than and inde
> pendently of the rituals.

For Livingstone, the myths and rituals share thematic elements and may be correlated to some extent, but not in a manner imagined by Gaster and others who followed his view of myth and ritual. The evidence does not support a direct one-to-one relationship between ritual activity in lines 1–29 and the narrative in lines 30–76.

Based on the preceding description of the text's contents, 1.23 shows both narrative attached to ritual and narrative embedded within ritual and allusions to narrative as expressed in spoken ritual expressions. I would regard lines 30–76 as narrative attached to lines 1–29. Indeed, the text as a whole is a scribal representation of ritual rubrics in lines 1–29 followed by a scribal addition of the narrative in lines 30–76. The scribal addition could have been based on a practice of reciting lines 30–76 on the occasion of the ritual represented in lines 1–29, but as it stands, there are no ritual instructions for such a recitation; and so lines 30–76 were transmitted scribally together with lines 1–29. At the same time, the ritual itself incorporates ritual recitation in line 16 and arguably in lines 8–11; the latter are explicitly said to be narrative recited within the ritual. The content of lines 8–11 and of line 16 do not correspond to lines 30–76; they are self-standing narratives relative to lines 30–76. In contrast, the mythic allusion in the goddess's epithet as the one who suckles the *'ilm n'mm* in lines 23–24 likely evokes the myth in lines 30–76, or some variant of this myth, or some piece of the myth or its variant. In sum, lines 1–29 reference a ritual event or setting (lines 1–7), with recitations and actions produced for this setting (lines 8–29). Some of these, in particular lines 8–11 and 16, show what may be regarded as alternative or additional mythologies brought into alignment with the ritual of lines 1–7. Such additional mythologies nonetheless fit into the larger, overarching theme of the feast of the Goodly Gods, reflected in the final recitation of this section in lines 23–27, which returns to, and therefore identifies with, the feast event of lines 1–7. The narrative of lines 30–76 offers a fuller version of the mythic worldview underlying the ritual setting of lines 1–7//23–27. The ritual of lines 1–7//23–27 is focused on the solution to the hungrily destructive gods in lines 30–76, and the various, additional components comport with this general picture.

2. The Royal Construction of Oppositions and Integration

Having sorted through the complex relations between the various myths and rituals, we may now turn to what the text as a whole represents. At the end of his theoretical considerations of 1.23, Xella (1973:106) summarizes his understanding of the text:

> Il mito de Šḥr e Šlm, operando una mediazone tra divino e umano, pone anche il seminato sotto la tutela degli dei. Il valore essenziale del frumento e della vite, alimenti fondamentali per gli uomini come per le divinità, ha il potere di attirare queste ultime fuori del deserto, dove hanno il proprio dominio, e di inserire nel cosmo divino anche terreni che l'uomo coltiva.

As Xella's comments nicely highlight, the text sets up binary oppositions between divinity and humanity and between desert and sown. The elements of ritual food and wine achieve what Xella well calls "mediazone," what I regard as ritual "reconciliation," or perhaps better "integration."[2] We may pursue the approach taken by Xella, based on the analysis in chapters 2 and 3 (especially their excursuses), as well as ancient Near Eastern scholarship and the fields of ritual studies and anthropology of religion. In particular, we may explore three sets of oppositions encoded in the text.

The Environmental Code: *MDBR* and *MDR'* and the Fall Interchange Period

Numerous scholars who have worked on this text have noted the central importance of this contrast for lines 52–76 (Xella 1973:96–106; Wyatt 1987:380–85). The *'ilm n'mm* are expelled from the company of El's family to the *mdbr* and enter the *mdr'* only after a long period of time and only after they are permitted to do so. This narrative representation of contrasting zones is in a sense effaced, as the *'ilm n'mm* are permitted to pass from one zone to the other, if only for the duration of the sacred meal. I argued in chapter 2 that the invitation to these gods in lines 1–7 and 23–24 ritually performs or invokes what the narrative describes or evokes. In both contexts, these *'ilm n'mm*, who do not belong at home in the sown, are integrated within it for the duration of the banquet. The hunt of Rahmay in line 16 also expresses passage from one zone to another and back, in her going out to the *mdbr* to hunt for game that presumably is brought back into the *mdr'*. It might be argued that the *mdbr* as a source for game appears implicitly in line 16, yet explicitly a zone of barrenness in lines 65–68. Thus this zone is polyvalent, both positive and negative. Xella (1973:105–6) comments in

---

2. I wish to thank Dr. Beate Pongratz-Leisten for suggesting this latter term.

this vein: "il deserto è tutto il territorio non coltivato, luogo sacro e puro (*mdbr qdš*) dove operano divinità e forze che trascendono l'uomo."

In their hunt for food, the goddess and the Goodly Gods cross the boundaries of these zones. For the time of the ritual meal, expressed in both narrative and ritual action, the two zones are linked, if not integrated, via food and wine. The integration is in a sense reexpressed in terms of the experience of the seasonal cycle. The time of year when this ritual is set is the fall-interchange period, standing between the ebbing of the dry season and the onset of the rainy season. The shift in season marks an intersection between two times, which in the Baal mythology is expressed as conflict with Death. In 1.23, there is no such conflict of deities mythologized. Nor does 1.23 show any surrender to the power of Mot, as putatively expressed by the ritual in CAT 1.127.30 (see Pardee 2002:131).[3] Unlike elimination rituals, which send a domesticated animal out to the dangerous power in the outback, 1.23 invites the dangerous power of the outback into the sown. There is little effort at appeasing such power along the lines of elimination rites. Instead, the season, with its yield of produce, becomes the time when life can include the power of destruction (though perhaps in a weakened state). The approaching fall equinox likewise signals the shift from one order to another, and so the signs of the times, both on earth and in the heavens, mark a moment of plenty. The time of seasons and constellations thus expresses intersection of the temporal order, and within the context of this temporal reconciliation spatial opposition is momentarily erased.

THE CODE OF DIVINITY: THE *'ILM N'MM* AND EL'S ASTRAL FAMILY

The contrast between the two spatial zones corresponds to the contrast in types of divinities presented in the text. The literary parallelism between the two sets of births in lines 49–64 draws attention to both their similarities and their differences. Both sets of births are sired by El and the same pair of females. Accordingly, Shahar and Shalim and the *'ilm n'mm* enjoy the same origins. However, it is also clear that their natures are significantly different. The contrasting uses of the term **'db* in lines 54 and 64 suggest the difference between the order of sacrifice with the birth of Shahar and Shalim versus the unbounded monstrous appetite of the *'ilm n'mm*.

The difference in literary treatment points to the deeper contrast in divine natures, between the household of El versus the destructive power of the *'ilm*

---

3. Loretz and Janowski have argued that this is an elimination ritual; see Loretz 1985:35–57; Janowski and Wilhelm 1993; and Janowski, "Azazel," *DDD* 128–31; Wright 1987; cf. Borowski 2002c:418, with references to the pertinent literature. However, Pardee (1997:293 n. 27) has expressed doubts about this interpretation for 1.127.30.

n'mm who are not "at home" with El. His household, as represented by Shahar and Shalim as well as the reference to Shapshu, is fundamentally astral in character. In contrast, the figures of the *'ilm n'mm* are themselves neither astral nor "at home." The opposition between the two sets of pairs is in fact magnified by the literary parallelism in their presentation.

The opposition between the two pairs and what they represent is strongly marked in the text; their reconciliation in the text is not. By the same token, the reconciliation or at least meeting of the two sets of divinities seems to be indicated by the entry of the *'ilm n'mm* into the space belonging to the beneficial deities, El and his astral family. The text's emphasis falls on the *'ilm n'mm* and their entry into the sown. The other gods, in the narrative of lines 30–76, recede into the background as the *'ilm n'mm* assume center stage. This hardly means, however, that the beneficial deities no longer inhabit this cosmos. The ritual instructions seem to bear out this reading, as the "dwellings of the gods" (line 19) indicate a place for the beneficial deities in the ritual. Correspondingly, these same deities have their homes generally associated with cultivated regions, in other words the sown to which the *'ilm n'mm* gain access. For this cultic moment, the two sets of deities occupy the same ritual space. In the ritual and the main narrative, the sets of divine opposites meet.

The Alimentary Code: Herbs in Dairy and the Meat of the Hunt

Related to the two preceding codes is the code represented by the components of the meal (Xella 1973:94–96). The "coriander in milk, mint in curd" in line 14 figures in the larger meal of food and wine. As noted in chapter 2, the alimentary ingredients in line 14 do not look like a meal or an entire sacrificial offering on par with the invitation in line 6. I infer this reconstruction from what I take to be implicit to line 16 in the following, fifth section (lines 16–18): the goddess goes off to hunt and presumably returns with the game to be used as an offering, to be given to the gods invited to eat and drink in the first section (lines 1–7). Lying behind this mythological allusion in line 16, then, is the securing of meat for the food. If this is true, the fourth and fifth sections (lines 13–15 and 16–18) presuppose a meal combining the meat of the hunt and dairy products with herbs.

With this interpretation of the text, it may be said that Ginsberg's instincts about it furnishing the "Canaanite" backdrop to the biblical prohibition against "boiling a kid in its mother's milk" (Exod 23:19; 34:26; Deut 14:21) were perhaps right after all. However, the terms in which the comparison was cast were misplaced. The generation of Ginsberg and his contemporaries saw the biblical world as standing in conflict and opposition to the so-called Canaanites allegedly represented by the Ugaritic texts. Since the mid-1970s, most scholars see no general religious *Kulturkampf* between contemporaneous Canaanite and Israelite cultures based on what is related in the Ugaritic and biblical texts. Instead, this religious conflict was often a matter of inner-Israelite developments. On one level, 1.23 does provide a very general "Canaanite" (or better, West Semitic) backdrop to the biblical prohibition against "boiling a kid in its mother's milk" (Exod 23:19; 34:26; Deut 14:21), but the more immediate backdrop to these prohibitions is Israelite (cf. Gen 18:8; Deut 32:14).

Ginsberg's approach focuses on some of the elements in the meal and overlooks the potential importance of other components, not to mention the overall combination that they represent. It is the total combination of elements that may express the symbolic sensibilities of the culture. For help in this area, we may turn to anthropological research on foodways. In the words of Claude Lévi-Strauss, culinary practices show the capacity "to elaborate abstract ideas and combine them in the form of propositions" (1969:1). Mary Douglas, followed by a number of biblical scholars such as Jacob Milgrom, has developed a number of oppositional categories for biblical rules for animals included and excluded in the dietary laws of Lev 11 and Deut 14 (for full discussion and critique, see Houston 1993; Kunin 2004). Kunin's discussion applies structuralist (or, in his own terms, "neo-structuralist") categories to the dairy-meat prohibitions.[4]

One can see a similar trend among a number of French classicists who, under the influence of structuralist anthropology, have explored the symbolic cultural values expressed by cuisine in ancient Greek texts. A programmatic statement was forwarded by Marcel Detienne (1989), and, in the same volume, Jean-Pierre Vernant (1989) explored a number of correlations between culinary items and cultural perceptions (e.g., cultivated grains are to culture as wild plants are to nature). Vernant (1981, 1989) has used this approach to explore what he has called the "alimentary codes" of Greek cuisine in Hesiod's *Theogony* and *Works and Days*. The following exploration is aimed at decoding the alimentary code of 1.23 and related biblical texts in connection to their cultural settings.

Thematically, the food in 1.23 reflects, on the one hand, ingredients gathered (coriander and mint), added to other elements processed from domesticated crop (wine) and domesticated animals (milk and butter), and, on the other hand, game that derives from outside the domesticated sphere. In short, the ingredients of the meal correspond to the combination of different sorts of divine participants as well as the different zones to which they belong. CAT 1.23 expresses in a series of binary categories an overall view of divine-

---

4. As noted in the discussion in chapter 2, Kunin uncritically entertained Ginsberg's theory of Israelite rejection of Canaanite practice. Apart from this mistaken notion, Kunin pays little attention to the cultural practices involved in these codes.

human reality. The dietary components correspond to the destructive and beneficial deities, who correspond further to the *mdbr* and the *mdrʿ*. In short, the food elements in 1.23.14 and 16 are expressive of binary oppositions that come together in a manner that is reminiscent of Claude Lévi-Strauss's binary opposition between "the raw and the cooked." The correlation reflected by the alimentary elements in 1.23.14 reflects intersection between opposing realms of human experience. There is a further theoretical point expressed through the alimentary element of the wine. Arguably the most celebrated part of the meal, the wine is a prototypical product of domesticated species and human labor. This product marks the ultimately domesticate character of the entire enterprise over and against the various sources represented by the components of the food.

This picture of alimentary elements in 1.23 belongs, broadly speaking, to a larger tradition of foodways in the Ugaritic texts as well as early biblical tradition. Xella (1978) offers a fine comparative analysis of 1.17 V and Gen 18, which highlights the offerings of meat for divine guests. The combination of dairy and meat represents a further specification of the meal hospitality in Gen 18:8. Deuteronomy 32:14 also reflects the wealth of meat and dairy that the fertile environment, blessed by divinity, can produce (though with some differences in detail that are noted below). As Gaster noted, CAT 1.23 perhaps presents what Exod 23:19 and 34:26 explicitly label firstfruits (cf. Deut 14:21–22), but the Ugaritic and earlier biblical sources, on the one hand, and the legal biblical sources in Exodus, on the other hand, differ over the proper substances to be used for offering the yield of the season. In 1.23 as well as 1.17 V, Gen 18:8, and Deut 32:14, dairy and meat may be combined; for Exod 23:19 and 34:26, these are to be kept separate. There is no "Canaanite" polemic implicit to the biblical verses, as Ginsberg imagined. Instead, the biblical prohibitions are to be situated more immediately against the backdrop of the situation within ancient Israel. One further difference involves the season: 1.23 is clearly set in the fall interchange period, while the biblical prohibitions appear to be tied to the spring.

In order to identify the symbolic significance of these differences, it is necessary to include some consideration of the settings of the different texts. To begin with 1.23, the meat in this text deriving from the goddess's hunt (in line 16) is undomesticated.[5] The case of 1.23 hardly represents the general situation

---

5. As discussed in chapter 2 (specifically at line 14), it is possible that the dairy and meat elements appear together in line 14, if one were to apply to this line the finding of Heckl (2001) and Sasson (2002, 2003), who read BH *ḥlb* as "fat" rather than "milk" in the biblical prohibitions (see Guillaume 2002). If this approach were correct, then Ugaritic *ḥlb* and *ḥmʾat* in 1.23.14 would combine animal fat with some sort of dairy product. Even if the point were not to apply to Ugaritic *ḥlb*, which is a dairy product (as suggested by the internal parallelism in line 14), then the meat of

for sacrifice in ancient Ugarit. In view of the setting (outside the temple setting) and the recipients of the offering (nonbeneficial deities), this text constitutes a departure from what otherwise appears as the Ugaritic norm. Compared to the Ugaritic ritual texts, this one is decidedly different, which can be appreciated better by probing the relationship between the alimentary elements in the text and the recipients and zones named later in the text. The ingredients in 1.23 reflect a combination of ingredients gathered (coriander and mint) and processed from domesticated animals (fat/milk and butter), to be added to game (meat) that derives from outside the domesticated sphere. In short, the ingredients of the meal correspond to the combination of divine participants as well as the zones to which they belong. Like Levi-Straus's "raw and cooked," the alimentary components represent binary oppositions that come together, matching the meeting of the destructive and beneficial deities who belong to the *mdbr* and the *mdrʿ* yet meet in the ritual moment presented by 1.23. Finally, the components in lines 14–16 include neither fowl nor fish, in keeping with the theme expressed in lines 62–63, that the *ʾilm nʿmm* devour the fowl of the sky and the fish from the sea.

To highlight some further features of the dietary elements in 1.23, it may be useful to compare some biblical texts showing overlapping features in their alimentary codes. Like 1.23, Gen 18:8 combines meat and dairy products, but its alimentary code differs in one important respect. In Gen 18, it is clear that the meat derives from domesticated animals and not from the hunt. In 18:7, Abraham goes to the flock to select the animal for the meal; he is not described as hunting. Compared to 1.23, Gen 18:7–8 represent a different code, one that is expressive of the two basic sorts of alimentary yields provided by the pastoral economy of domesticated flocks, namely, their meat and their dairy products (Sarna 1989:129). Missing from this biblical passage are the animals of the hunt. Along with its general references to dairy and meat, Deut 32:14 includes honey, oil, and wine (cf. Gen 27:27–28). This verse differs from both 1.23 and Gen 18:7–8, insofar as it does not explicitly distinguish between domesticated and undomesticated animals. So it would appear that the distinction was not significant to the biblical author; therefore, even if undomesticates are involved, this distinction is not important in the expression of the verse's alimentary code. In contrast, 1.23.16 alludes to the undomesticated component of the meal.

The biblical verses prohibiting the boiling of the kid in its mother's milk (Exod 23:19; 34:26; Deut 14:21) show yet a further alimentary code. While 1.23

---

the hunt symbolized by line 16 in conjunction with the ingredients of line 14 would nonetheless point to the presence of dairy and meat at the feast. Either way, 1.23 combines domesticated and undomesticated components.

combines alimentary components from domesticated and undomesticated species, the biblical prohibitions differentiate between elements derived from domesticated sources. The alignment of alimentary offerings in the biblical verses relative to 1.23 may be traced to their different settings. The offering in 1.23 is outside in the sown, the intersection point between the steppe and urban (temple) home. The offering of firstfruits in Exod 23:19 and 34:26 is situated in a different type of venue, at "the house of Yahweh your god." Accordingly, the setting in the biblical verses is a domesticated one, and correspondingly the presentation of alimentary elements reflects an order involving domesticated species. In contrast, 1.23 reflects an intersection of domesticated and undomesticated, and this is reflected in its dietary elements. In the biblical prohibitions, there is no game from the hunt as in 1.23; rather, the meat in Exod 23:19 and 34:26 derives from the firstfruits of the domesticated herd. The setting thus fits the alignments of alimentary elements: 1.23 combines domesticated and undomesticated components in the sown, while Exod 23:19 and 34:26 differentiate between elements all derived from domesticated sources in the domestic setting of the god's house (temple). This approach helps to address further the alimentary code in Gen 18:7–8 relative to these texts. Like Gen 18:7–8, the biblical prohibitions mention the two products produced of the flocks, but unlike this story, they separate the dietary elements. Genesis 18:7–8, like 1.23, is not played out in a temple setting, but well outside it.

This distinction may reflect a further difference about the nature of the deities mentioned. 1.23 presupposes two classes of deities ritually present, with the focus decidedly falling on the threatening *'ilm n'mm*. In contrast, Exod 23:19 has no destructive power in mind, and if anything can be garnered from the verse's context, only one god is ritually in view. The theme of the offering made to destructive divine power in 1.23 in the sown is unparalleled in the Ugaritic ritual corpus. Instead, the beneficial deities are viewed as the usual recipients of offerings in the Ugaritic sacrificial texts, and this is the situation also in Exod 23:19 (note the interpretive lens of verse 13) and 34:26.[6]

There may be a corresponding observation to be made about how divinity operates in the different temporal settings of the firstfruits offerings. The autumnal offerings in the sown in 1.23 focus on the destructive deities moving from the outback in the sown, the home of the beneficial gods; in an inverse direction, the goddess goes out from the sown to the outback to hunt. Accordingly, the combination of alimentary elements points to the different realms that also mark different types of deities. In short, the food components stand for

---

6. Exceptions to this generalization are the elimination rituals noted above, p. 15 n. 18 and p. 152 n. 3.

the combination of beneficial deities and destructive deities; in other words, life and death. In contrast, the vernal firstfruits of the biblical verses point to one temple view of the beneficial divinity. Accordingly, the biblical verses separate the beneficial god from destructive powers. It is the god of life to whom the gifts of the firstfruits are devoted.

We might speculate further that the prohibition against the kid's destruction in the mother's own milk encodes the separation of death from life in the relationship of the kid and its mother. The biblical calendars appear to set the prohibitions in the context of the spring, and it may be that the kid was typically thought to have a springtime birth.[7] To be destroyed in a manner connected with its own mother, especially shortly following its own birth, affirms the preservation of the life-giving relationship. It does not prohibit the slaughter of the kid by itself, as this would deny the basic premise of meat slaughter in the sacrificial system. Instead, it acknowledges, in separating the alimentary components of the herd, a separation of death from the expression of the mother-offspring relationship. This acknowledgment in turn communicates the beneficial nature of the deity who maintains a separation from death within the priestly temple-cult.[8] Sometimes the biblical prohibitions (or at least Deut 14:21) are interpreted as humanitarian expressions (see Houston 1993:257–58; Tigay 1996:140). While possible (up to a point), this interpretation does not account for the cultic formulation and setting of these laws. The cultic settings apparent between these biblical prohibitions and 1.23 encode symbolic understandings of death and life: where 1.23 represents death and life in relation to one another, the biblical prohibitions separate them. Indeed, 1.23 contains not one but two treatments of death and destruction, which are explored further in the next section.

The Twin Sides of Death and Destruction

Two pictures, represented by Death in lines 8–11, on the one hand, and, on the other hand, the narrative and invocations of the ʾilm nʿmm, point to two radically different treatments of the cosmos's destructive power. In lines 8–11, Death is destroyed like a vine that is cut down. In lines 30–76, the cosmic destructive forces are admitted into the realm of life and plenty usually reserved for the beneficial gods (which I take to be El and his astral family). Accordingly, the text as a whole represents the threat of destructive power in two strikingly opposing

---

7. This observation was brought to my attention by Richard Averbeck.

8. I am not suggesting that this separation of life and death is the general view of ancient Israel or even of the Israelite priestly cult in general, only that the texts indicate that it was one such priestly view; there may have been others that approximate what we see in 1.23.

modes: a force to be defeated, expressed by the violence of the harvest, but also a power to be admitted to the same harvest.

We may say that these two pictures correspond to two sides of harvest: the pruning, binding, and cutting of the grapes on the vine brings their death, which in turn provides life, abundance, and well-being for those who benefit from their yield. In short, life feeds on the destruction of death, if only for the moment of the harvest and its ritual celebration. Personified Death, in lines 8–11, is a "ritual victim," while in lines 1–2 and 23–24 as well as lines 70–76, the destructive forces of the *'ilm n'mm* can be allowed to savor the plenty produced through death. Whereas lines 8–11 offer one theology of death, that the death of death allows life, in the larger narrative and implicit to the invitations to the feast, we glimpse an extremely different viewpoint, which in terms of the text's focus in lines 1–7//23–27 and 30–76 looms over the whole text: destructive forces can enter the realm of life and momentarily be unthreatening, as the larger celebration of life overshadows the threat of destruction. Where other texts highlight the loss of life paid at the hands of Death (1.6 II), we might say that 1.23 presents the reduction of death and destruction by the overwhelming force of life.

THE ROYAL CONSTRUCTION OF COSMIC DUALITY AND UNITY IN 1.23.30–76

The two sides of death and destruction as well as the oppositions of space, divinity, and alimentary elements noted above resonate with further forms of duality in lines 30–76 that commentators have long noted. There is first of all two unnamed females who call for their two parents (lines 30–33). Their courtship by El is expressed as two parallel alternatives, as to whether the females are to experience him as a father or as a man/husband (lines 39–49). Following El's acquisition of the two females, his sexual relations with them results in two parallel sets of births (lines 49–59). The initial set of births produces two named gods, Shahar and Shalim (lines 49–54), while the second yields apparently two more gods, the unnamed *'ilm n'mm* (lines 55–61). Following their births, their appetite is expressed in terms of their two lips, one stretching below to the underworld (possibly, earth), while the other extends to the heavens (possibly, sky); this appetite also consumes the animals of sky and sea and then moves in two directions, right and left (lines 61–64). These divinities then progress through two zones, first (lines 64–69) in the steppe or outback (*mdbr*) and then (lines 70–76) in the cultivated region, called the sown (*mdr'*).

The presentation, particularly appreciated by Xella (1973) and Hettema (1989–90), builds a series of dual structures that are ultimately interlocking. In addition, one might view the literary presentation as itself a statement about reality in narrative form. The ancients did not write systematic treatises about ontology. In Kunin's words (2004:105 n. 3), "mythology ... is a creator of ontology." Instead, the ancient texts expressed relations and causation in reality, through a narration of divine familial ties. In 1.23, the author(s) narrated reality in line 30–76 (and also, as I have surmised, in line 16 and perhaps other lines as well). The reality that is narrated in lines 30–76 is a series of binary oppositions, one unfolding from the prior one. The beginning of these unfolding oppositions is provided with a divine origin, in the form of the paired wives and the double sets of births. This paired cosmic reality is manifest both in the heavens in the phenomena of Dawn and Dusk, and it can be experienced in the reality of the terrestrial level, in the regions of the outback and the sown. In sum, reality is experienced on the cosmic and terrestrial planes as a series of oppositions.

While perceptible or lived reality is conveyed in binary pairing, the cosmos is not presented ultimately as a dualistic reality. The reality is given a single point of origin, narrated in the figure of El, the creator-god. He is the author or point of origin of the pairs of women and their double-sets of twin offspring. The reality also has a single end-point, narrated in the inclusion of the *'ilm n'mm* into the zone belonging to the beneficial deities (lines 70–76) and celebrated in the ritual to which these gods are invited (lines 1–7, 23–27). It may be said that the beginning and end-points signal a vision of reality that is ultimately monistic. Origins and destiny are ultimately monistic, despite the experience of paired oppositions standing between these two points. All told, the text dramatizes a series of cosmic dualities emanating from a single cosmic origin, a picture characteristic of ancient Near Eastern theogonies. This mythological structure arguably corresponds analogically to later neo-Platonic theories of divine emanation. An important difference between this text and later philosophical accounts of reality is that 1.23 expresses its theory of cosmic reality embedded within its rituals and myths.

Modern scholarship, utilizing its own arsenal of theory, tends to assume that texts only presuppose a theoretical perspective. However, some ancient texts do more than presuppose a theoretical outlook. Instead, they manifest the construction of their own theory about ritual that goes beyond what appears to have been used traditionally in the culture to which they belong. In a number of texts, including 1.23, the representation of ritual practice is also the locus for ritual theory. In this connection, a well-known characterization of ritual by the anthropologist Clifford Geertz (1966:28; cited also in Bell 1992:27) is applicable to 1.23: "In a ritual, the world as lived and the world as imagined, fused under a single set of symbolic forms, turns out to be the same world." Lines 30–76 narrate or evoke a view of reality, or more accurately, a constructed view of it, while the ritual material performs or invokes the similarly constructed end-point of cosmic unity. The ritual dwells momentarily in monistic reality, in contrast to life outside of ritual, which is represented as duality. The ritual performance in

1.23 celebrates and its ritual narratives express the vision that a single ultimate reality lies behind the oppositional perceptions and experiences of life. In short, the "claim" of 1.23 is that its ritual performs an overcoming of the duality of human experience, perhaps most fundamentally its sense of separateness from the gods themselves. In this ritual, not only different sorts of divinities but also gods and humans cross a fundamental divide in reality in coming together. Quite correctly then, Wright (2001:47) focuses on ritual as the locus for the meeting of divinities and humans (see also Xella 1973:94–95).

This sort of mediation or reconciliation is in fact what modern ritual theorists have often regarded as the very definition of ritual. This area of study, especially developed by anthropologists such as Victor Turner and Clifford Geertz, as well as the scholar of religion, Catherine Bell, provides help for thinking further about the nature of the oppositions in 1.23 and their mediation. The remainder of this section represents a reflection on 1.23 in light of anthropological theory on ritual.

Victor Turner (cited in Bell 1992:21) could characterize ritual as "the special paradigmatic activities that mediate or orchestrate the necessary and opposing demands of both *communitas* and the formalized social order." In contrast, Bell (1992:37, 42) resists this view of ritual (see also the comments of Kunin 2004:15–16). Bell would see ritual as a construct of power generated by the production of ritual, not simply a straightforward etic interpretation of ritual. In the case of 1.23, in both rituals and narrative, contrasts are well drawn and arranged. Here Bell's reflections on ritual practices are applicable (1992:98–99):

> ritual practices spatially and temporally construct an environment organized according to schemes of privileged opposition. The construction of this environment and the activities within it simultaneously work to impress those schemes upon the bodies of participants.... Through the orchestration in time of loose but strategically organized oppositions, in which a few oppositions quietly come to dominate others, the social body internalizes the principles of the environment being delineated. Inscribed within the social body, these principles enable the ritualized person to generate in turn strategic schemes that can appropriate other sociocultural situations.

We certainly cannot know all of the ritual and social mechanisms underlying "the principles of the environment" or the "strategic schemes" within the royal ritual of ancient Ugarit. At the same time, we may observe a number of oppositions that can be recognized as "in-forming" the ritualistic participants' social and political sense of reality. In other words, 1.23 broadly conforms to Bell's view of ritualization, where she suggests (Bell 1992:104) that

> ritualization not only involves setting up of oppositions, but through the privileging built into such an exercise it generates hierarchical schemes to produce a loose sense of totalitiy and systematicity. In this way, ritual dynamics afford an experience of 'order' as well as the 'fit' between this taxonomic order and the real world of experience.

These oppositions apply to the divine forces evoked in the rituals and in the narrative; they also apply to a number of other features in 1.23 (as described in the preceding sections). The oppositions are, however, not manifest on the level of human participants. In other words, there are no human "opponents" in the ritual corresponding to the *'ilm n'mm*.

Like the binary oppositions, their reconciliation or integration in 1.23 is a construct of the text's users, in this context the royal parents and their royal officials. The text offers the construction of reconciliation as the apparent "natural outcome" of oppositions. The fundamental divide between deities and humans overcome in this text applies on the human side only to the royal parents and personnel who oversee and control the ritual; lesser mortals are nowhere in view. The mythic narrative evokes El as the point of origins, in the larger ritual context overseen by the royal couple and personnel. The text as a whole serves to link the identities of El and the king as the principal markers and movers of reconciliation over and against the binary oppositions of space and time. Across these oppositions, El and the king together represent unity within hierarchy of the divine and human orders. In short, 1.23 expresses royal power by connecting the cosmic origins in the figure of El with the present reality in the person of the king; their linkage together asserts an ideal of unity over the varied orders of experience captured in the binary oppositions. In Geertz's words (1966:34), "The acceptance of authority that underlies the religious perspective that the ritual embodies thus flows from the enactment of the ritual itself." The ritual of 1.23 disguises its own discourse of power, in its representation of natural plenty. In what Bell (1992:82) characterizes as the "fundamental 'misrecognition'" of what ritual practice does, 1.23 offers a picture of beauty and wonder of the moment of plenty that actually serves to elevate the human powers overseeing this plenty. Additionally, the text masks the fact that the human agents named in it did not produce this plenty, yet they profited from the labor of those who did perform the labor but go unmentioned by the ritual.

Even as the text disguises social facts about its participants, it also aligns them. Again, in Bell's words (1992:141),

> Ritualization always aligns one within a series of relationships linked to the ultimate sources of power. Whether ritual empowers or disempowers one in some practical sense, it always suggests the ultimate coherence of a cosmos in which one takes a particular place. This cosmos is experienced as a chain of

states or an order of existence that places one securely in a field of action and in alignment with the ultimate goals of all action.

The power of the royal participants is not achieved simply by coercion or some form of social control. Bell (1992:171–223) is particularly critical of this assumption. The following comments of Bell (1992:200, 213) are germane:

> the establishment and maintenance of power of kings or the power of capitalism has to be rooted in preexisting forms of behavior, socialized bodies, and local relations of power, which could not be mere projections of the central power and still effectively maintain and legitimate that power…. The traditionalism, authority, dramaturgy of ritual power can be as fragile as they can be impressive and enduring.

In the case of 1.23, royal power is expressed by casting traditional forms of ritual practice (sacrifice in lines 1–7//23–27) and mythic worldviews (narrative and images of the divine meal in lines 70–76) in terms that favor their royal patrons. At a minimum, this is evident from their patronage being ritually proclaimed (lines 1–7). Linking human and divine levels, royal patronage of the divine meal engenders a form of social mediation that moves the fulcrum-point of perceived reality in favor of the coherent royal worldview generated in the text: "All levels of social experience—body, home, community, and cosmos—were brought into a reinforcing conformity with one another" (Bell 1992:210). The proposed homology of roles between the royals and the mythological figures of lines 30–76 would represent a dramatic example of producing such a cosmic coherence. In many other texts, El may be the patron of the king and a comparable patriarch, but 1.23 further reinforces the identification of god and king. In particular, the text presents the king corresponding to El holding ultimate oversight over the sown, with the royal servants under the authority of the king mentioned in lines 7 and 26 corresponding to the watchman of the sown in lines 68–76.[9] If the king may be said to promote an identification of himself with El, the rituals and myths of 1.23 follow the lines characterized by Bell (1997:129) for ritual across a wide variety of cultures: "The king's cult creates the king, defines kingliness, and orchestrates a cosmic framework within which the social hierarchy headed by the king is perceived as natural and right."

Further focus on the monarchy may be inferred from the lack of any mention of priestly functionaries in the text. This is not to say that they are not there in the background; indeed, one may infer that the "I" of line 1 is such a figure. At

---

9. As an alternative, the king himself has been correlated with the watchman of the sown; see Clemens 2001:715 n. 556, 1026 n. 1884.

the same time, the omission underscores the importance of the human parties who are explicitly mentioned, namely, the royals and their servants. 1.23 shows a further form of textual silence, namely, the omission of people outside royal circles. Marshall Sahlins (1972:215) offers a comment that applies to 1.23: "Food dealings are a delicate barometer, a ritual statement as it were, of social relations, and food is thus employed instrumentally as a starting, a sustaining, or a destroying mechanism of sociability."[10] On the most explicit level, the ritual and narrative about meals in 1.23 arguably constitutes a barometer of social relations. The social relations are not those of the royal circle and the wider society; instead, they involve the royal circle and the divine sphere. By implication, the text highly privileges the royals over all other human parties.

These unnamed parties might be signaled by the physical setting invoked by the text. The rituals and myths take place in the sown (cf. CAT 4.149.14–16; Trujillo 1973:192–93) instead of the customary setting of royal ritual, namely, the temple. By taking place in this setting, perhaps this text implicitly asserts royal patronage over its subjects who work the sown to the benefit of the monarchy. In short, the royal patronage of the ritual in the sown ritually reenacts royal authority over the sown and those of the society who operate in the sphere. We might suggest that the royal rehearsing of a drama of Death in lines 8–11 or destructive forces' entry to the edge of the sown from the periphery in lines 70–76 signals an inverse expression of royal hegemony moving from the center of the sown out to its edge. In any case, ritualization in 1.23.1–29 may achieve privileging of the royals over the unnamed others of the society whom they rule, but it also ultimately expresses a single worldview that includes them implicitly, by naming and describing a center or home for the society more generally as well as the threat posed by death and the agricultural plenty to be shared by all. Ultimately, everyone in the society is in the sown, at home. In this way, 1.23 generates a symbolic universe expressing both social differentiation and coherence, or in other words, unity in hierarchy.

3. In Closing

A comparison of the Baal Cycle (1.1–1.6), Aqhat (1.17–1.19), or Kirta (1.14–1.16) show widely differing configurations of the relationship between myths and rituals. Although the myth and ritual approach has largely passed from scholarly discussions, the problems that it sought to address have not. The rituals in 1.23 show a highly complex relationship with its myths. The myths themselves seem to incorporate or evoke only one ritual element in its description, namely,

---

10. I thank Kevin McGeough for bringing this discussion of Sahlins to my attention.

the sacrifice in the sown. And even in this case, we have no knowledge as to the priority or original relationship between the ritual and the myth of the offering in the sown. Here we may contrast Aqhat, for which Wright (2001) has nicely demonstrated the depth of ritual elements. Wright (2001:229) explains the preponderance of ritual in Aqhat and offers an insightful comparison with Kirta and the Baal Cycle:

> The tale is primarily about the interaction of human and deities. In the cultural world of the ancient Near East, these interactions were viewed as occurring and being facilitated by ritual events. Thus, it would be natural for an author to employ ritual to describe the interaction of gods and humans in narrative. This hypothesis is supported by the similar preponderance of ritual in the Kirta tale, which also treats commerce between the human and divine spheres. This hypothesis also explains the more limited occurrence of human-divine ritual in the Ba'l cycle, which deals with matters only on the divine plane (though we often find deities interacting with each other there in ritual contexts).

To return to 1.23, it is evident that lines 30–76 as a unit stands closer to the Baal Cycle than Aqhat or Kirta in terms of its use of ritual elements. Like the Baal Cycle, 1.23.30–76 shows the divine meal as a central scene for deities. Yet this comparison addresses only lines 30–76. Clearly what 1.23 entails as a whole is considerably more complex.

Wright's comments alert us to the range of ritual in literary myth. At the same time, the issue at hand for 1.23 is not myth incorporating ritual elements. While 1.23 contains a literary text akin to the Baal Cycle, Kirta or Aqhat, the text as a whole shows a set of very different relationships between myths and rituals: rituals incorporating different mythic elements; and myth thematically paralleling ritual (to some degree), yet with no ritual in it. In constructing a symbolic world by a complex set of relationships between actual rituals and myths centered on the offering in the sown, the text contains a variety of mythic themes and ritual actions. In the end, it is evident that every text requires its own examination and appreciation for the way that it constructs its symbolic universe. The myths and rituals in 1.23 stand both on their own and in tandem, and they do in a way unattested in any other Ugaritic text. Lines 30–76 are not an explanatory myth for lines 1–29 (or its parts); instead, lines 30–76 evoke a narrative representation of the world invoked by the lines in 1–29 that share its content in abbreviated ritual forms, in particular the dominant ritual of lines 1–7//23–27.

CAT 1.23 also differs markedly from other Ugaritic texts in terms of its multiple visions of life and death as well as various means to express them. Its combination of the different viewpoints and ways to communicate them is unique for the Ugaritic corpus. Although 1.23 is quite a short text relative to the

Baal Cycle, Kirta, or Aqhat, it betrays significant insights into the nature of the cosmos that are every bit as compelling as what is presented in these longer and better-known works. Both the Baal Cycle and 1.23 claim that the death of death permits life (see P. L. Watson 1972). At the same time, these texts make this assertion in radically different ways. Moreover, each text contributes additional ideas about life and death. Further assessment of the mythologies of death and life in 1.23, relative to other texts from Ugarit and beyond, remains a matter for another study.[11]

---

11. I hope to address this question in the third volume of the commentary on the Baal Cycle (*UBC* 3).

Ackerman, S. 1993. "The Queen Mother and the Cult in Ancient Israel." *JBL* 112:385–401.

Aistleitner, J. 1953. "Götterzeugung in Ugarit und Dilmun (SS und Ni. 4561)." *Acta Orientalia Academiae Scientiarum Hungaricae* 3:285–311.

Aitken, K. T. 1989. "Word Pairs and Tradition in an Ugaritic Tale." *UF* 21:17–38.

Albright, W. F. 1928–29. "The Second Season at Tell Beit Mirsim." *AfO* 5:119–20.

————. 1934. "The North-Canaanite Poems of Al'êyân Ba'al and the 'Gracious Gods.'" *JPOS* 14:101–40.

————. 1938. "Was the Patriarch Terah a Canaanite Moon-God?" *BASOR* 71:35–40.

Allman, M. 2000. "Eucharist, Ritual and Narrative: Formation of Individual and Communal Moral Character." *Journal of Ritual Studies* 14/1:60–68.

Almagro-Gorbea, M. 1983. "Pozo Moro: El monumento orientalizante, su contexto socio-cultural y sus parallelos en la arquitectura funeraria ibérica." *Madrider Mitteilungen* 24:197–201.

Anderson, G. A. 1991. *A Time to Mourn, A Time to Dance.* University Park: Pennsylvania State University Press.

Arnaud, D. 1986. *Recherches au pays d'Aštata, Emar VI.3: textes sumériens et accadiens, Texte.* Paris: Éditions Recherche sur les Civilisations.

Arnold, P. P. 2000. "Eating and Giving Food: The Material Necessity of Interpretation in Thai Buddhism." *Journal of Ritual Studies* 14/1:6–22.

Attridge, H. W., and R. A. Oden Jr. 1976. *The Syrian Goddess (De Dea Syria) Attributed to Lucian.* SBLTT 9, Graeco-Roman Religion Series 1. Missoula, Mont.: Scholars Press.

————. 1981. *Philo of Byblos / The Phoenician History: Introduction, Critical Text, Translation, Notes.* CBQMS 9. Washington, D.C.: Catholic Biblical Association of America.

Averbeck, R. E. 2003. "Myth, Ritual, and Order in 'Enki and the World.'" *JAOS* 123: 757–71.

————. 2004. "Ancient Near Eastern Mythography as It Relates to Historiography in the Hebrew Bible: Genesis 3 and the Cosmic Battle." Pages 328–56 in *The Future of Biblical Archaeology, Reassessing Methodologies and Assumptions: The Proceedings of a Symposium August 12-14, 2003 at Trinity International University.* Edited by J. K. Hoffmeier and A. Millard. Grand Rapids: Eerdmans.

Baeten, E. M. 1996. *The Magic Mirror: Myth's Abiding Power.* SUNY Series in the Philosophy of the Social Sciences. Albany: State University of New York Press.

Barton, G. A. 1934. "A Liturgy for the Celebration of the Spring Festival at Jerusalem in the Age of Abraham and Melchizedek." *JBL* 53:61–78.

Bell, C. 1992. *Ritual Theory, Ritual Practice.* Oxford: Oxford University Press.

————. 1997. *Ritual: Perspectives and Dimensions.* Oxford: Oxford University Press.

Berlin, A. 1985. *The Dynamics of Biblical Parallelism.* Bloomington: Indiana University Press.

Bidmead, J. 2002. *The Akîtu Festival: Religious Continuity and Royal Legitimation in Mesopotamia*. Gorgias Dissertations: Near Eastern Studies 2. Piscataway, N.J.: Gorgias.

Biggs, R. D. 1967. *ŠÀ.ZI.GA, Ancient Mesopotamian Potency Incantations*. Texts from Cuneiform Sources II. Locust Valley, N.Y.: Augustin.

Binger, T. 1997. *Asherah: Goddesses in Ugarit, Israel and the Old Testament*. JSOTSup 232. Copenhagen International Seminar 2. Sheffield: Sheffield Academic Press.

Blake, F. R. 1951. *A Resurvey of Hebrew Tenses*. Scripta Pontificii Instituti Biblici 103. Rome: Pontifical Biblical Institute.

Blau, J. 1977. *An Adverbial Construction in Hebrew and Arabic: Sentence Adverbials in Frontal Position Separated from the Rest of the Sentence*. The Israel Academy of Sciences and Humanities Proceedings, 6/1. Jerusalem: Israel Academy of Sciences and Humanities.

Blau, J., and S. E. Loewenstamm. 1970. "Zur Frage der scriptio plena im Ugaritischen und Verwandtes." *UF* 2:19–33.

Bordreuil, P., and D. Pardee. 1989. *Concordance*. Vol. 1 of *La trouvaille épigraphique de l'Ougarit*. RSO 5. Mémoire 86. Paris: Éditions Recherche sur les Civilisations.

————. 2004. *Manuel d'ougaritique*. 2 vols. Paris: Geuthner.

Borowski, O. 2002a. *Agriculture in Iron Age Israel*. Boston: American Schools of Oriental Research.

————. 2002b. "Animals of the Literatures of Syria-Palestine." Pages 289–306 in Collins 2002.

————. 2002c. "Animals of the Religions of Syria-Palestine." Pages 405–24 in Collins 2002.

Bottéro, J. 1995. *Textes culinaires Mésopotamiens/Mesopotamian Culinary Texts*. Mesopotamian Civilizations 6. Winona Lake, Ind.: Eisenbrauns.

————. 2004. *The Oldest Cuisine in the World: Cooking in Mesopotamia*. Translated by T. L. Fagan. Chicago: University of Chicago Press.

Bowen, N. R. 2001. "The Quest for the Historical *Gĕbîrâ*." *CBQ* 63:597–618.

Brown, M. L. 1987. " 'Is it Not?' or 'Indeed!': *HL* in Northwest Semitic." *Maarav* 4/2: 201–19.

Caubet, A. 2002. "Animals in Syro-Palestinian Art." Pages 211–34 in Collins 2002.

Caquot, A., M. Sznycer, and A. Herdner. 1974. *Mythes et legendes*. Vol. 1. of *Textes ougaritiques*. LAPO 7. Paris: Cerf.

Civil, M. 1983. "Enlil and Ninlil: The Marriage of Sud." *JAOS* 103:43–66.

Clemens, D. M. 2001. *Ugaritic and Ugarit Akkadian Texts*. Vol. 1 of *Sources for Ugaritic Ritual and Sacrifice*. AOAT 284/1. Münster: Ugarit-Verlag.

Clifford, R. J. 1975. "Recent Scholarly Discussion of CTCA 23 (UT 52)." Pages 99–105 in vol. 1 of *Society of Biblical Literature 1975 Seminar Papers*. Missoula, Mont.: Scholars Press.

————. 1983. "Isaiah 55: Invitation to a Feast." Pages 27–35 in *The Word of the Lord Shall Go Forth: Essays in Honor of David Noel Freedman in Celebration of His Sixtieth Birthday*. Edited by C. L. Meyers and M. O'Connor. Winona Lake, Ind.: Eisenbrauns.

————. 1999. *Proverbs*. OTL. Louisville: Westminster John Knox.

Cohen, C. 1996. "The Ugaritic Hippiatric Texts." *UF* 28:105–53.

Collins, B. J., ed. 2002. *A History of the Animal World in the Ancient Near East*. HdO 1/64. Leiden: Brill.

Cooper, J. S. 1993. "Sacred Marriage and Popular Cult in Early Mesopotamia." Pages 81–96 in *Official Cult and Popular Religion in the Ancient Near East: Papers of the First Col-

loquium on the Ancient Near East—The City and Its Life Held at the Middle Eastern Culture Center in Japan (Mitaka, Tokyo), March 20-22, 1992. Edited by E. Matsushima. Heidelberg: Universitätsverlag.

Cross, F. M. 1968. "Jar Inscriptions from Shiqmona." *IEJ* 18:226–33 = Cross 2003:286–89.

————. 1973. *Canaanite Myth and Hebrew Epic.* Cambridge: Harvard University Press.

————. 1998. *From Epic to Canon: History and Literature in Ancient Israel.* Baltimore: The Johns Hopkins University Press.

————. 2003. *Leaves from an Epigrapher's Notebook: Collected Papers in Hebrew and West Semitic Palaeography and Epigraphy.* HSS 51. Winona Lake, Ind.: Eisenbrauns.

Cunchillos J.-L., and J.-P. Vita, eds. 1995. *Concordancia de palabras ugaríticas en morfología desplegada.* Vol. 2 of *Banco de datos filológicos semíticos noroccidentales.* Madrid: Institución Fernando el Católico.

Cutler, B., and J. MacDonald 1982. "On the Origin of the Ugaritic Text KTU 1.23." *UF* 14:33–50.

Dahood, M. 1966. *Psalms I: 1–50.* AB 16. Garden City, N.Y.: Doubleday.

————. 1969. "Ugaritic-Hebrew Syntax and Style." *UF* 1:15–36.

Delcor, M. 1967. "Two Special Meanings of the Word יד in Biblical Hebrew." *JSS* 12:238–40.

Detienne, M. 1981. *L'invention de la mythologie.* Paris. Translated as *The Creation of Mythology.* Translated by M. Cook. Chicago: University of Chicago Press, 1986.

————. 1989. "Culinary Practice and the Spirit of Sacrifice." Pages 1–22 in *The Cuisine of Sacrifice among the Greeks.* Edited by M. Detienne and J. P. Vervant. Translated by P. Wissing. Chicago: University of Chicago Press.

Dietrich, M., and O. Loretz. 1977. "Ug. *mšt'lt* (KTU 1.23: 31.35.36)." *UF* 9:342–43.

————. 1993. "Zur Debatte über die Lautentwicklung *z - d* im Ugaritischen (*zr'/dr'* 'säen', *db/'db* 'legen, setzen')." *UF* 25:123–32.

————. 1998. "Beschwörung gegen die Schädlichen Naturkrafte (KTU 1.23)." Pages 350–57 in *Rituale und Beschwörungen II.* Edited by O. Kaiser et al. TUAT 2/3. Gütersloh: Gütersloher Verlagshaus.

————. 1999. "Keret, der leidende 'König der Gerechtigkeit': Das Wortpaar *ṣdq* ∥ *yšr* als Schlüssel zur Dramatik des Keret-Epos (KTU 1.14 I 12–21a)." *UF* 31:133–64.

————. 2000. "Ugaritisch *qîl G* "fallen" und seine abgeleiteten Stämme Š und Št." *UF* 32:177–94.

————. 2002. "Die Wurzel *'db/'db* und ihre Ableitungen im Ugaritischen." *UF* 34:75–108.

————. 2003. "Die ugaritisch Wortpaare *dm∥mm'* und *brkm∥ḥlqm* im Kontext westsemitischer anatomischer Terminologie." *UF* 35:141–79.

Dietrich, M., and W. Mayer. 1996. "Festritual für die Palastgöttin Pidray: Der hurro-ugaritische KTU 1.132." *UF* 28:165–76.

Dijkstra, M. 1994. "The Myth of Astarte, the Huntress (1.92)." *UF* 26:113–26.

————. 1998. "Astral Myth of the Birth of Shahar and Shalim (KTU 1.23)." Pages 265–87 in *"Und Mose schrieb dieses Lied auf": Studien zum Alten Testament und zum Alten Orient. Festschrift für Oswald Loretz zur Vollendung seines 70. Lebenjahres mit Beiträgen von Freunden, Schülern und Kollegen.* Edited by M. Dietrich and I. Kottsieper. AOAT 250. Münster: Ugarit-Verlag.

Dobrusin, D. L. 1981. "The Third Masculine Plural of the Prefixed Form of the Verb in Ugaritic." *JANES* 13:3–10.

Doty, W. G. 2000. *Mythography: The Study of Myths and Rituals.* 2nd ed. Tuscaloosa: University of Alabama Press.

Dussaud, R. 1933. "Les Phéniciens au Negeb et en Arabie d'après un texte de Ras Shamra." *RHR* 108:5–49.

Edmunds, L. 1990. "Introduction: The Practice of Greek Mythology." Pages 1–20 in *Approaches to Greek Myth*. Edited by L. Edmunds. Baltimore: The Johns Hopkins University Press.

Eliade, M. 1991. "Toward a Definition of Myth." Pages 3–5 in vol. 1 of *Mythologies*. Edited by Y. Bonnefoy. Chicago: University of Chicago Press.

Fisher, M. 1969. "Lexical Relations between Ethiopic and Ugaritic." Ph.D. diss., Brandeis University.

Fitzgerald, A. 1967. "Hebrew *yd* = 'Love' and 'Beloved.' " *CBQ* 29:62–68.

———. 2002. *The Lord of the East Wind*. CBQMS 34. Washington, D.C.: Catholic Biblical Association of America.

Fleming, D. 1991. "The Voice of the Ugaritic Incantation Priest (RIH 78/20)." *UF* 23:141–54.

———. 1992. *The Installation of Baal's High Priestess at Emar: Window on Ancient Syrian Religion*. HSS 42. Atlanta: Scholars Press.

———. 2000. *Time at Emar: The Cultic Calendar and the Rituals from the Diviner's House*. Mesopotamian Civilizations 11. Winona Lake, Ind.: Eisenbrauns.

Foley, C. M. 1980. "The Gracious Gods and the Royal Ideology of Ugarit." Ph.D. diss., McMaster University.

———. 1987. "Are the 'Gracious Gods' *bn šrm*? A Suggested Restoration for KTU 1.23:1–2." *UF* 19:61–74.

Fontenrose, J. 1966. *The Ritual Theory of Myth*. Berkeley and Los Angeles: University of California Press.

Foster, B. R. 1993. *Before the Muses: An Anthology of Akkadian Literature*. 2 vols. Bethesda, Md.: CDL.

Frayne, D. 1985. "Notes on the Sacred Marriage Rite." *BiOr* 42:5–22.

Frazer, J. G. 1890. *The Golden Bough*. New York: Macmillan.

Frevel, C. 1995. *Aschera und der Ausschliesslichkeitsanspruch YHWHs*. BBB 94. Weinheim: Athenäum.

Gai, A. 1982. "The Reduction of Tenses (and Other Categories) of the Consequent Verb in North-West Semitic." *Or* 51:254–56.

Gaselee, S. 1917. *Achilles Tatius*. Loeb Classical Library. London: William Heinemann; New York: G. P. Putnam's Sons.

Gaster, T. H. 1934. "An Ancient Semitic Mystery-Play from a Cuneiform Tablet Discovered at Ras-esh-Shamra." *Studi e Materiali di Storia delle Religioni* 10:156–64.

———. 1946. "A Canaanite Ritual Drama, the Spring Festival at Ugarit." *JAOS* 66:49–76.

———. 1947. "The Canaanite Poem of the Gracious Gods, Line 12." *JAOS* 67:326.

———. 1977. *Thespis: Ritual, Myth, and Drama in the Ancient Near East*. New York: Norton.

Geertz, C. 1966. "Religion as a Cultural System." Pages 1–46 in *Anthropological Approaches to the Study of Religion*. Edited by M. Banton. ASA Monographs 3. London: Tavistock.

Ginsberg, H. L. 1935. "Notes on the Birth of the Beautiful Gods." *JRAS*:45–72.

———. 1982. *The Israelian Heritage of Judaism*. Texts and Studies of the Jewish Theological Seminary of America 24. New York: Jewish Theological Seminary of America.

Good, R. M. 1982. "Metaphorical Gleanings from Ugarit." *JJS* 33:55–59.

———. 1986. "Hebrew and Ugaritic *nḥt*." *UF* 16:153–56.

Gordon, C. H. 1949. *Ugaritic Literature: A Comprehensive Translation of the Poetic and Prose Texts*. Scripta Pontificii Instituti Biblici 98. Rome: Pontificium Institutum Biblicum.

————. 1966. *Ugarit and Minoan Crete: The Bearing of Their Texts on the Origins of Western Culture.* New York: Norton.

————. 1988. "Ugaritic *RBT/RABĪTU.*" Pages 127–32 in *Ascribe to the Lord: Biblical and Other Studies in Memory of Peter C. Craigie.* Edited by L. Eslinger and G. Taylor. JSOT-Sup 67. Sheffield: Sheffield Academic Press.

Grabbe, L. L. 1976. "The Seasonal Pattern and the 'Baal Cycle.' " *UF* 8:57–63.

Gray, J. 1965. *The Legacy of Canaan.* Revised ed. VTSup 5. Leiden: Brill.

Greenfield, J. C. 1964. "Ugaritic *mdl* and Its Cognates." *Bib* 45:527–34 = Pages 847–54 in *'Al Kanfei Jonah: Collected Studies of Jonas C. Greenfield on Semitic Philology.* Edited by S. M. Paul, M. E. Stone, and A. Pinnick. Leiden: Brill; Jerusalem: Magnes, 2001.

————. 1979. "The Root *šql* in Akkadian, Ugarit and Aramaic." *UF* 11:89–93 = Pages 731–33 in *'Al Kanfei Jonah: Collected Studies of Jonas C. Greenfield on Semitic Philology.* Edited by S. M. Paul, M. E. Stone, and A. Pinnick. Leiden: Brill; Jerusalem: Magnes, 2001.

————. 1987. "The Epithets *RBT//ṮRRT* in the KRT Epic." Pages 35–37 in *Perspectives on Language and Text: Essays and Poems in Honor of Francis I. Andersen's Sixtieth Birthday, July 28, 1985.* Edited by E. W. Conrad and E. G. Newing. Winona Lake, Ind.: Eisenbrauns. = Pages 898–900 in *'Al Kanfei Jonah: Collected Studies of Jonas C. Greenfield on Semitic Philology.* Edited by S. M. Paul, M. E. Stone, and A. Pinnick. Leiden: Brill; Jerusalem: Magnes, 2001.

Greenstein, E. L. 1976. "A Phoenician Inscription in Ugaritic Script?" *JANES* 8:49–57.

Guillaume, P. 2002. "Thou Shall Not Curdle Milk with Rennet." *UF* 34:213–15.

Gulde, S. 1998. "KTU 1.23—Die Beschwörung der *Agzrm bn ym.*" *UF* 30:289–334.

Hallo, W. W. 1987. "The Birth of Kings." Pages 45–52 in *Love and Death in the Ancient Near East: Essays in Honor of Marvin H. Pope.* Edited by J. H. Marks and R. M. Good. Hamden, Conn.: Four Quarters.

Haran, M. 1978. "Seething a Kid in Its Mother's Milk." *ErIsr* 14:12–18.

————. 1985. "Das Böcklein in der Mich seiner Mutter und das saügende Muttertier." *TZ* 41:135–59.

Harris, S. N. 1997. "Ritual: Communication and Meaning." *Journal of Ritual Studies* 11/1:35–44.

Heckl, R. 2001. "Ḥelaeb oder ḥālāb? Ein möglicher Einfluss der frühjüdischen Halacha auf die Vokalisation des MT in Ex 23,19b; Ex 34:34:26b; Dtn 14,21b." *ZAH* 14:144–58.

Heltzer, M. 1980. "Der ugaritische Text KTU 4.751 und das Festmahl (?) der Dienst-leute des Königs." *UF* 12:413–15.

————. 1990. "Vineyards and Wine in Ugarit." *UF* 22:119–35.

Hettema, T. L. 1989–90 " 'That It May be Repeated'. A Narrative Analysis of KTU 1.23." *JEOL* 31:77–94."

Hoffner, H. A., Jr. 1964. "An Anatolian Cult Term in Ugaritic." *JNES* 23:66–68.

Horwitz, W. J. 1974. "Some Possible Results of Rudimentary Scribal Training." *UF* 6:75–83.

Houston, W. 1993. *Purity and Monotheism: Clean and Unclean Animals in Biblical Law.* JSOT-Sup 140. Sheffield: Sheffield Academic Press.

Huehnergard, J. 1987. *Ugaritic Vocabulary in Syllabic Transcription.* HSS 32. Atlanta: Scholars Press.

————. 2002. "*izuzzum* and *itūlum.*" Pages 161–85 in *Riches Hidden in Secret Places: Ancient Near Eastern Studies in Memory of Thorkild Jacobsen.* Edited by T. Abusch. Winona Lake, Ind.: Eisenbrauns.

Hunger, H., and D. Pingree. 1989. *MUL.APIN: An Astronomical Compedium in Cuneiform*. AfO 24. Horn, Austria: Berger & Söhne.

Jacobsen, T. 1976. *The Treasures of Darkness: A History of Mesopotamian Religion*. New Haven: Yale University Press.

———. 1987. *The Harps That Once...: Sumerian Poetry in Translation*. New Haven: Yale University Press.

Janowski, B., and G. Wilhelm. 1993. "Ber Bock, der die Sünden hinausträgt: Zur Religionsgeschichte des Azazel-Ritus Lev 16,10.21f." Pages 109–69 in *Religionsgeschichtliche Beziehungen zwischen Klainasien, Nordsyrien und dem Alten Testament im 2. und 1. vorchristlichen Jahrtausend*. Edited by B. Janowski, K. Koch, and G. Wilhelm. OBO 129. Göttingen: Vandenhoeck & Ruprecht.

Jørgensen, K. E. Jordt, et al. 1980. *Fauna and Flora of the Bible*. 2nd ed. UBS Handbook Series. New York: United Bible Societies.

Kapelrud, A. 1952. *Baal in the Ugaritic Texts*. Copenhagen: Gad.

Keel, O. 1980. *Das Böcklein in der Milch seiner Mutter und Verwandtes*. OBO 33. Fribourg: Universitätsverlag; Göttingen: Vandenhoeck & Ruprecht.

Kellerman, G. 1986. "The Telepinu Myth Reconsidered." Pages 115–24 in *Kaniššuwar: A Tribute to Hans Güterbock on His Seventy-Fifth Birthday, May 27, 1983*. Edited by H. A. Hoffner Jr. and G. M. Beckman. AS 23. Chicago: Oriental Institute of the University of Chicago.

Kennedy, C. 1981. "The Mythological Reliefs from Pozo Moro, Spain." Pages 209–16 in *Society of Biblical Literature 1981 Seminar Papers*, 20. Chico, Calif.: Scholars Press.

Kirk, G. S. 1971. *Myth: Its Meaning and Functions in Ancient and Other Cultures*. Cambridge: Cambridge University Press.

———. 1974. *The Nature of Greek Myths*. Harmondsworth: Penguin. Repr., London: Penguin, 1990.

Knauf, E. A. 1988. "Zur Herkunft und Sozialgeschichte Israels: 'Das Böckchen in der Milch seiner Mutter.'" *Bib* 69:153–69.

Komoróczy, G. 1971. "Zum mythologischen und literaturgeschichtlichen Hintergrund der Ugaritischen Dichtung 'ŠŠ.'" *UF* 3:75–80.

Kosmala, H. 1964. "Mot and the Vine: The Time of the Ugaritic Fertility Rite." *ASTI* 3:147–51.

Kramer, S. N. 1969. *The Sacred Marriage Rite: Aspects of Faith, Myth, and Ritual in Ancient Sumer*. Bloomington: Indiana University Press.

Krecher, J. 1992. "UD.GAL.NUN versus 'Normal' Sumerian: Two Literatures or One?" Pages 285–303 in *Literature and Literary Language at Ebla*. Edited by P. Fronzaroli. Quaderni di Semitistica 18. Florence: Dipartimento di Linguistica, Università di Firenze.

Kühne, C. 1973. "Ammishtamru und die Tochter der 'Grossen Dame.'" *UF* 5:175–84.

———. 1974. "Mit Glossenkeilen markierte fremde Wörter in akkadischen Ugarittexten." *UF* 6:157–67.

Kunin, S. D. 2004. *We Think What We Eat: Neo-structuralist Analysis of Israelite Food Rules and Other Cultural and Textual Practices*. JSOTSup 412. New York: T&T Clark.

Lambert, W. G. 1975. "The Problem of the Love Lyrics." Pages 98–135 in *Unity and Diversity: Essays in the History, Literature, and Religion of the Ancient Near East*. Edited by H. Goedicke and J. J. M. Roberts. Baltimore: The Johns Hopkins University Press.

Lambert, W. G., and A. R. Millard. 1969. *Atra-ḫasîs: The Babylonian Story of the Flood*. With the Sumerian Flood Story by M. Civil. Oxford: Clarendon.

Landsberger, B. 1966. "Einige unerkannt gebliebene oder verkannte Nomina des Akkadischen." *WO* 3:246–70.

Lapinkivi, P. 2004. *The Sumerian Sacred Marriage in the Light of Comparative Evidence.* SAAS 15. Helsinki: Helsinki University Press.

Lehmann, M. R. 1953. "A New Interpretation of the Term שדמות." *VT* 3:361–71.

Leick, G. 1994. *Sex and Eroticism in Mesopotamian Literature.* London: Routledge.

Levenson, J. D. 1997. *Esther: A Commentary.* OTL. Louisville: Westminster John Knox.

Lévi-Strauss, C. 1969. *The Raw and the Cooked.* Translated by J. and D. Weightman. New York: Harper & Row.

Levine, B. A., and J. M. de Tarragon. 1993. "The King Proclaims the Day: Ugaritic Rites for the Vintage (*KTU* 1.41//1.87)." *RB* 100:76–115.

Lichtenstein, M. H. 1968. "The Banquet Motifs in Keret and in Proverbs 9." *JANES* 1/1:19–31.

————. 1977. "Episodic Structure in the Ugaritic Keret Legend: Comparative Studies in Compositional Technique." Ph.D. diss., Columbia University.

Lipiński, E. 1970. "Banquet en l'honneur de Baal. CTA 3 (VAB), A, 4–22." *UF* 2:75–88.

————. 1983. "The 'Phoenician History' of Philo of Byblos." *BiOr* 40:305–10.

————. 1986. "Fertility Cult in Ancient Ugarit." Pages 207–15 in *Archaeology and Fertility Cult in the Ancient Mediterranean: Papers presented at the First International Conference on Archaeology of the Ancient Mediterranean, the University of Malta 2–5 September 1985.* Edited by A. Bonanno. Amsterdam: Grüner.

Livingstone, A. 1986. *Mystical and Mythological Explanatory Works by Assyrian and Babylonian Scholars.* Oxford: Clarendon.

Lloyd, J. B. 1990. "The Banquet Theme in Ugaritic Narrative." *UF* 22:169–93.

Loewenstamm, S. E. 1973. "Lexicographical Notes on 1. *ṭbḫ*; 2. *hnny/hlny*." *UF* 5:209–11.

Loretz, O. 1971. "Psalmenstudien." *UF* 3:101–15.

————. 1985. *Leberschau, Sündenbock, Asasel in Ugarit und Israel.* UBL 3. Altenberge: CIS-Verlag.

————. 1993. "Ugaritisch-hebräich *ḫmr/ḥmr* und *msk* (/*mzg*): Neu- und Mischwein in der Ägäis und in Syrien-Palästinas." *UF* 25:247–58.

Macdonald, M. N. 2000. "Food and Gender in the Highlands of Papua New Guinea." *Journal of Ritual Studies* 14/1:23–31.

Marcus, D. 1974. "Ugaritic Evidence for 'The Almighty/the Grand One'?" *Bib* 55:404–47.

Margalit, B. 1981. "The Ugaritic Creation Myth." *UF* 13:137–45.

————. 1995. "K-R-T Studies." *UF* 27:215–315.

Márquez Rowe, I. 2000. "The King of Ugarit, His Wife, Her Brother, and Her Lovers: The Mystery of a Tragedy in Two Acts Revisited." *UF* 32:365–83.

Marsman, H. J. 2003. *Women in Ugarit and Israel: Their Social and Religious Position in the Context of the Ancient Near East.* OTS 49. Leiden: Brill.

Mattila, R. 2002. *Assurbanipal through Sin-šarru-iškun.* Part 2 of *Legal Transactions of the Royal Court of Nineveh.* SAA 14. Helsinki: Helsinki University Press.

McLaughlin, J. L. 2001. *The marzēaḥ in the Prophetic Literature: References and Allusions in Light of the Extra-Biblical Evidence.* VTSup 86. Leiden: Brill.

Merlo, P. 1996. "Über die Ergänzung <št> in KTU 1.23:59." *UF* 28:491–94.

Mettinger, T. N. D. 2001. *The Riddle of Resurrection: "Dying and Rising Gods" in the Ancient Near East.* CBOT 50. Stockholm: Almqvist & Wiksell.

Milgrom, J. 1985. "An Archaeological Myth Destroyed: 'You Shall Not Boil a Kid in Its Mother's Milk.'" *BAR* 1/3:48–55.

Miller, C. L. 1999. "Patterns of Verbal Ellipsis in Ugaritic Poetry." *UF* 31:333–72.

Miller, P. D., Jr. 1970. "Ugaritic *ǵzr* and Hebrew *ʿzr II.*" *UF* 2:159–75.

Montgomery, J. A. 1913. *Aramaic Incantation Bowls from Nippur*. Philadelphia: University Museum.

———. 1934. "Ras Shamra Notes. II." *JAOS* 54:60–66.

———. 1942. "Ras Shamra Notes. VII: The Ugaritic Fantasia of the Gracious and Beautiful Gods." *JAOS* 62:49–51.

Moor, J. C. de. 1972. *New Year with Canaanites and Israelites*. 2 vols. Kamper Cahiers 21–22. Kampen: Kok.

———. 1987. *An Anthology of Religious Texts from Ugarit*. Nisaba 16. Leiden: Brill.

———. 1990. "Loveable Death in the Ancient Near East." *UF* 22:233–45.

Moor, J. C. de, and P. van der Lugt. 1974. "The Spectre of Pan-Ugaritism." *BiOr* 31:3–26.

Moran, W. L. ed. and trans.1992. *The Amarna Letters*. Baltimore: The Johns Hopkins University Press.

Mullen, E. T., Jr. 1980. *The Divine Council in Canaanite and Early Hebrew Literature*. HSM 24. Chico, Calif.: Scholars Press.

Nielsen, D. 1936. *Ras Šamra Mythologie und biblische Theologie*. Abhandlungen für die Kunde des Morgenlandes 21/4. Leipzig: Deutsche morgenländische Gesellschaft.

Nissinen, M. 2001. "Akkadian Rituals and Poetry of Divine Love." Pages 93–136 in *Mythology and Mythologies: Methodological Approaches and Intercultural Influences*. Edited by R. M. Whiting. Melammu Symposia II. Helsinki: Neo-Assyrian Text Corpus Project.

Oden, R. A., Jr. 1977. *Studies in Lucian's* De Syria Dea. HSM 15. Missoula, Mont.: Scholars Press.

———. 1979. "Theoretical Assumptions in the Study of Ugaritic Myths." *Maarav* 2/1:43–63.

Olmo Lete, G. del. 1995. "The Sacrificial Vocabulary at Ugarit." *SEL* 12:37–49.

Olyan, S. M. 1988. *Asherah and the Cult of Yahweh in Israel*. SBLMS 34. Atlanta: Scholars Press.

Owen, D. I. 1995. "Pasuri-Dagan and Ini-Tessup's Mother." Pages 573–84 in *Solving Riddles and Untying Knots: Biblical, Epigraphic, and Semitic Studies Presented to Jonas C. Greenfield*. Edited by Z. Zevit, S. Gitin, and M. Sokoloff. Winona Lake, Ind.: Eisenbrauns.

Pardee, D. 1975. "The Preposition in Ugaritic." *UF* 7:329–78.

———. 1978. "Letters from Tel Arad." *UF* 10:289–336.

———. 1987. "'As Strong as Death.'" Pages 65–69 in *Love and Death in the Ancient Near East: Essays in Honor of Marvin H. Pope*. Edited by J. H. Marks and R. M. Good. Guilford, Conn.: Four Quarters.

———. 1997a. "The Baʿlu Myth." *COS* 1.86:241–74.

———. 1997b. "Dawn and Dusk." *COS* 1.87:274–83.

———. 1997c. "Ugaritic Extispicy." *COS* 1.82:291–93.

———. 2000a. "Animal Sacrifice at Ugaarit." *Topoi*, Supplement 2: 321–31.

———. 2000b. *Les textes rituels*. 2 vols. RSO 12. Paris: Éditions Recherche sur les Civilisations.

———. 2002. *Ritual and Cult at Ugarit*. SBLWAW 10. Atlanta: Society of Biblical Literature.

———. 2005. "On Psalm 29: Structure and Meaning." Pages 153–83 in *The Book of Psalms: Composition and Reception*. Edited by P. W. Flint and P. D. Miller Jr. VTSup 99. Leiden: Brill.

———. forthcoming. "RIH 98/02: A Preliminary Presentation of a New Song to Athtartu." In *Ugarit at Seventy-Five: Its Environs and the Bible*. Edited by K. L. Younger. Winona Lake, Ind.: Eisenbrauns.

Parker, S. B. 1989. *The Pre-biblical Narrative Tradition: Essays on the Ugaritic Poems* Keret *and* Aqhat. SBLRBS 24. Atlanta: Scholars Press.

Parpola, S. 1987. *Letters from Assyria and the West*. Part 1 of *The Correspondence of Sargon II*. SAA 1. Helsinki: Helsinki University Press.

Paul, S. M. 2005. *Divrei Shalom: Collected Studies of Shalom M. Paul on the Bible and the Ancient Near East 1967–2005*. CHANE 23. Leiden: Brill.

Pentiuc, E. J. 2001. *West Semitic Vocabulary in the Akkadian Texts from Emar*. HSS 49. Winona Lake, Ind.: Eisenbrauns.

Pongratz-Leisten, B. 1994. *Ina šulmi îrub: Die kulttopographie und ideologische Programmatik der akîtu-Prozession in Babylonien und Assyrien im I. Jahrtausend v. Chr.* Baghdader Forschungen 16. Mainz am Rhein: von Zabern.

————. 2000. "Hieros Gamos." *RGG*[4] 3:1730–31.

————. forthcoming. "Alliances between the Gods and the King and the Transfer of Divine Knowledge." In *Sacred Marriages in the Biblical World*. Edited by M. Nissinen and R. Uru. Winona Lake, Ind.: Eisenbrauns.

Pope, M. H. 1947. "A Note on Ugaritic *ndd-ydd*." *JCS* 1:337–41 = Pope 1994:359–63.

————. 1955. *El in the Ugaritic Texts*. VTSup 5. Leiden: Brill.

————. 1977. *Song of Songs: A New Translation with Introduction and Commentary*. AB 7C. Garden City, N.Y.: Doubleday.

————. 1978. "Mid Rock and Scrub, a Ugaritic Parallel to Exodus 7:19." Pages 146–50 in *Biblical and Near Eastern Studies: Essays in Honor of William Sanford LaSor*. Edited by G. Tuttle. Grand Rapids: Eerdmans = Pope 1994:45–50 [with "An Afterthought (22/12/92) on 'Mid rock and Scrub' "].)

————. 1979. "The Ups and Downs of El's Amours." *UF* 11:701 8.

————. 1987. "The Status of El at Ugarit." *UF* 19:219–33.

————. 1994. *Probative Pontificating in Ugaritic and Biblical Literature: Collected Essays*. Edited by M. S. Smith. UBL 10. Münster: Ugarit-Verlag.

Porter, J. R 1981. "Genesis XIX:30–38 and the Ugaritic Text of ŠḤR & ŠLM." Pages 1–8 in *Proceedings of the Seventh World Congress of Jewish Studies: Studies in the Bible and the Ancient Near East Held at the Hebrew University of Jerusalem 7–14 August 1977*. Jerusalem: World Union of Jewish Studies.

Prattis, I. 2001. "Understanding Symbolic Process—Metaphor, Vibration, Form." *Journal of Ritual Studies* 15/1:38–54.

Rainey, A. F. 1965. "The Military Personnel of Ugarit." *JNES* 24:17–27.

————. 1971. "Observations on Ugaritic Grammar." *UF* 3:151–72.

————. 1995. Review of M. Dietrich and O. Loretz, *Mantik in Ugarit*. *UF* 27:704–6.

Ratner, R., and B. Zuckerman. 1985. "On Reading the 'Kid in the Milk' Inscription." *BAR* 1/3:56–58.

————. 1986. " 'A Kid in Milk'? New Photographs of KTU 1.23, Line 14." *HUCA* 57: 15–60.

Reiner, E. 1995. *Astral Magic in Babylonia*. TAPS 85/4. Philadelphia: American Philosophical Society.

Rendsburg, G. A. 1987. "Modern South Arabian as a Source for Ugaritic Etymologies." *JAOS* 107:623–28.

Renfroe, F. 1992. *Arabic-Ugaritic Lexical Studies*. ALASP 5. Münster: Ugarit-Verlag.

Renger, J. 1972–75. "Heilige Hochzeit. A. Philologisch." *RlA* 4:251–59.

Rinaldi, G. 1968. "*jmjn (jāmîn)* 'la destra.'" *Bibbia e Oriente* 10:162.

Ringgren, H. 1979. "Ugarit und das Alte Testament: Einige methodologische Erwägungen." *UF* 11:719–21.

Rochberg, F. 2004. *The Heavenly Writing: Divination, Horoscopy, and Astronomy in Mesopotamian Culture.* Cambridge: Cambridge University Press.

Rosenthal, F. 1940. Review of C. Virolleaud, *La déesse 'Anat. Or* 9:290–95.

Rundin, J. S. 2004. "Pozo Moro, Child Sacrifice, and the Greek Legendary Tradition." *JBL* 123:425–47.

Sahlins, M. 1972. *Stone Age Economics.* Chicago: Aldine.

Sarna, N. M. 1989. *The JPS Torah Commentary: Genesis.* Philadelphia: Jewish Publication Society.

Sasson, J. M. 2002. "Ritual Wisdom? On 'Seething a Kid in Its Mother's Milk.'" Pages 294–308 in *Kein Land für sich allein: Studien zum Kulturkontakt in Kanaan, Israel/Palästina und Ebirnâri für Manfred Weippert zum 65. Geburtstag.* Edited by U. Hübner and E. A. Knauf. OBO 186. Fribourg: Universitätsverlag; Göttingen: Vandenhoeck & Ruprecht.

————. 2003. "Should Cheeseburgers Be Kosher?" *BRev* 19/6:41–43, 50–51.

Schloen, J. D. 1993. "The Exile of Disinherited Kin in *KTU* 1.12 and *KTU* 1.23." *JNES* 52:209–20.

Segert, S. 1986. "An Ugaritic Text Related to the Fertility Cult (*KTU* 1.23)." Pages 217–24 in *Archaeology and Fertility Cult in the Ancient Mediterranean: Papers Presented at the First International Conference on Archaeology of the Ancient Mediterranean, the University of Malta 2–5 September 1985.* Edited by A. Bonanno. Amsterdam: Grüner.

Selms, A. van. 1970. "Yammu's Dethronement by Baal: An Attempt to Reconstruct Texts UT 129, 137 and 68." *UF* 2:252–68.

Seow, C. L. 1989. *Myth, Drama, and the Politics of David's Dance.* HSM 44. Atlanta: Scholars Press.

Shedl, C. 1964. "Psalm 8 in ugaritischer Sicht." *FuF* 38:183–85.

Sivan, D. 1997. *A Grammar of the Ugaritic Language.* HdO 1/28. Leiden: Brill.

Skelley, C. J. 1994. *Dictionary of Herbs, Spices, Seasonings, and Natural Flavorings.* New York: Garland.

Smith, J. Z. 1969. "The Glory, Jest and Riddle: James George Frazer and the Golden Bough." Ph. D. diss., Yale University Press.

————. 1978. *Map is Not Territory: Studies in the History of Religions.* Studies in Judaism in Late Antiquity 23. Leiden: Brill.

————. 1989. "Dying and Rising Gods." Pages 521–27 in vol. 4 of *The Encyclopedia of Religion.* Edited by M. Eliade. New York: Macmillan.

Smith, M. S. 1990. *The Early History of God: Yahweh and the Other Deities of Ancient Israel.* San Franciso: Harper & Row.

————. 1994a. "Myth and Myth-Making in Ugaritic and Israelite Literatures." Pages 293–341 in *Ugarit and the Bible: Proceedings of the International Symposium on Ugarit and the Bible, Manchester, September 1992.* Edited by G. J. Brooke, A. H. W. Curtis, and J. F. Healey. Ugaritisch-Biblische Literatur 11. Münster: Ugarit-Verlag.

————. 1994b. *The Ugaritic Baal Cycle. Vol. 1: Introduction with Text, Translation and Commentary of KTU 1.1–1.2.* VTSup 55. Leiden: Brill.

————. 1997. "Psalm 8:2b–3: New Proposals for Old Problems." *CBQ* 59:637–41.

————. 1998a. "The Death of 'Dying and Rising Gods' in the Biblical World: An Update, with Special Reference to Baal in the Baal Cycle." *SJOT* 12/2:257–313.

————. 1998b. "A Potpourri of Popery: Marginalia from the Life and Notes of Marvin H. Pope." *UF* 30:645–64.

————. 1999. "Grammatically Speaking: The Participle as a Main Verb of Clauses (Predicative Participle) in Direct Discourse and Narrative in Pre-Mishnaic Hebrew." Pages 278–332 in *Sirach, Scrolls and Sages: Proceedings of a Second International Symposium on the Hebrew of the Dead Sea Scrolls, Ben Sira and the Mishnah, Held at Leiden University, 15-17 December 1997*. Edited by T. Muraoka and J. F. Elwolde. STDJ 33. Leiden: Brill.

————. 2001. *The Origins of Biblical Monotheism: Israel's Polytheistic Background and the Ugaritic Texts*. Oxford: Oxford University Press.

————. forthcoming. "Recent Study of Israelite Religion in Light of the Ugaritic Texts." In *Ugarit at Seventy-Five: Its Environs and the Bible*. Edited by K. L. Younger. Winona Lake, Ind.: Eisenbrauns.

Soldt, W. H. van. 1990. "Fabrics and Dyes at Ugarit." *UF* 22:321–57.

————. 1991. *Studies in the Akkadian of Ugarit: Dating and Grammar*. AOAT 40. Kevelaer: Butzon & Bercker; Neukirchen-Vluyn: Neukirchener.

Staal, F. 1978. "The Meaninglessness of Ritual." *Numen* 26:2–22.

————. 1989. *Rules without Meaning*. New York: Lang.

Stager, L. E. 1982. "The Archaeology of the East Slope of Jerusalem and the Terraces of the Kidron." *JNES* 41:11–21.

Steiner, R. C. 2000. "Does the Biblical Hebrew Conjunction -w Have Many Meanings, One Meaning, or No Meaning at All?" *JBL* 119:249–67.

Stol, M. 2000. *Birth in Babylonia and the Bible: Its Mediterranean Setting*. Cuneiform Monographs 14. Groningen: Styx.

Talmon, S. 1976. "Wilderness." *IDBSup* 946–49.

————. 1997. "*Miḏbār; ʿărāḇâ*." *TDOT* 8:87–118.

Thompson, R. C. 1949. *A Dictionary of Assyrian Botany*. London: British Academy.

Tigay, J. H. 1996. *The JPS Torah Commentary: Deuteronomy*. Philadelphia: Jewish Publication Society.

Toorn, K. van der. 2000. "Cuneiform Documents from Syria-Palestine: Texts, Scribes, and Schools." *ZDPV* 116:97–113.

————. forthcoming. *Scribal Culture and the Making of the Hebrew Bible*.

Touissant-Samat, M. 1992. *A History of Food*. Translated by A. Bell. Oxford: Blackwell.

Tropper, J. 1991. "Finale Sätze und *yqtla*-Modus im Ugaritischen." *UF* 23:341–52.

————. 1994. "Die enklitische Partikel -*y* im Ugaritischen." *UF* 26:473–82.

Tropper, J., and E. Verreet 1988. "Ugaritisch *ndy, ydy, hdy, ndd* und *d(w)d*." *UF* 20:339–50.

Trujillo, J. I. 1973. "The Ugaritic Ritual for a Sacrificial Meal Honoring the Good Gods (Text CTA: 23)." Ph.D. diss., The Johns Hopkins University.

Tsevat, M. 1978. "Comments on the Ugaritic Text UT 52." *ErIs* 14:24*–27*.

Tsumura, D. T. 1973. "The Ugaritic Drama of the Good Gods: A Philological Study." Ph.D. diss., Brandeis University.

————. 1974. "A Ugaritic God Mt-w-šr and His Two Weapons." *UF* 6:407–13.

————. 1978a. "A Problem of Myth and Ritual Relationship: CTA 23 (UT 52):56–57 Reconsidered." *UF* 10:387–95.

————. 1978b. "The Vetitive Particle ya and the Poetic Structure of Proverb 31:4." *Annual of the Japanese Institute* 4:23–31.

————. 1981. "Ritual Rubric or Mythological Narrative?—CTA 23 (UT 52):56–57 Reconsidered." Pages 9–16 in *Proceedings of the Seventh World Congress of Jewish Studies:*

Studies in the Bible and the Ancient Near East Held at the Hebrew University of Jerusalem 7–14 August 1977. Jerusalem: World Union of Jewish Studies.

———. 1999. "Kings and Cults in Ancient Ugarit." Pages 215–38 in *Priests and Officials in the Ancient Near East: Papers of the Second Colloquium on the Ancient Near East—The City and Its Life Held at the Middle Eastern Culture Center in Japan (Mitaka, Tokyo)*. Edited by K. Watanabe. Heidelberg: Winter.

Van de Mieroop, M. 1999. *Cuneiform Texts and the Writing of History*. London: Routledge.

Veldhuis, N. 1991. *A Cow of Sîn*. Library of Oriental Texts 2. Groningen: Styx.

Vernant, J. P. 1981. "Sacrificial and Alimentary Codes in Hesiod's Myth of Prometheus." Pages 57–79 in *Myth, Religion, and Society: Structuralist Essays*. Edited by R. L. Gordon. Cambridge: Cambridge University; Paris: Editions de la Maison des Sciences de l'Homme.

———. 1989. "At Man's Table: Hesiod's Foundation Myth of Sacrifice." Pages 21–86 in *The Cuisine of Sacrifice among the Greeks*. Edited by M. Detienne and J. P. Vervant. Translated by P. Wissing. Chicago: University of Chicago Press.

Verreet, E. 1984. "Beobachtungen zum ugaritischen Verbalsystem." *UF* 16:307–21.

———. 1986. "Beobachtungen zum ugaritischen Verbalsystem III." *UF* 18:363–86.

Versnel, H. S. 1990. "What's Sauce for the Goose Is Sauce for the Gander: Myth and Ritual, Old and New." Pages 25–90 in *Approaches to Greek Myth*. Edited by L. Edmunds. Baltimore: The Johns Hopkins University Press.

Vicente, M. B. 2003. "Pozo Moro Monument." Pages 56–57 in *Museo Arqueológico Nacional*. English edition. Electa Art Guides. Barcelona: Electa.

Virolleaud, C. 1933. "La naissance des dieux gracieux et beaux: Poème phénicien de Ras-Shamra." *Syria* 14:128–51.

Voigt, R. 1990. "Probleme der Ugaritistik." *UF* 22:399–414.

Walls, N. H., Jr. 1992. *The Goddess Anat in the Ugaritic Myth*. SBLDS 135. Atlanta: Scholars Press.

———. 2001. *Desire, Discord and Death: Approaches to Ancient Near Eastern Myth*. ASOR Books 8. Boston: American Schools of Oriental Research.

Watson, P. L. 1972. "The Death of 'Death' in the Ugaritic Texts." *JAOS* 92:60–64.

Watson, W. G. E. 1977. "Ugaritic and Mesopotamian Literary Texts." *UF* 9:273–84.

———. 1979. "The PN *yṣb* in the Keret Legend." *UF* 11:807–9.

———. 1982. "Trends in the Development of Classical Hebrew Poetry: A Comparative Study." *UF* 14:265–77.

———. 1986. "Internal Parallelism in Ugaritic Verse." *UF* 17:345–56.

———. 1990. "Abrupt Speech in Ugaritic Narrative Verse." *UF* 22:415–20.

———. 1993a. "The Goddesses of Ugarit: A Survey." *SEL* 10:47–59.

———. 1993b. "Number Parallelism Again." *UF* 25:435–40.

———. 1994. "Aspects of Style in KTU 1.23." *SEL* 11:3–8.

———. 2000. "Non-Semitic Words in the Ugaritic Lexicon (V)." *UF* 32:567–75.

Weinfeld, M. 1983. "Divine Intervention in War in Ancient Israel and in the Ancient Near East." Pages 121–47 in *History, Historiography and Interpretation: Studies in Biblical and Cuneiform Literatures*. Edited by H. Tadmor and M. Weinfeld. Jerusalem: Magnes.

Welch, J. W. 1974. "Chiasmus in Ugaritic." *UF* 6:421–36.

Westenholz, J. G. 2000. *Cuneiform Inscriptions in the Collection of the Bible Lands Museum Jerusalem: The Emar Tablets*. Cuneiform Monographs 13. Groningen: Styx.

Wiggermann, F. 1992. *Mesopotamian Protective Spirits. The Ritual Texts.* Cuneiform Monographs I. Groningen: Styx.

———. 1996a. "Scenes from the Shadow Side." Pages 207–20 in *Mesopotamian Poetic Language: Sumerian and Akkadian.* Edited by M. E. Vogelzang and H. L. J. Vanstiphout. Cuneiform Monographs 6. Groningen: Styx.

———. 1996b. "Transtigridian Snake Gods." Pages 33–55 in *Sumerian Gods and Their Representations.* Edited by I. L. Finkel and M. J. Geller. Groningen: Styx.

Wiggins, S. A. 1993. *A Reassessment of 'Asherah': A Study According to the Textual Sources of the First Two Millennia B.C.E.* AOAT 235. Kevelaer: Butzon & Bercker; Neukirchen-Vluyn: Neukirchener.

———. 1996. "Shapsh, Lamp of the Gods." Pages 327–50 in *Ugaritic, Religion and Culture: Proceedings of the International Colloquium on Ugarit, Religion and Culture, Edinburgh, July 1994. Essays Presented in Honour of Professor John C. L. Gibson.* Edited by N. Wyatt, W. G. E. Watson, and J. B. Lloyd. UBL 12. Münster: Ugarit-Verlag.

Wilson, E. J. 1991. "Ugaritic *'d* and an Unusual Use of Sumerian ID." *Akkadica* 74–75:48–53.

Wright, D. P. 1987. *The Disposal of Impurity: Elimination Rites in the Bible and in Hittite and Mesopotamian Literature.* SBLDS 101. Atlanta: Scholars Press.

———. 2001. *Ritual in Narrative: The Dynamics of Feasting, Mourning, and Retaliation Rites in the Ugaritic Tale of Aqhat.* Winona Lake, Ind.: Eisenbrauns.

Wyatt, N. 1976. "Atonement Theology in Ugarit and Israel." *UF* 8:415–30.

———. 1977. "The Identity of *mt wšr.*" *UF* 9:379–81.

———. 1986. "Killing and Cosmogony in Canaanite and Biblical Thought." *UF* 17: 375–86.

———. 1987. "Sea and Desert: Symbolic Geography in West Semitic Religious Thought." *UF* 19:375–89.

———. 1992a. "A New Look at Ugaritic *šdmt.*" *JSS* 37:149–53.

———. 1992b. "The Pruning of the Vine in KTU 1. 23." *UF* 24:425–27.

———. 1996. *Myths of Power: A Study of Royal Myth and Ideology in Ugaritic and Biblical Traditions.* UBL 13. Münster: Ugarit-Verlag.

———. 1998. *Religious Texts from Ugarit: The Words of Ilimilku and His Colleagues.* Biblical Seminar 53. Sheffield: Sheffield Academic Press.

———. 2001. "Dennis Pardee, *Les Texts Rituels* (RSO 12, Paris 2000), An Appraisal." *UF* 33:696–706.

———. 2002. *Religious Texts from Ugarit: The Words of Ilimilku and His Colleagues.* 2nd ed. Biblical Seminar 53. Sheffield: Sheffield Academic Press.

———. 2004. "Androgyny in the Levantine World." Pages 191*–98* in *Teshûrôt LaAvishur, Studies in the Bible and the Ancient Near East in Hebrew and Semitic Languages: Festschrift Presented to Prof. Yitzhak Avishur on the Occasion of His 65th Birthday.* Edited by M. Heltzer and M. Malul. Tel Aviv: Archaeological Cennter Publications.

———. 2005a. "Androgyny in the Levantine World." Pages 151–88 in *The Mythic Mind: Esssays on Cosmology and Religion in Ugaritic and Old Testament Literature.* London: Equinox.

———. 2005b. "Marriage, Mayhem and Murder: An Everyday Story of Royal Folk." Pages 231–51 in *"There's such Divinity doth Hedge a King": Selected Essays of Nicolas Wyatt on Royal Ideology in Ugaritic and Old Testament Literature.* Society for Old Testament Study Monographs. Hants, England: Ashgate.

Xella, P. 1973. *Il mito di Šḥr e Šlm: Saggio sulla mitologia ugaritica.* Studi semitici 44. Rome: Istituto di Studi del vicino oriente, Università di Roma.

―――. 1976. *Problemi del mito nel vicino oriente antico.* Annali [Istituto Orientle di Napoli] supplemento 7. Napoli: Istituto orientale di Napoli.

―――. 1978. "L'épisode de Dnil et Kothar (KTU 1.17=CTA 17 v 1–31) et Gen. xviii 1–17." *VT* 28:483–88.

―――. 2003. "Problemi attuali nello studio delle Religioni: I. – Recenti dibattiti sulla methodologia." *Studi e Materiali di Storia delle Religioni* 69 (ns XXVII/1):219–66.

Yon, M., and D. Arnaud, eds. 2001. *Études ougaritiques I. Travaux 1985-1995.* RSO 14. Paris: Éditions Recherche sur les Civilisations.

Young, D. W. 1977. "With Snakes and Dates: A Sacred Marriage Drama at Ugarit." *UF* 9:291–314.

Zamora, J. A. 2000. *La vid y el vino en Ugarit.* Banco de datos filológicos semíticos nord-occdentales: Monografías 6. Madrid: Consejo de investigaciones científicas.

Zevit, Z. 2001. *The Religions of Ancient Israel: A Synthesis of Parallactic Approaches.* New York: Continuum.

Zijl, P. J. van. 1972. *Baal: A Study of Texts in Connexion with Baal in the Ugaritic Texts.* AOAT 10. Kevelaer: Butzon & Bercker; Neukirchen-Vluyn: Neukirchener.

Index of Primary Sources

Apocrypha and Pseudepigrapha

1 Maccabees
6:34   46 n. 20

Ben Sira
34:30   37 n. 8
37:27   37 n. 8
39:26   46

1 Enoch
86   13

New Testament

Matthew
23:23   55

Luke
11:42   55

John
15:1–8   47

Revelation
14   47
14:14–20   47

Texts from Ugarit

CAT/KTU
1.1 IV   61
1.1 IV 14–15   60
1.1–1.6   5, 10, 164
1.2 I 14   105
1.2 I 15   105
1.2 I 20   105
1.2 I 31   105
1.2 I 43   45
1.2 III 22   91
1.2 IV   42, 106
1.2 IV 11   61, 90
1.2 IV 18   61, 90
1.2 IV 19   38
1.2 IV 19–20   37
1.2 VI 11   60
1.2 VI 19   60
1.3 I   32, 36, 60

1.3 I 4–8   114
1.3 I 5   36
1.3 I 8   114
1.3 I 8–11   114
1.3 I 16   36
1.3 I 18–19   114
1.3 I 20   52
1.3 I 22   97
1.3 I 24   103
1.3 II 5–7   97
1.3 II 15–16   81
1.3 II 18   97
1.3 II 19–20   115–16
1.3 II 29–30   116
1.3 II 39–40   102
1.3 III 1   97
1.3 III 7   103
1.3 III 10   97
1.3 III 19–20   97
1.3 III 31   33
1.3 III 40   97
1.3 III 41   103
1.3 IV 12   97
1.3 IV 40   91
1.3 IV 40–41   100 n. 43
1.3 IV 48–53   62
1.3 IV 50–53   94
1.3 IV 51   103
1.3 V 6–7   74
1.3 V 17–18   48
1.3 V 32–33   92, 93
1.3 V 39–44   62
1.3 V 41–44   94
1.4 I 13–14   100 n. 43
1.4 I 14–18   94
1.4 I 21   100 n. 43
1.4 I 22   79
1.4 II   77
1.4 II 3–4   82
1.4 II 3–10   77
1.4 II 3–11   82
1.4 II 5–7   82
1.4 II 8–9   56, 82
1.4 II 10–11   82
1.4 II 28–29   100 n. 43
1.4 II 31   100 n. 43
1.4 III–IV   3 n. 1
1.4 III 14   105

Other Near Eastern Inscriptions

Classical Authors